Fly for Less

Flying Clubs and Aircraft Partnerships

Fly for Less
Flying Clubs and Aircraft Partnerships

Geza Szurovy

TAB BOOKS
Blue Ridge Summit, PA

Disclaimer. All material in this book, including the appendices, is intended and should be used as a source of general information only. The contents, including all forms and tables, are not to be relied upon as specific legal, insurance, financial, or maintenance advice, or for specific aircraft operations. It is the reader's responsibility to seek the services of appropriate attorneys at law, insurance, financial, and maintenance professionals for advice regarding specific transactions or operations. It is the user's responsibility to ensure that all forms used meet all legal and other requirements regarding intended use. Readers are reminded of the pilot in command's responsibility to consult all official sources of information relevant to every aspect of a proposed flight and personally assure compliance with all laws, regulations, and procedures. Readers are also reminded that the law varies from state to state in the United States, reinforcing the need for the services of an attorney in any specific situation.

FIRST EDITION
FIRST PRINTING

© 1992 by **Geza Szurovy**.
Published by TAB Books.
TAB Books is a division of McGraw-Hill, Inc.

Library of Congress Cataloging-in-Publication Data

Szurovy, Geza.
    Fly for less : flying clubs and aircraft partnerships / by Geza
Szurovy.
      p. cm.
    Includes index.
    ISBN 0-8306-3850-4 (h)   ISBN 0-8306-3851-2 (p)
    1. Private flying—Societies, etc. 2. Airplanes—Purchasing.
3. Joint ownership of personal property. I. Title.
TL713.5.S98 1992
629.133'340422'068—dc20   92-15745
                                         CIP

TAB Books offers software for sale. For information and a catalog, please contact TAB Software Department, Blue Ridge Summit, PA 17294-0850.

Acquisitions Editor: Jeff Worsinger
Book Editor: Norval G. Kennedy
Director of Production: Katherine G. Brown
Book Design: Jaclyn J. Boone
Photos by author unless noted otherwise.
Cover design and illustration by Denny Bond, East Petersburg, PA   AV1

For Bob Schuette
Airplane Partner Extraordinaire

Contents

Part II   Partnerships

Acknowledgments

AIRCRAFT PARTNERSHIPS AND FLYING CLUBS are the only reason why I have been able to do some of the flying that remains most vivid in my mind. To the K.I.M. Flying Club, the Regie der Luchtwegen, the MIT Soaring Association, Greater Boston Soaring, the Mashonaland Flying Club, the Tiger Club, 3 Romeo Whiskey, the New England Escadrille, and my partners in 8 Bravo Mike and 6 Papa Echo, thanks for the memories.

The Aircraft Owners and Pilots Association was most helpful in granting permission to reproduce three standard AOPA sample documents pertaining to flying clubs: sample articles of incorporation, sample bylaws, and sample flight rules. The samples are in the appendices.

(AOPA is general aviation's premiere watchdog in Washington, an advocate before the FAA and other government institutions. In addition to representing general aviation's interests, AOPA provides valuable membership benefits to pilots and aircraft owners. Among the services offered is advice related to most aspects of operating and owning aircraft, chart and flight planning services, and advice and counsel on aviation law and medicine. AOPA partner organizations provide aviation insurance, aircraft financing, title search and escrow services, and a variety of other programs. The organization's monthly publication, *AOPA Pilot*, is an outstanding aviation magazine. Additional information about the association is available by calling 1-800-USA-AOPA.)

In writing this book, I have also benefited greatly from the generous comments, advice, and critique offered with great enthusiasm by members of the flying community exceptionally knowledgeable about the topic at hand, particularly concerning the more specialized areas of aviation insurance, finance, law, and maintenance. Special thanks are due to Sam Peoples of Multibank Aviation, Norwood Airport, Massachusetts; Grace Smith and Joe Rowland of Aero Insurance, Hanscom Field, Massachusetts; Lew McMahon, Esq., of Green McMahon and Heed, Keene, New Hampshire; Matt Thurber and Anne Enman of the West Valley Flying Club, Palo Alto, California; Jud Milgram; Dave Nadler; and Anne.

And last but not least thanks to my editors, Jeff Worsinger for believing in an idea, and Norval Kennedy for working so hard to polish it.

Foreword

IF YOU'RE LIKE MOST PILOTS, you'll do anything to fly.

From washing airplanes to hanging around at the airport, hoping another pilot will offer to share a flight; taking a bag lunch to work for a month so you can enjoy a solitary hour in the cool smoothness of sunrise to practice touch-and-goes; persuading the local mechanics to let you help break in a new engine.

And the more you fly, the more you want to fly. It's addictive, no question about it. Your friends might express an occasional interest in going flying, but few of them can understand the way your heart beats faster when you first hear the low-pitched buzz of a Cherokee or a Skylane, then look up and see it silhouetted against the bright blue sky. Or the constant urge that makes you stop and wander around every airport you pass by, wondering who all those airplanes belong to and why they aren't flying, and thinking for the thousandth time that you ought to start a business offering to help owners keep their airplanes healthy by flying their airplane more than occasionally, and your only expense would be the cost of fuel.

The hour or so a month you're able to rack up fills your logbook pages ever so slowly. Every time that you add another entry, it seems that you'll never finish that first logbook; never be able to afford to take that flying trip through the western U.S. you've always dreamed about (and you have the charts to prove it); never fly that hot Mooney 252 you've lusted after; or take up the challenge of taildragging in antique biplanes; or fulfill any of the flying dreams that hound you constantly.

Oh well, you think, if only I could just afford to fly that Archer a few more hours a month. Then I'd feel confident enough to take that trip to northern Idaho, plus I'd finally be able to start working on my instrument rating.

Just a few more hours a month, is that too much to ask for?

No, it isn't.

Opportunities for more flying time at reduced cost are out there and anyone can take advantage of them.

By reading this, you are taking the first step toward more affordable flying and toward achieving your flying dreams, which are encouraged by the author.

Geza Szurovy's book explains how, through aircraft partnerships or flying clubs, you can fly for less. A lot less. And you can use your savings to fly the same airplane a lot more, or fly bigger and faster airplanes as much as you used to fly that Skyhawk or Warrior.

By spreading the costs of ownership and operation among a greater number of like-minded pilots, you can fly for less.

While partnerships and flying clubs are not new, Geza's book is the only book available that details how to set up efficient and effective flying clubs and partnerships. You'll not only learn the advantages of both and when a partnership should be turned into a club, but you'll also learn how to avoid common pitfalls inherent in aircraft ownership and operation, and how to protect yourself from liability problems.

Of value to any potential owner is the chapter on how to determine operating costs on an annual and hourly basis. And any aircraft buyer will benefit from the chapter on how to purchase an airplane and how to make sure it is in excellent condition.

Geza is currently partners in a Piper Arrow III and has owned, either alone or in partnership, four other airplanes from a Grumman TR-2 to a homebuilt Long-EZE. An international businessman, Geza has written extensively about his travels for national newspapers and about flying in other countries in his first book, *The Private Pilot's Guide to Renting and Flying Airplanes Worldwide*. The book recently received the prestigious Aviation/Space Writers Association Award of Excellence. Geza's byline can also be found in a number of national aviation magazines, including *Private Pilot*, *Kitplanes*, *Soaring*, *AOPA Pilot*, and *Atlantic Flyer*. Geza has a DC-3 type rating and has flown more than 50 different types of airplanes and gliders.

A trend toward flying clubs and partnerships is on the increase and is offering a lower cost alternative to the typical FBOs. FBOs must build into their rental rate a reasonable profit margin. Nonprofit flying clubs and partnerships can operate the same aircraft at considerable savings over FBOs and at the same time keep the fleet in excellent shape for reasonable costs. The benefits accrue not only to the pilot, but also to the owners and operators of the airplanes, for their operating costs will be reduced and therefore cost of ownership reduced, too. This means more airplanes are available at lower costs, and that means more flying for you—more opportunities to make your dreams reality.

And that's what this book is all about.

Matt Thurber
Utica, Michigan

Matt Thurber was formerly the service manager for West Valley Flying Club in Palo Alto, California. He is an A&P with an IA, also holding ATP and CFII certificates. Thurber was formerly an associate editor at FLYING Magazine *and* Aviation International News.

Introduction

HE STOOD BY THE FENCE, watching the Skyhawk climb into the fresh morning air. It had been four long years since he had last advanced the throttle and felt the tense anticipation he so enjoyed at the beginning of every flight. "Power set, airspeed alive, power still set, rotate . . ." and then, as the airplane had settled into a steady climb providing options if the fan ever stopped, the tension had slowly yielded to a tranquil sense of wonder at the world unfolding below. That last flight had been perfect and he had entered the 201st hour in his logbook after he taxied back to the FBO and shut down. But then he and his wife had bought their first house and then came the kids, and $80 an hour for a Skyhawk was just too much. So now he brings the kids to the airport from time to time to watch the airplanes from the parking lot. And he imagines taxiing into position and advancing the throttle again. If only he could fly that Skyhawk for $45 an hour . . . .

Sound familiar? This is only one of many scenarios that keep pilots grounded or restrict their flying to fewer hours or more modest equipment than they would prefer. Yet at the same time there is a vast fleet of underutilized airplanes out there. Many of them are becoming an ever increasing financial burden on individual owners who would welcome a chance to spread the expenses around in these demanding economic times. With the right attitude, the news is good. If you are keen to find ways of doing more for less, of making more efficient use of those idle airplanes, there is tremendous scope for progress through nonprofit cooperative flying, through aircraft partnerships, and flying clubs.

The idea of cooperative flying is not new. Orville and Wilbur Wright's Flyer was without a doubt the first successful airplane partnership. In a recent debate, no fewer than 16 flying clubs vied for the title of being the oldest flying club in America. All the clubs predated 1941 and the unofficial winner was the University of Detroit Flying Club, dating back to the early 1920s. Outside the United States, where avgas has always cost two to four times as much, for many pilots, flying clubs or partnerships have been the only way to go. The escalating cost of flying steadily outpaces inflation; it is high time to develop cooperative flying to its full potential and let it claim a much greater share in the mainstream of American general aviation.

Part I
Fly for less

1

Options

COOPERATIVE FLYING VENTURES ARE FORMED primarily for economic reasons. The main objective is to do more flying for your buck. But depending upon the resources you have available, more flying for the buck can mean many things.

At the most basic level, it is the difference between flying or watching Skyhawks from the airport parking lot. If you are a licensed pilot who is now temporarily grounded, flying for less is finding the least expensive airplane to get back in the air. If you are one of these people who has never flown a light aircraft but tells every pilot that "I would be one, if only . . .," and means it, then flying for less is the least expensive dual option, wherever it might be. If you rent a Cherokee commercially for 50 hours a year because that is all you can afford, then flying for less is finding an alternative that allows you to fly more hours for the same amount of money. Or, if you are satisfied with 50 hours a year, it allows you to accomplish that objective for less money. So far, flying for less has meant quantity; quantity of hours flown and quantity of money.

But flying for less also means quality. More flying for the buck can mean flying a Mooney for the same amount of money you now spend on a Cherokee. It might mean flying a Citabria and a Beech Sierra the same amount of total hours you spend in the commercially rented Cherokee for the same amount of money. It might mean affording an IFR rating when other options for the same amount of time and money would keep you VFR. And flying for less can also be, and most often is, a compromise between quality and quantity, such as flying fewer hours in a Bonanza when the other option is more hours in a Skyhawk.

The permutations are endless, but the common thread in flying for less is comparing the hourly rate for the aircraft and related expenses with the contents of the cash pot you have available for flying. Cooperative flying will always be less expensive than sole ownership, and beyond a minimum number of hours flown, it will yield lower hourly rates than those offered by the commercial alternative.

Two basic options for nonprofit cooperative flying ventures are aircraft partnerships and flying clubs. This book is all about what they are, how to do your homework to decide which option is better for you, how to establish your choice, and how to run a cooperative flying venture.

PARTNERSHIPS

Partnerships (in some states, legally referred to as co-ownerships because of their nonprofit nature) are the simple form of cooperative flying. As the name implies, two or more partners get together and buy an airplane. Usually they own equal shares, do more or less the same sort of flying, and have equal voices in decisions. The partnership is truly a democracy. Compatibility, not only of personalities, but also in flying objectives is of paramount importance. The partnership can consider itself successful if all partners get the amount of flying they set out to accomplish in an airplane they really want, according to a schedule they initially envisioned.

The Cessna Skyhawk is an enduring favorite of cooperative flying ventures.

Partnerships vary in purpose. Many are formed to permit the participating partners to do some serious touring at considerable savings over commercial rates and with greater flexibility in aircraft availability. Others are organized by partners who want to learn to fly or upgrade their ratings, and seek a budget alternative to the commercial flying schools. Still others might be arranged to construct a home-built, sharing complementary building skills, or to own and fly a warbird or rare classic that would be prohibitively expensive for even the wealthiest single owner.

The number of partners greatly influences the character of the partnership. If a partnership grows, at some point it will reach a stage where it becomes too unwieldy to be run as a partnership and is much better off being transformed into a flying club.

FLYING CLUBS

The organization of the flying club is more complex than the partnership. It usually has legal status in the form of incorporation and owns airplanes in its own right (or it might lease the airplanes). Members join it to enjoy the benefits of renting its airplanes. Members might own a share of the flying club, but are not direct owners of shares in the aircraft.

The average flying club's greater number of members in comparison to partnerships makes it too big to be easily manageable without a significant delegation of responsibilities within the club. The flying club is more like a democratically elected government. Its members elect from among themselves officials for set periods of time to govern the club's affairs. There is also a greater need for more detailed procedures to keep all the members up to the same standards, and ensure an equitable distribution of aircraft availability. Because of the greater demands imposed on it by the greater number of members, the flying club also requires more recordkeeping and administration than the partnership.

Aircraft availability is lower and less flexible in the flying club (but often not by much), and there are a greater number of pilots who must all get along. Among the benefits, the most significant is financial. The cost of joining a flying club, even if you have to purchase a share, which is not always the case, is way below the capital investment required to buy your piece of a partnership. The cost of flying in a flying club is usually also well below the expenses of a partnership, especially if a member flies only between 50 and a 100 hours per year.

Other advantages are access to a greater variety of airplanes, or the chance for pilots on a budget too tight for a partnership to fly more expensive equipment.

Flying clubs come in all sizes and forms. Some place great emphasis on training. Others are formed exclusively to provide economical touring, and some aim for an agreeable balance. Certain clubs specialize in ragwing antiques, others are dedicated to soaring. A club might have only 15 or 20 members, other clubs' membership rosters might run into the hundreds. Many get by on volunteer help alone from the membership and others hire professional help.

The successful flying club is run as a friendly but no-nonsense business. For in spite of its nonprofit principles (it does not distribute profits to its shareholders), a flying club is a business. It has assets (the airplanes), it generates income (the airplane rentals), it has to be responsible for its liabilities (it has to pay its bills), and someone has to manage the whole cycle, just like a business.

Pilots who have little money to invest in a partnership might find that once they are settled into a well run flying club they will never want to fly under any other arrangement.

CHECKPOINTS

Regardless of your ultimate choice between partnership and flying club, you will have to deal effectively with similar issues to make your efforts successful.

Where to begin? Think of the venture as a cross-country flight. The issues you need to address are your checkpoints, and this book is your map. You need to choose your destination from the map, identify the checkpoints, plan your flight, and go out there and fly it. And you better not miss those checkpoints on the way.

The issues you will have to resolve are introduced below. The solutions will come later, and will differ greatly depending on your choice of partnership or flying club and a whole host of other factors. At this stage, the important thing is to develop an awareness of what you face. The points below will be recurring themes as you progress through the book. This trip, of sorts, shall do more than simply present catch-all solutions; perhaps more importantly, it shall provide a basis of understanding for you to devise your own solutions.

Evaluate your needs

"One foot up, the other foot down, that's the way to London town," so it is written in Mother Goose. For pilots contemplating a cooperative flying venture, the first step is to evaluate their needs. You learn how to sort out exactly what you want from flying to be able to rationally choose the most suitable option.

Financial analysis

A need is one thing, paying for it is another. The most difficulty in any form of aircraft ownership is sorting out exactly how much it will cost. Vague notions and partial information cause many pilots to discard options that might very well be affordable.

The cost of flying is dissected and explained in great detail. You learn how to evaluate the costs of owning and operating any aircraft, and how to translate those costs to the level of individual partners and flying club members. You are made aware of the importance of comparative financial analysis to devise the best solution. You are also provided with all the worksheets to enable you to make your own calculations. Then it is a simple matter of comparing the results to the pot of money you have standing by.

For aircraft costs, partnerships, and flying clubs, you are also presented with financial spreadsheet programs. You can set them up on your personal computer to enable you to analyze any aircraft type and partnership or club option by simply entering a handful of assumptions.

Forms of organization and operating rules

No cooperative venture can function effectively without a good understanding among the participants of how it is to be organized and run. These matters are best set out on paper to avoid misunderstandings, make it easier to run the operation, and also for legal reasons. Sound organization and rules up front eliminate problems down the road.

Beech Aircraft Corporation

The ageless V-35 Bonanza. A well maintained early model yields exceptional performance for the price.

For partnerships, the key document is the partnership agreement. An entire chapter is devoted to it, explaining its role and contents, and providing guidance on setting up your own agreement. Sample agreements are also provided.

The flying club needs additional documents. All aspects of the club's articles of incorporation, bylaws, operating rules, and rental agreements are discussed in detail. Sample documents are also provided.

Financing the aircraft

This section evaluates the pros and cons of borrowing to purchase the aircraft of the partnership or flying club. It explains the terms and conditions on which banks are willing to finance aircraft. It covers the credit decision process, and shows you how to apply for a loan with a good chance of approval.

While the banks evaluate you, you should also be comparing the terms and conditions offered by the banks to get the best deal. A worksheet is provided to help you evaluate and compare the options available.

Banks are only one source of financing; others, including partner and member financing, are also covered by this section.

Sample loan agreements are provided.

Insuring the aircraft

Insurance is a most important, and for most pilots, a most mysterious topic. The mystery is unraveled as you are walked through an insurance policy and learn how to assess your venture's requirements and how best to obtain the coverage you need. A worksheet to help you evaluate and compare options offered by insurers is presented.

Operations

A cooperative flying venture has to have an effective operations structure to function well. For partnerships, operations is mostly a matter of effective scheduling and fueling arrangements, but for the flying club, especially one with many members and a number of aircraft, there are other issues as well. This section covers the options.

Maintenance

Maintenance can be handled in many ways, and the alternatives present a variety of trade-offs. Owner maintenance, independent mechanics, full service maintenance shops, and full in-house maintenance are all discussed, as applicable to partnerships or flying clubs.

Recordkeeping and administration

Accountability is essential for all cooperative flying ventures, not only to keep the participants informed, but especially to enable the venture to function from day to day. Recordkeeping and administrative techniques are discussed and a sampling of forms is provided for guidance, covering financial records and statements, as well as aircraft flight and maintenance records.

Buying the aircraft

An extensive section takes you through buying an aircraft, from initial research to closing the deal. This is the final step when establishing a cooperative flying venture because for the best results possible, you should have everything set up and ready to go before you actually buy the aircraft.

Seller questionnaires, prepurchase inspection checklists, a flight test checklist, and a closing checklist are provided.

So much for the checkpoints. Now it is time to move on to learning the approach you should use in evaluating your options, and turning your plans into reality.

2

The approach

WHEN MOST PILOTS FIRST CONSIDER a cooperative flying venture, our ideas are vague and rather disorganized. We have an uneasy sense of not even knowing where to begin. We all seek facts. But most of us don't even realize that we also seek something equally important, a method, an organized, analytical approach without which the facts might mislead us or make little sense. Both issues shall be addressed in comprehensive detail:

- An analytical approach to evaluate cooperative flying ventures, utilizing the tools that make sense of the facts.
- Numerous factual examples of the various aspects of cooperative flying ventures.

Within this structure the book progresses from the general to the specific, treating partnerships and flying clubs in separate, self-contained sections.

The key to devising the best solution for your needs and pocketbook is to take to heart the analytical approach and rigorously apply it to your own circumstances. You can put together an outstanding cooperative flying venture simply by shoehorning the factual examples onto your situation. But you are likely to realize much greater benefits if you treat the factual examples only as illustrations of the results you can achieve by a way of thinking. Be flexible and creative. Let your mind race. Dare ask the unthinkable. Are you a closet DC-3 fanatic on a Cherokee budget? Well, how do 25 shareholders in a DC-3 compare to two partners in a Warrior? You have nothing to lose and everything to gain by gathering and rigorously analyzing the facts. And after the DC-3 analysis, a Mooney with six partners will look just as attainable as the Warrior with two.

THE IMPORTANCE OF A "CAN DO" ATTITUDE

Creativity and flexibility are unleashed to greatest effect by an upbeat, positive attitude. Let it be your rule to first define without constraints the airplane and kind of flying you really want to do. Then consider the resources you have or need to marshal to make it happen. Treat constraints as hurdles to be knocked out of the way, not as automatic deal breakers. Explore all alternatives, no matter how far fetched, to make the numbers work.

Make it your goal to continue analyzing every possible scenario until you find a structure that works for your budget. Even if some of the results might be unrealistic, it will be a lot of fun to run the numbers and a valuable learning experience. And as you analyze various options you will be surprised to find how little it sometimes takes in additional commitment by another partner or two to put you all in that antique Stearman instead of something more conventional.

STEP 1. YOUR INITIAL OBJECTIVE

Your point of departure should be that anything is possible. Set yourself the highest goal. Identify the airplane you really want to fly, admit to yourself how much you would want to fly it, be honest about your ability to fly it, and only then move on to analyzing what it would take financially and otherwise. Never discard an opinion at the outset because you think it will not work financially.

Setting your initial objective implies doing a lot of information gathering on the aircraft models you are considering. While the primary focus of this book is on the various aspects of cooperative flying arrangements, be sure to also read early in your search the section on how to research, find, and buy an airplane.

STEP 2. DOLLARS AND SENSE

The book's central point is that financial reasons motivate pilots to seek cooperative flying opportunities; thus, the ability to accurately assess the costs of flying is crucial to determining the option best for you.

The simple, easy-to-use financial model for determining flying costs is one of the most important tools presented in this book. Once you have a good idea of your initial objective, you should plan to give your undivided attention to using this model to figure out what you can afford. Do the calculations for as many scenarios as it takes to make the numbers work. Worksheets are provided in the appendix. Vary the airplane options, the number of partners, the hours flown, the amount borrowed to finance the airplane, and whatever else you can think of; however, you must be careful to keep your assumptions realistic. You can adjust at will the variables over which you have control, such as the number of partners, the amount of money you want to borrow, or the number of hours you want to fly, but you must be careful to obtain, and leave unchanged, accurate figures for variables beyond your control, such as fuel prices and aircraft fuel consumption.

The financial model will be an especially powerful tool if you can work spreadsheets on a personal computer. The model is designed in spreadsheet form to be set up on a personal computer. The program is written for Excel, but is also compatible with Lotus and other popular spreadsheets (the program is found in the appendices). It is so structured that once it is set up, you need only to enter a handful of clearly defined assumptions—monthly tiedown costs, the

The Beech Musketeer is a good, low-cost compromise to simultaneously meet training and touring needs.

price of fuel, the size of your aircraft loan, your annual insurance payment, TBO, and the like—and the computer does the rest. It automatically calculates all costs for up to 15 pilots. Change one assumption, and the model is immediately adjusted to reflect the new cost structure. The variations you can run in an evening are far more than you will need.

STEP 3. PARTNERSHIP OR FLYING CLUB?

Your initial financial analysis will determine from a financial perspective how many partners it would take to afford the type airplane you selected. If the number of partners is beyond six or seven, you might be better off forming or joining a flying club. A flying club financial analysis model that analyzes the costs of operating a flying club is presented to evaluate this option. Nonfinancial considerations should be taken into account at this time to decide between partnership or flying club. Having made your decision, you can move into the next phase, the nuts and bolts work of establishing the cooperative flying venture of your choice.

STEP 4. ESTABLISHING A COOPERATIVE FLYING VENTURE

In this phase, you will have to first reconsider in greater detail the financial aspects of your choice, and then you are ready to make it happen. You will have to make a serious commitment to the venture with a like-minded group of people, hammer out the details, and acquire an airplane or perhaps several, if you are forming a club with more than one airplane. Focus upon two things, based upon personal perspective:

- Acceptability of the aircraft your group is acquiring. Does it meet all the criteria you set during your evaluation and is it priced right?
- Compatibility with your partners or fellow club members.

If you sense the slightest problem in either case, don't commit yourself to anything until you can resolve whatever is bothering you.

Be prepared for a lot of hard work. It will be worth the effort because how you implement your choice will determine how well it functions. When your partner or fellow club member sheepishly shows up at your door with a crumpled piece of wing under his arm is not the time to realize you should have had a partnership agreement or club bylaws.

When you actually buy the aircraft depends upon a variety of factors, but in general, you had better have the cooperative flying details all worked out and agreed to before you sign on the dotted line.

STEP 5. GOING FLYING

This is the big payoff, the reason for all your hard work. And if you did a thorough job, and adhere to the commitments to which you all agreed, by this stage your cooperative flying venture should be on autopilot.

3

Compelling numbers

CONSIDER THESE FACTS: If you were to rent a Piper Arrow for 100 hours per year from a commercial operator, it would cost $9,000. If you were to dip into the piggy bank and buy that Arrow alone, the 100 hours would cost $12,175 (excluding the purchase cost). But find three partners and you'll be flying that Arrow 100 hours for only $5,867; or get together with 14 other ambitious budget fliers, form an Arrow club, and fly 100 hours for only $3,343.

The most convincing reason for you to form an airplane partnership or a nonprofit flying club is to substantially reduce your flying costs in comparison to owning an airplane alone or renting one from a commercial operator. The savings are so significant that for many of us a partnership or a flying club might mean the difference between flying or being grounded. For those of us on a more generous flying budget, the reduced costs allow us to fly a more complex airplane in a partnership or a flying club for the same amount of money we would have to spend on owning a simpler airplane alone or renting it commercially.

Because your decision to form a partnership or a flying club is motivated by cost savings, you must be able to compare the costs of a variety of alternatives to choose the best option. To make these comparisons, you must clearly understand the costs of flying. Do not be intimidated by financial figures. If you can calculate courses, wind correction angles, headings, fuel burns, and estimated times of arrival, you will have already mastered the simple math necessary to calculate the cost of flying. The logical building block approach you use for navigational calculations also works best for financial calculations. First, you have to have a framework of analysis. Next, you have to calculate the individual components within this framework, and finally you have to combine the individual components to get the bottom line, the magic number that tells you how much you would spend on one particular alternative compared to others.

This chapter will give you the tools to analyze the costs of flying. It will take you step-by-step through the various cost components, and will show you why multiple ownership is such a compelling alternative to owning alone or renting commercially. It is important to become comfortable with the basic financial model developed in this chapter. It will be used throughout the book as we

Piper Aircraft Corporation, Monte Rankin

The forgiving Arrow is a good complex aircraft choice for the cooperative flying venture.

explore the various partnership and flying club alternatives, and will be your most valuable analytical tool in making your own decisions about how many partners to have and what equipment to buy.

For those of you with basic computer spreadsheet skills, appendix A-3 and A-4 shows the layout and formulas for the financial model on Excel. It is a very simple process and will enable you to run any number of scenarios by simply changing a few numbers in the assumptions.

THE FRAMEWORK OF ANALYSIS

In analyzing your flying expenses, you will select an aircraft type, you will estimate the hours you would like to fly it per year, and you will calculate what your expenses will be under several options: rental from a commercial operator, owning the airplane by yourself, and owning the airplane with a number of partners. Within your ballpark objectives, you should analyze numerous options to home in on the best deal for you. Keep an open mind. Vary the aircraft types and the number of partners liberally. And don't be surprised to find that with an extra partner or two you can afford a Beech Sierra on a budget that made you think only of a Cessna 172. That is the whole point of doing this analysis.

Any operator incurs two types of expenses when flying an airplane: fixed and operating.

Fixed expenses are expenses which you have to pay regardless of the hours flown by the airplane (such as insurance and state fees). They are commonly measured annually.

Operating expenses are expenses incurred directly as a result of operating an airplane (examples are fuel and oil). They are commonly measured hourly.

Total flying expenses (the combination of fixed and operating expenses) are measured two ways: hourly and annually.

To find out how much it costs to fly per hour, the *total hourly expenses*, divide the annual fixed expenses by the hours you plan to fly during the year (to get hourly fixed expenses), and add this amount to the hourly operating expenses. Total hourly expenses are important because this is the figure you will compare among the options you are considering to determine the least expensive hourly rate. It is also the only measure in which commercial rental rates are expressed.

To find out how much it costs you to fly for the entire year, the *total annual expenses*, multiply the total hourly expenses by the number of hours you plan to fly. Total annual expenses are important because this is the total amount you will spend for the whole year. This is the figure you will compare, option by option, with your yearly total flying budget.

Let's begin to build the financial expenses model block by block (Table 3-1). We will list the single owner and partnerships of two, three, and four. Expenses are per person. The expense numbers we will use are for a normally aspirated Piper Arrow III. The commercial rental expense will be listed later, after we have established the expenses of ownership. Let's start with fixed expenses. Note that for fixed expenses the partnership expenses are simply the single owner expense divided by the number of partners. This assumes that all partners share fixed expenses equally, which is usually the case in partnerships.

Table 3-1.

NUMBER OF PILOTS	1	2	3	4
ANNUAL FIXED EXPENSES				
Tiedown/Hangar	900.00	450.00	300.00	225.00
Insurance	1,500.00	750.00	500.00	375.00
State Fees	120.00	60.00	40.00	30.00
Annual	750.00	375.00	250.00	187.50
Maintenance	1,000.00	500.00	333.33	250.00
Loan Payments	3,443.30	1,721.65	1,147.77	860.83
Cost of Capital non-cash	1,750.00	875.00	583.33	437.50
Total Fixed Expenses / yr	9,463.30	4,731.65	3,154.43	2,365.83

Tiedown/hangar

This is simply what you pay for aircraft storage. You are usually billed monthly by the airport, so multiply the monthly fee by 12 to get this annual expense.

Insurance

This is your annual insurance bill. It can vary widely from insurer to insurer and depends upon the extent of coverage you choose and the level of experience the pilots have. Call several insurance companies for competing quotes, or work through your broker, and enter the total figure of the best quote.

State fees

This is a collective category for various state fees and taxes for the year, and will vary from state to state. Call your state aeronautics commission for the details. Typical state fees are annual registration fees and excise taxes. Your local FBO and private owners at your airport are also good sources of information if you are unfamiliar with these fees.

Annual

This is the cost of the annual inspection only. It is the flat fee your mechanic charges to inspect your type of airplane. Anything he finds that needs to be fixed is extra, and should be entered under *maintenance*. This annual expense is usually listed as a separate item on the total bill you get, including anything that had to be fixed as a result of the inspection when your airplane is annualed. It is entered separately because it is a yearly flat fee that you know you will have to spend no matter what. To obtain this figure, ask your mechanic for his annual fee for your type of aircraft.

Maintenance

There are two schools of thought on the appropriate category for maintenance expense. One holds that maintenance is strictly an operating expense, not a fixed expense, to be reserved against entirely per flying hour. The other school holds that some maintenance has to be done every year, regardless of whether or not the airplane flies. The latter school believes that some regular maintenance should be estimated every year, in addition to maintenance covered by the maintenance reserve per hour. The model presented here subscribes to the latter approach.

This category covers the costs of the maintenance work that is typically done in one year on your airplane regardless of whether it flies or not. It is an estimate, as actual maintenance expenses will vary from year to year depending on how many unforeseen expensive maintenance costs you were hit with during the

The Seguin Geronimo delivers outstanding twin performance at a bargain price.

year. Annual maintenance expenses will be higher for older aircraft and a good mechanic can usually give you some indication of any imminent major expenses as a result of normal wear and tear.

It is up to you if you want to reserve all maintenance in this category, or split it between this category and hourly engine and maintenance reserves, or reserve entirely on an hourly basis. In introducing the model, we choose to split maintenance expense between the two categories.

Loan payments

This is the amount you fork over to your friendly banker for letting you think that you own the airplane. It is your monthly bank payment multiplied by 12. To get it, call your banker and request a quote based on how much you want to borrow and for how long. This example assumes $20,000 borrowed for 10 years at prevailing interest rates, which works out to $287 per month, or $3,443 per year. Borrowing is expensive.

The Excel model has the payment formula built into it. You only enter the loan amount, interest rate, and maturity into the assumptions and the model will calculate the annual payment. Alternatively, you can use a financial calculator or call your banker for a monthly payment amount that you can multiply by 12.

Cost of capital (noncash)

For those of us who are not financiers, this item might not be immediately clear, but it is very easy and important to understand. When we bought the airplane, we put a big chunk of *capital* (often called *down payment* or *equity*) into it. Had we not bought the airplane, we would have presumably left the money in the bank, where it would have earned interest, thereby increasing in value. When we decided to buy the airplane, we accepted to forego this increase in our capital, so it is a cost. It is not a cash cost because we do not have to pay it out of our pocket. Rather, it is money that was not put in our pocket to begin with, but would have been put there had we left the money in the bank, instead of sensibly buying an airplane with it. It is an amount by which we are poorer at the end of the year, so it is an expense.

This amount is calculated by taking the capital you have in the airplane (in this case $25,000, which is the $45,000 purchase price minus the $20,000 bank loan) and figuring out how much it would have earned, had it been left in the bank (in this case $25,000 at 7 percent, the going rate for a certificate of deposit, or $21,750).

Because this is not a cash item, it is tempting to simply ignore it and many people do, but they are fooling themselves. If you ignore the cost of your capital, you are not making a realistic comparison with the commercial rental rates of your FBO.

Total fixed expenses/year

This amount is simply the total of the individual entries. To recap, total fixed expense is the amount of money you will have to spend on an airplane regardless of how little or how much you fly it.

Before we move on to the next block, hourly operating expenses, notice how dramatically fixed expenses per person decline with the increase in the number of partners (Table 3-1).

As you can see in Table 3-2, hourly operating expenses remain the same regardless of the number of partners. The airplane will eat a constant amount of fuel and oil and suffer the same wear and tear in an hour of flying regardless of how many partners own it. The figures are presented for up to four partners here because this is also how they are presented in the complete model to make the math work when you are ready to calculate total expenses. Let's consider each component of operating expenses and how it is calculated.

Table 3-2.

HOURLY OPERATING EXPENSES				
Fuel	20.00	20.00	20.00	20.00
Oil	0.13	0.13	0.13	0.13
Engine Reserve	5.00	5.00	5.00	5.00
General Maint Res	2.00	2.00	2.00	2.00
Total Op Exp / hr	27.13	27.13	27.13	27.13

Fuel

This is the amount of money your airplane burns in fuel per hour. It is calculated by taking the cost of one gallon of fuel and multiplying it by the number of gallons your airplane uses in one hour (in this case, 2×10).

Oil

This is the cost of the oil your airplane uses in one hour. It is calculated by taking the price of a quart of oil and dividing it by the number of hours your airplane takes to use one quart of oil (in this case $1/qt \div 0.13$ qt/hr).

Engine reserve

One of the biggest expenses in the life of your airplane is the overhaul of its engine at the recommended overhaul time (if you are lucky and it lasts that long). Many a pilot has been grounded because he or she didn't have the wheelbarrow full of cash that was needed for the overhaul when the time came. The engine reserve expense forestalls such an embarrassment. This amount is the money set aside for each hour of flying to build up a reserve specifically earmarked for overhauling the engine. It is a cash expense because it should be paid into a bank account where it accumulates until overhaul time. It is not intended for any engine maintenance other than overhaul, and the temptation to raid it should be resisted.

How much you decide to reserve is up to you. At a minimum you should take the cost of a major overhaul and divide it by the number of hours the engine is expected to run before overhaul. In the example, the Arrow was purchased with a zero time engine that is expected to run 2,000 hours when it will be overhauled for $10,000. So, $10,000 \div 2,000 = \$5$/hr. If you buy the airplane with 1,000 hours and it is expected to run another thousand, you would have to reserve $10 per hour. Or, you could establish a bank account with a $5,000 deposit to cover the first 1,000 hours and reserve $5 per hour for the remaining time. The choice is yours. Just don't get caught short.

General maintenance reserve

This expense is similar to the engine reserve, except it is intended to ensure the availability of funds for general maintenance and airframe refurbishment. Do not confuse this reserve with the fixed maintenance expenses that cover an estimated amount of maintenance that has to be done every year, regardless of whether or not the airplane flies. A yearly $1,000 expense is estimated for maintenance for this Arrow under fixed expenses. The $2 reserve per hour will build a maintenance reserve in addition to that. If not used, it will build a surplus to be used for maintenance and care including eventual airframe refurbishment.

This general reserve may also be more readily raided in a pinch for extraordinary expenses, such as a radio meltdown not covered by insurance.

Many people use this reserve to meet all routine maintenance expenses and stash away a much bigger amount into it. They run a surplus in years of low maintenance and replenish the account with assessments in years of high maintenance. It is a disciplined way to ensure that routine maintenance money is available when needed. If you elect to do this rather than treat a part of routine maintenance under fixed expenses, then your entry into the fixed expense maintenance budget would be zero.

Total hourly operating expenses

This figure is the sum of the components of operating expenses. This completes the definition of the expense modules.

Total hourly expenses (given number of hours flown)

We can now move on to combining the individual expenses to calculate total hourly expenses and total annual expenses and make comparisons to the commercial rental rate (Table 3-3).

Table 3-3.

TOTAL HOURLY EXPENSES				
50 Hours	216.39	121.76	90.21	74.44
100 Hours	121.76	74.44	58.67	50.78
150 Hours	90.21	58.67	48.15	42.90
Hourly Commercial Rental	90.00	90.00	90.00	90.00

To recap, total hourly expenses are the fixed expenses for the year divided into the number of hours flown during the year (to get hourly fixed expenses), plus the hourly operating expenses. Examine a three-person partnership at 50 hours: total hourly expenses per partner are $3,154.43 (the annual fixed expenses)/50 hours (the hours flown) + $27.13 (the hourly operating expenses), which equals $90.21.

Total hourly expenses will be higher if you fly fewer hours because your fixed expenses, being spread over fewer hours, will be higher per hour.

The hourly commercial rental rate is simply the rate charged by your FBO for the same type of airplane.

As you can see, owning alone you will have to fly more than 150 hours a year in this case to break even. Getting a partner significantly reduces the expenses and puts each partner comfortably ahead of the rental option at 100 hours, and three partners or more match the rental option by flying as little as 50 hours each.

Now all that remains is to see how much you will spend in total for the year under the various options, and compare these amounts to how much you have available. We will look at total annual expenses for 50, 100, and 150 hours of flying time (Table 3-4).

Table 3-4.

TOTAL ANNUAL EXPENSES

50 Hours,	Own	10819.55	6087.90	4510.68	3722.08
	Own cash only	9069.55	5212.90	3927.35	3284.58
	Rent	4500.00	4500.00	4500.00	4500.00
100 Hours,	Own	12175.80	7444.15	5866.93	5078.33
	Own cash only	10425.80	6569.15	5283.60	4640.83
	Rent	9000.00	9000.00	9000.00	9000.00
150 Hours,	Own	13532.05	8800.40	7223.18	6434.58
	Own cash only	11782.05	7925.40	6639.85	5997.08
	Rent	13500.00	13500.00	13500.00	13500.00

The total annual expenses for a given number of hours flown are the total hourly expenses for the hours flown (remember, this figure already takes into account your fixed expenses) multiplied by the hours flown. Examine the three-person partnership again: Total annual expenses for each partner flying 50 hours are $90.21 (the total hourly expenses at 50 hours flown) × 50 hours = $4,510.68.

That might be clear and straightforward, but what is this "cash only" business? This is a refinement that tells you how much cash you will spend out of pocket for the year. Remember the cost of capital (the noncash amount you are losing because your capital isn't earning money in the bank because you used it to buy the airplane)? Remember how we said this was not money out of your pocket, but money not put into your pocket? While it is costing you $4,510.68 to fly this airplane 50 hours in a three-person partnership, $583.33 of this amount is not money you are spending, but money you are not receiving. So, as long as you are willing to not receive this amount, you need only $3,927.35 in cash for the year to afford 50 hours of flying the Arrow in a three-person partnership.

The total annual expenses tell you how to best spend the cash you have for the year. Suppose you have $5,500 available in cash. For that amount, you could rent an Arrow for a little more than 50 hours. Or, with one partner, you could each fly 50 hours and avoid the restrictions and hassles of rental. Or, in a three-person partnership, you could fly 100 hours. You have just doubled your annual flying time for the same amount of cash. Is the tradeoff of having to deal with two other partners instead of just one worth it? It sure is to me, but you decide.

Now that you have become comfortable with the various blocks of the model, take a look at the next table. It is the entire model, designed to calculate your per person flying costs for groups of up to 15 people. Use copies of the blank form in appendix A-1 (Aircraft Expense Worksheet) to calculate the costs of your own personal options. Better still, turn to appendix A-3 and A-4 and set up the model on Excel or Lotus 1-2-3, or have someone do it for you (it is very easy to do for anyone who has even the most basic familiarity with spreadsheets). Once set up, all you have to do is change the handful of variables in the assumption blocks as appropriate and the spreadsheet will instantly calculate everything for you (Table 3-5).

One more important point for pilots interested in forming a flying club: As with airplane performance, a chart can be worth a thousand numbers. Take a look at Table 3-6. It charts the total hourly expenses per person of flying the Arrow for 50, 100, and 150 hours, and it reveals a trend very important to flying clubs. When you get beyond 10 people, the difference between total hourly expenses at 50 hours, 100 hours, and 150 hours is dramatically reduced. This is because the fixed expenses are spread out among so many people that the operating expenses assume a much greater portion of total expenses per person.

As we have seen, operating expenses do not change per hour and are paid by the hour every time the airplane flies. This lends itself naturally to a flying club structure where relatively low per person annual dues and fees are used to meet fixed expenses and the hourly rental rate is changed to meet operating expenses. This method ensures that fixed expenses for the year are always met, regardless of the hours flown by the aircraft, and is the key to the successful flying club.

You are now familiar with the tools of honestly calculating how much it really costs you to fly. Bear in mind that the method is important, not the numbers used here to illustrate the method. The assumptions we made are real life, but they apply to a specific neck of the woods at one particular point in time. Use them for guidance as we explore the various multiple ownership options and equipment choices, but gather the numbers relevant to your environment and make your own realistic assumptions. Be creative and inquisitive, and run the model again and again; ideally, you will find a way to afford the airplane you really want to fly.

Table 3-5.

FLYING EXPENSES PER PERSON, SINGLE ENGINE FOUR SEAT COMPLEX, 200HP.

NUMBER OF PILOTS	1	2	3	4	5	6	7	8	9	10	11	12	13	14	15
ANNUAL FIXED EXPENSES															
Tiedown/Hangar	900.00	450.00	300.00	225.00	180.00	150.00	128.57	112.50	100.00	90.00	81.82	75.00	69.23	64.29	60.00
Insurance	1,500.00	750.00	500.00	375.00	300.00	250.00	214.29	187.50	166.67	150.00	136.36	125.00	115.38	107.14	100.00
State Fees	120.00	60.00	40.00	30.00	24.00	20.00	17.14	15.00	13.33	12.00	10.91	10.00	9.23	8.57	8.00
Annual	750.00	375.00	250.00	187.50	150.00	125.00	107.14	93.75	83.33	75.00	68.18	62.50	57.69	53.57	50.00
Maintenance	1,000.00	500.00	333.33	250.00	200.00	166.67	142.86	125.00	111.11	100.00	90.91	83.33	76.92	71.43	66.67
Loan Payments	3,443.30	1,721.65	1,147.77	860.83	688.66	573.88	491.90	430.41	382.59	344.33	313.03	286.94	264.87	245.95	229.55
Cost of Capital (non-cash)	1,750.00	875.00	583.33	437.50	350.00	291.67	250.00	218.75	194.44	175.00	159.09	145.83	134.62	125.00	116.67
Total Fixed Expenses / yr	9,463.30	4,731.65	3,154.43	2,365.83	1,892.66	1,577.22	1,351.90	1,182.91	1,051.48	946.33	860.30	788.61	727.95	675.95	630.89
HOURLY OPERATING EXPENSES															
Fuel	20.00	20.00	20.00	20.00	20.00	20.00	20.00	20.00	20.00	20.00	20.00	20.00	20.00	20.00	20.00
Oil	0.13	0.13	0.13	0.13	0.13	0.13	0.13	0.13	0.13	0.13	0.13	0.13	0.13	0.13	0.13
Engine Reserve	5.00	5.00	5.00	5.00	5.00	5.00	5.00	5.00	5.00	5.00	5.00	5.00	5.00	5.00	5.00
General Maint Res	2.00	2.00	2.00	2.00	2.00	2.00	2.00	2.00	2.00	2.00	2.00	2.00	2.00	2.00	2.00
Total Op Exp / hr	27.13	27.13	27.13	27.13	27.13	27.13	27.13	27.13	27.13	27.13	27.13	27.13	27.13	27.13	27.13
TOTAL HOURLY EXPENSES															
50 Hours	216.40	121.76	90.22	74.45	64.98	58.67	54.17	50.79	48.16	46.06	44.34	42.90	41.69	40.65	39.75
100 Hours	121.76	74.45	58.67	50.79	46.06	42.90	40.65	38.96	37.64	36.59	35.73	35.02	34.41	33.89	33.44
150 Hours	90.22	58.67	48.16	42.90	39.75	37.64	36.14	35.02	34.14	33.44	32.87	32.39	31.98	31.64	31.34
Hourly Commercial Rental	90.00	90.00	90.00	90.00	90.00	90.00	90.00	90.00	90.00	90.00	90.00	90.00	90.00	90.00	90.00
TOTAL ANNUAL EXPENSES															
50 Hours, Own	10819.80	6008.15	4510.93	3722.33	3249.16	2933.72	2708.40	2539.41	2407.98	2302.83	2216.80	2145.11	2084.45	2032.45	1987.39
Own (cash only)	9069.80	5213.15	3927.60	3284.83	2899.16	2642.05	2458.40	2320.66	2213.53	2127.83	2057.71	1999.28	1949.83	1907.45	1870.72
Rent	4500.00	4500.00	4500.00	4500.00	4500.00	4500.00	4500.00	4500.00	4500.00	4500.00	4500.00	4500.00	4500.00	4500.00	4500.00
100 Hours, Own	12176.30	7444.65	5867.43	5078.83	4605.66	4290.22	4064.90	3895.91	3764.48	3659.33	3573.30	3501.61	3440.95	3388.95	3343.89
Own (cash only)	10426.30	6569.65	5284.10	4641.33	4255.66	3998.55	3814.90	3677.16	3570.03	3484.33	3414.21	3355.78	3306.33	3263.95	3227.22
Rent	9000.00	9000.00	9000.00	9000.00	9000.00	9000.00	9000.00	9000.00	9000.00	9000.00	9000.00	9000.00	9000.00	9000.00	9000.00
150 Hours, Own	13532.80	8801.15	7223.93	6435.33	5962.16	5646.72	5421.40	5252.41	5120.98	5015.83	4929.80	4858.11	4797.45	4745.45	4700.39
Own (cash only)	11782.80	7926.15	6640.60	5997.83	5612.16	5355.05	5173.40	5033.66	4926.53	4840.83	4770.71	4712.28	4662.83	4620.45	4583.72
Rent	13500.00	13500.00	13500.00	13500.00	13500.00	13500.00	13500.00	13500.00	13500.00	13500.00	13500.00	13500.00	13500.00	13500.00	13500.00

ASSUMPTIONS:

Hangar/Month:	75.00	Insurance/yr:	1500.00	State Fees/yr:	120.00	Annual:	750.00
Fuel Cons (gal/hr):	10.00	Fuel Cost ($/gal):	2.00	Oil Cons (qt/hr):	0.13	Oil Cost ($/qt):	1.00
Aircraft Value:	45000.00	Loan O/S:	20000.00	Loan Interest Rate:	12.00%	Loan/Inv Term (yrs):	10
Engine MOH Cost:	10000.00	Gen Maint Res/hr:	2.00	Com. Rental/hr:	90.00		

Maintenance/yr:	1000.00
Time Before OH:	2000.00
Cost of Capital Rate:	7.00%

Table 3-6.

Total Hourly Aircraft Expenses, Per Pilot Per Hour Flown

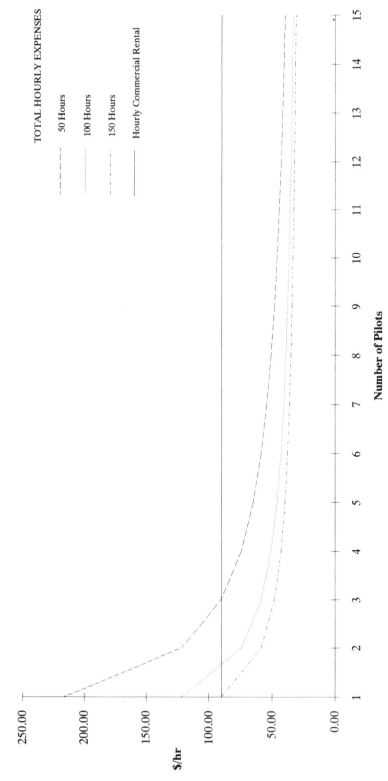

4

Partnership or flying club?

YOU HAVE SEEN THE NUMBERS and you like what they tell you. You are convinced that through some cooperative arrangement you, too, can fly in a manner that would be beyond your reach on your own. But to be successful, a cooperative flying arrangement must be analyzed and planned just as carefully as any major decision. In fact, it is a more complex task to evaluate cooperative flying options than to assess your choices as sole owner. In addition to equipment and financial considerations, you now have to also evaluate the human factor, compatibility with your potential partners or fellow club members. Sole ownership is "I, me, and myself." Partnerships and flying clubs are "us." The difference cannot be emphasized enough. Flexibility, tolerance, respect for group decisions and the needs of all members, and the ability to deliver on commitments made are essential to successful group flying. There are also limits to flexibility and tolerance; how well you fit into a particular group is so important. If you go berserk when someone leaves the fuel strainer in the left-side pocket instead of the right-side pocket, you shouldn't even think of joining the Flying Pigpens.

In evaluating your options it is important to first clearly define your goals: What would you like in equipment, and what commitment do you want to make in financial resources and time? An understanding of these objectives will enable you to decide if a partnership or a flying club is more suitable for you. Once you choose in principle between partnership or club, the real work of organizing one or finding one with the best fit begins. It is at this stage that analyzing the human factors becomes as important as equipment, financial, and time commitment considerations.

In this chapter, we ask the key questions that will help you evaluate if a partnership or a flying club would best meet your needs. Similar chapters in the aircraft partnerships and flying clubs sections of this book will then ask further questions in more detail about options within these forms of cooperative flying. This will help you focus on all the important considerations in making your ultimate choice.

How much money do I want to spend as an initial investment?

The answer to this question might decide the issue for you right up front. While a partnership saves a bundle over sole ownership, you still have to shell out thousands of dollars just to buy your piece of the airplane. A flying club, on the other hand, requires a much smaller individual investment, even if you have to buy a share of it. If you are forming a new flying club with 10 to 15 members, the initial individual contributions will be well below the amount required per person in a two to four person partnership for the same airplane. If you decide to join an established flying club, chances are that initiation fees will be minimal compared to a partnership investment.

How many hours would I like to fly annually?

Partnership expenses per hour decline substantially as the number of hours you fly per year increases. Flying club hourly rental expenses are constant, and because of the low capital investment and modest monthly fees, the total hourly expenses per person hardly decline with an increase in hours; thus, if you plan to fly only a modest number of hours per year, the per hour costs of a partnership might be more than you want to spend even if you are willing to cough up the initial investment; you might get more for your money in a flying club.

How much money do I want to spend annually on upkeep and other costs?

Annual expenses beyond the initial capital expenditure are an important consideration. You might have the capital to invest, but do you have the money to fork over year after year for your partnership share of insurance, taxes, fried radios, misbehaving airplane bits, and the ever increasing cost of annuals? Sure, you might also face an assessment in a flying club for a major expense, but it would be so much less because it is spread around so much more.

What kind of flying do I want to do?

Do you want an airplane at your beck and call on a moment's notice for week-long trips to the hinterland? A small partnership with flexible partners might be the best choice for you. Or do you want to go on frequent, short, local flights or longer trips with notice given far in advance? Then a flying club might be equally accommodating for lower expenses. Do you want to fly fewer hours in a complex airplane such as a Bonanza or a Seneca, instead of a lot of hours in a Warrior? It might be possible in a specialty flying club, or a very big flying club with a lot of airplanes for the same amount of money you would spend on the Warrior partnership.

The sporty, economical TR-2 is a delight to fly for pilots who enjoy the challenge of precise handling.

Do I want to fly a variety of airplanes?

If you want access to a variety of airplanes, a well established flying club with a big fleet might be a better alternative than a partnership. Or you might want to round up a greater number of pilots and form a new flying club with more than one airplane.

Am I prepared to volunteer my time to help set up and run a flying club?

A flying club might serve your purposes better than a partnership, but to set one up is a big job. It might require a much greater time commitment from its officers than a small partnership requires of its partners. If you join an already established club and are content to submit yourself to its hopefully enthusiastic and diligent officers, this might not be an issue. But if you are going to take an active role in setting up a flying club from scratch, stand by to spend most of your free time doing it for at least the first year or two.

Can I accept decisions by an elected board of directors, or do I want to be directly involved in decisions?

Flying clubs are not actual democracies. Sure, you elect the officers, but once elected, they make all the important decisions during their term, and there is no congress or judiciary to provide checks and balances. You might get elected yourself to influence decisions, but that is a big commitment. Or you might vote them out of office at the next election if enough members are as unhappy with them as you are, but during their term, you generally have to live with whatever they decide. You could vote with your feet, but then you wouldn't be flying and who wants that? The point is that flying clubs are inevitably somewhat political. If this is in line with your personality, you are all set. But if you are generally fed up with politicians at work and at the local, state, and federal level, a small, compatible partnership might be a better alternative.

Are there enough like-minded people around me who would want to form a flying club?

Even if the flying club alternative appears more attractive, you have to have enough interested people to form one. Resist the temptation to approach people who don't fully meet your flying standards, just to get the membership figure up to where you want it. The ensuing headaches would take a lot of the fun out of what you are supposedly doing for fun.

Are there any flying clubs in my area that would meet my needs?

If the flying club option makes more sense to you, check around carefully to see what clubs already operate in your area. Forming a new club is a much bigger job than joining an established, well run organization that meets your needs.

Are there any partnerships in my area looking for new members?

The same is true for partnerships. If one fits the bill and is looking for an additional partner, joining it might be a convenient shortcut to rustling up potential partners and finding an airplane to buy. But beware of the human factor—Will I fit into a group already accustomed to each other?—and treat your investment in the partnership's airplane as the brand new purchase it is.

Part II
Partnerships

5

Ask the right questions

WHEN WE EXPLORED THE CHOICE between partnership or flying club, we asked a series of questions to help us decide which of these forms of cooperative flying best suited our needs. But our decision was only the beginning. It merely set us up to explore in greater detail the options within our choice to find the best solution in view of our flying goals, budget, and personality.

The questions below are presented by topic, and selected questions are equally valid in several categories. They will help you focus on all the important aspects of forming or joining an aircraft partnership. They will get you on the right track. Consider them carefully and be innovative. Form further questions of your own. The more thoughtful questions you ask, the more informed your ultimate decision will be.

The best way to use this section is to read it before doing any serious analysis and planning of a partnership; get a flavor for the things to consider. Don't be too concerned if you are unsure about the answers; subsequent chapters offer the tools to figure them out. Then, as your partnership takes shape, refer to the questions again, and have your potential partners answer them independently. Iron out the small differences in your respective responses and beware of the big ones.

THE AIRPLANE

What kind of an airplane do I want? We all have a favorite airplane we would like to own and fly. Don't be constrained by cost when you first answer this question. You are considering a partnership to see if you can find a way to fly your dream airplane regardless of cost. So, think big. Choose the airplane you have always wanted and see if you can build a partnership around it to make the dollars and cents work.

Ask yourself if the airplane you want is suited for the kind of flying you plan to do. Do you mostly want to fly long distances, work on ratings, or cruise over the neighborhood? An aerobatic biplane might have great sex appeal but it might not be the best choice for long cross-country trips with your spouse, unless you

The Aerospatiale Tobago is steadily increasing in popularity since its introduction from France in the 1980s.

are both the barnstorming type. Alternatively, you might soon tire of the six-seat Cherokee if your family isn't interested in touring and your partners only want to fly to the local coffee shops. This is not to say that utility alone should be the deciding factor. Just be fully aware of the compromises you might be making.

Be realistic about your flying skills and compare that to the airplane that your heart and soul want. Be honest with yourself about the additional training you might need, and be willing and able to learn.

How much equipment do I want in the airplane now, and later? Extra equipment is expensive. It can dramatically increase the cost of a basic airplane. It also might be a bone of contention among partners. You might not want the $5,000 loran package for the weekend VFR flying you plan to do. But your partner, who will fly on business during the week, rain or shine, might think otherwise. It is generally easy to establish initial equipment standards based on need and the size of your purse when you buy the airplane.

Where a partnership is more likely to experience friction is on deferred equipment purchases. Caught up in the excitement of buying the airplane, it is tempting to say that you will worry about buying new avionics later, just to close the deal. But are you putting off the decision about additional equipment, or are you in agreement on what to get later and when to get it? The distinction is important. If it is the decision you put off, you might be setting up the partnership for a disagreement later.

Do I have any special requirements of the airplane? Are you going to use the airplane for any special purpose such as aerial photography or towing gliders? Do you need a tow hook, or do you want to cut camera ports into the fuselage? Assess the additional cost and effort of meeting any special requirements, and make sure your partners are fully aware of your intentions.

The sleek Mooney MSE is the latest in the long line of these highest performance four seaters.

FINANCES

How much do I have to invest in the airplane? We have already addressed this question briefly when we made the choice between partnership and flying club. Now is the time to sharpen your pencil and come up with a final figure for how much you have available to invest in the airplane. This figure should be strictly the amount you are willing to fork over on day one to buy the airplane. The annual cost of operating it should be considered separately.

How much financing am I willing to consider? If your partnership's resources are insufficient to buy the airplane of your choice and you are unwilling to increase the number of partners, you can still avoid going downmarket if you are willing to finance part of the airplane. A number of banks nationwide specialize in aircraft finance, and individual pilots with excess money to invest might also be a source of financing. Partners might finance other partners. Recognize two potential drawbacks to financing the partnership: it is expensive (interest payments are the hefty premium for using someone else's money), and it might make partners liable for each other's financial performance (if you can't pay your share, the bank can go after your partners). If one partner finances others in the partnership, the borrowing partners might feel like second-class citizens.

Financing the partnership is a viable option, but be sure to understand the additional costs and obligations it requires.

Would I accept financing from other partners, or would I be willing to finance them? When not all partners have the cash to buy the airplane, one partner might offer to finance another rather than go to a bank. The bank will want all partners to be liable for the loan and will want to take the airplane as collateral. The partner who has enough cash to pay for his share of the airplane and to finance another partner might not wish to cosign for a loan from a bank for a variety of reasons, and might not want to see the bank take the airplane as collateral. The downside of one partner financing the other is potential friction in operating the partnership because of the direct financial obligation.

If you do finance a partner or accept financing from one, do it only under commercial terms and conditions, and document the arrangement with a loan agreement put together by a lawyer.

How much can I spend annually on the airplane? The amount of money you and your partners have to invest defines the kind of airplane you can afford to buy. The amount of money you can spend on it annually tells you if you can afford to keep it flying. You should have a good idea of the annual lump sum you can spend on flying before you carefully analyze how much you need to spend under a variety of partnership scenarios to fly the airplane of your choice.

Will my annual budget allow me the amount of flying I want? You might find that your annual budget allows you to fly the airplane, but not as much as you would like. If this is the case, you have to decide between quality and quantity. You may accept fewer flying hours, or you may go down market or increase the number of partners to cut the costs per hour.

PARTNERSHIP STRUCTURE

How many partners do I need to fly the airplane I want? Once you have an idea of your budget and you run the numbers on the total costs of buying and flying the airplane you want, it will become clear to you how many partners you will need to make the partnership work financially. If this number coincides with the number of partners you had in mind independent of financial considerations, you are all set. If not, it is time to tweak the numbers and review options until you find the best compromise.

Do I want all partners to own equal shares of the airplane? Occasionally a group of individuals would so much like to fly an airplane that not all of them can equally afford, that a more well-off partner might be willing to own a larger share of the airplane. In principle, this is a good solution because everyone ends up flying an airplane that otherwise none of them could afford, even in partnership. But in practice it might spell trouble. For the partners who invested less, this arrangement sounds like a free lunch, and we all know there is no such thing. Inevitably, the partner with the greater investment will expect some form of repayment, be it a greater say in decisions, explicit or implicit scheduling preference, or extra work on the airplane by the other partners.

In spite of the potential pitfalls, this form of ownership can work well under certain conditions. It can be especially successful when the partner with the lower share has a skill from which the partnership can benefit. A&P mechanics and instructors often are welcomed minority partners. It can also work well for related partners who have a good family relationship beyond the partnership. A brother or sister that flies a lot on business during the week might be happy to let another sibling fly on the weekends on a minority share. The trick is to clearly establish the rules.

Should partners pay annual fixed expenses such as insurance and tie down pro rata according to time flown, or in equal shares? If the amount of time partners fly the airplane varies greatly, the payment of annual fixed expenses becomes an issue. By paying equal amounts, do partners who fly less subsidize partners who fly more? One school of thought says yes, and recommends a pro rata splitting of these costs, which can be a formidable administrative task. Another school of thought says no, on the theory that these expenses are a cost of owning the airplane regardless of how much you fly, and should be borne equally. It is up to you and your partners to choose.

How do I want to keep track of expenses, and who will do the accounting? Expenses can be done on the back of an envelope, which will drive most partners crazy, and it can be done on an accounting software program with weekly statements in triplicate. The practical answer lies somewhere in the middle. Accounts are important and one partner should be in charge of keeping the numbers. All partners should agree on how the accounts should be maintained, and the partner keeping them shouldn't hesitate to request assistance if the numbers begin to get the better of him. Keeping the accounts accurately and up to date requires a lot of discipline and not everyone is cut out for the job. Be patient with the partner saddled with the task, but don't let it get out of hand.

Do I want to resolve partnership disputes by simple majority or consensus? This is a very important question, and a matter of choice. If the partners' personalities can handle simple or two thirds majority with no hard feelings, it makes the resolution of disputes easy. A unanimous (consensus) decision might be more difficult to obtain, but leaves far less room for hard feelings.

Do I want to hold regularly scheduled partnership meetings, or are sporadic ''as needed'' meetings enough? This is a matter of choice. Larger partnerships might want regularly scheduled meetings, small ones can easily meet informally at the airport coffee shop. Just make sure all partners are on the same wavelength.

INSURANCE

How much insurance do I want on the airplane? The partners have to agree on the amount of insurance coverage they want on the airplane. Agreement on hull insurance, the replacement cost of the airplane, is usually easy to agree upon. Liability insurance can be more ticklish. The more protection you want from liability lawsuits, the higher the rate. The more personal assets that you have to protect (property that the courts would confiscate to compensate a victim) the higher level of liability insurance you will want. A partner worth considerably less than another might be reluctant to pay for high liability coverage.

Insurance premiums can be an issue when one partner is in a higher risk category than another partner because of less experience, age, or detrimental record of any sort. You may work out a pro rata arrangement, or you might find it simpler to split the cost equally anyway. The choice is yours, just make sure you are all comfortably in agreement with whatever you decide.

Another insurance issue to consider is whether any of the partners plans to use the airplane for commercial purposes from which he alone benefits. Commercial rates are considerably higher than noncommercial rates, and you will certainly want to work out some pro rata arrangement.

OPERATIONS AND SAFETY

When and for how long at a time will I and my partners use the airplane from a scheduling standpoint? It is important to have a general idea of airplane use patterns because if conflicts arise, the partnership will quickly break down. Be especially careful to assess intended use during the weekends. Some pilots like frequent short flights on the weekend, others like to take turns disappearing with the airplane for the whole weekend.

Be on the lookout for potential partners whose need for the airplane is complementary to yours. If you are a weekend flyer try to find someone who flies mostly during the week.

What arrangement will we have to pay for fuel? How will we ensure that each partner pays for the fuel he or she used? This is an important detail. Mixups about fuel charges and empty tanks when full tanks are expected are a major source of headaches for partnerships; however, alternatives are available. Make sure that all partners are comfortable with the selected method and are committed to observing it.

Am I comfortable with my partners' intended use of the airplane? The issue (short of illegal use) is one of wear and tear. If your flying is mostly leisurely touring, do you want a partner who will use the airplane mostly for training? Would you feel comfortable allowing a partner to tow gliders in an airplane that you wanted to fly aerobatically?

Do I have a problem with allowing qualified nonpartners borrowing the airplane from time to time? This can be a tricky question because it means lending your airplane to friends or friends of your partners from time to time. The benefit to you is marginal because unless you are commercially insured, you cannot accept any compensation for wear and tear. On the other hand, a partner might have a special relationship with someone outside the partnership to whom loan of the airplane is warranted. A potential problem outside the partnership is where do you draw the line? If you lend to one friend, why not the others? It is perhaps best to have a strict policy of not lending the airplane to nonpartners.

Allowing qualified nonpartners to do the flying when you or another partner are also on board in a pilot's seat is easier to deal with. Just check insurance implications and have well established procedures for the accompanying partner to assume control at any time—"I have the airplane."

MAINTENANCE

Do I want to work on the airplane or have a shop do everything on it? This is a question of expense. Many partnerships come to grief over arguments about unnecessary or unnecessarily expensive maintenance. Handing the airplane keys to the flashiest FBO on the field at annual time or in case of trouble is fine as long as every member feels that way and the partnership has a mountain of money. It is wise to have a clause in the partnership agreement that requires the partners to consult with each other before committing the partnership to an expense that exceeds a particular amount.

THE HUMAN FACTOR

Do I have a lot of time to devote to the partnership? Do I want to be at the airport a lot, fussing over the airplane? This is a time and a personality issue. If you have less time to spend taking care of the airplane than your partners expected, you could have a problem. If you are the kind of person who constantly finds something on the airplane to fuss over instead of flying it, and your partners are not, they might become annoyed with you.

Do I want to constantly add equipment to the airplane? Are you one of these people who always is on the lookout for the newest gizmo with which to adorn the panel at great cost? Your partners might be happy with the way the airplane is equipped, and they might not be in a financial position to fork over a check every time you visit the pilot shop. If you are a gadget freak, be sure to find like-minded partners.

Are the aesthetics of the airplane important to me? This is an important personality question. If you want to rush out and get a paint job or an interior because the old one is beginning to fade, you will not be happy with partners who take good mechanical care of the airplane but care little about aesthetic appearance.

Am I a detail-oriented letter of the law fussbudget, or do I just want to get the job done? Within the letter of the law a variety of alternatives are available in flying the airplane and taking care of it. Flying is a schizophrenic affair. It demands engineering precision from people with an artistic bent. To fly a 747 by the numbers is engineering. To fly a Stearman well is art. To some degree, all of us who fly are combined engineers and artists. But too much of one personality can aggravate too much of the other. If you are intolerant of equally accepted alternative in-flight procedures to the procedures that you prefer, if you insist that the seat belt straps be just so when you leave the airplane, or if you are sensitive about the tie-down knots, be sure to get like-minded partners.

Am I laid back about scheduling, or do I want a highly structured scheduling system? Depending upon the use of the airplane and the number of partners, informal phone calls to schedule the airplane might suffice, or you might need a rigid booking system. Be sure to understand your needs and also your preferences. Some pilots like a formal scheduling system even when an informal arrangement would do. Others prefer to muddle through even when they should have a well organized answering service.

What skills do I and my partners bring to the partnership? This is a very important question. Partners with applicable skills can save a partnership a bundle. Perhaps the ideal partnership is between an A&P mechanic, a lawyer, an accountant, an avionics technician, and a CFII. You get the idea. Be on the lookout for potential partners who are mechanically inclined or are good with numbers and accounts, or have ratings from which other partners can also benefit.

Would I feel comfortable with partners who are considerably more experienced than I am? Less experienced partners can learn a lot from partners with more experience, but, depending upon the respective personalities, might end up feeling stifled and ill at ease instead. Pay particular attention to personality issues if there is big difference in experience levels among partners.

Would I feel comfortable with partners who are much better off financially than I am? Partners who are well to do and are quick to spend freely might make you feel uncomfortable if you are in a different financial league, even if they have the best intentions.

Do I want to socialize with my partners, or do I want the partnership primarily for financial convenience? It is worthwhile for all partners to have similar attitudes about socializing with one another. Otherwise it is inevitable that someone will be the odd person out.

Are my potential partners' answers to these questions in line with mine? This, perhaps, is the most important question of them all. Potential partners should answer the questions independently and everyone should get together in a group to compare notes.

6

Analyze the numbers

TOOLS FOR ANALYZING AIRCRAFT COSTS are presented in chapter 3. This chapter demonstrates by example how to employ these tools with the greatest degree of flexibility to ensure maximum coverage of the partnership options available to you for a given amount of money. The computer spreadsheet extends to 15 pilots, but to keep things simple, the examples presented here are for up to six partners. All the examples share basic assumptions:

- Hangar/tiedown per month: $80
- State fees per year: $120
- Fuel costs: $2/gal
- Oil costs: $2.50/qt
- Loan outstanding: 50 percent of aircraft purchase price
- Loan interest rate: 10 percent
- Loan maturity: 10 years
- Cost of capital: 7 percent

To demonstrate how loan payments enter into the equation, it is assumed that 50 percent of the purchase price is borrowed, a fairly common practice in partnerships. The rest of the assumptions are entered for each aircraft separately at the bottom of each table.

From the standpoint of acquiring the aircraft, the common link is purchase price, the amount of capital required per partner per option. From the standpoint of operating the partnership, the common link, the bottom line, is total hourly expense per option:

(Per partner annual fixed expenses ÷ number of hours flown) + hourly operating expenses, shown for 50 hours, 100 hours, and 150 hours per partner.

Five basic ways to examine options are calculated. The simplest case, and a good place to start, is investigating one airplane type to determine how the costs per partner are reduced as the number of partners increases. You can assess how much that Skyhawk will cost with two, three, or four partners.

The second option is to take a given number of partners and determine the per partner costs of a variety of airplanes. If there are three of you, you can determine how much it would cost to get a Sierra instead of a Musketeer.

The third option is to intermingle the first two choices, by comparing different aircraft types for a different number of partners. This option allows you to see if a Mooney with five partners is going to cost the same as a Skyhawk with two partners, for the same number of hours flown.

The fourth option is a variation of the third option. You compare different types of aircraft for a different number of partners, but for a different number of hours flown. This alternative enables you to compare the costs of flying the Mooney with five partners for 50 hours per year per partner to flying the Skyhawk with two partners for 100 hours per year each.

The fifth option is to compare the costs of different aircraft types, all of which deliver the same performance. If your objective is to fly four seats at 120 knots, this analysis helps you identify the least costly choice from among all the aircraft types out there fitting your requirement. An early Arrow II will perhaps do just as well as a later model Sierra, for considerably less.

A word about the numbers used in the examples: Particular aircraft types have been in production or were in production for years or decades and are on the used market at a wide range of prices. In addition, aircraft prices and the costs of operating, insuring, and caring for them fluctuate significantly over the years. The numbers presented are real-world and at one time applied to particular aircraft chosen from the wide selection available on the used market; however, the numbers might not necessarily represent current conditions. They demonstrate how to perform an analysis with your up-to-date numbers.

One aircraft type
Given number of hours flown per partner
Variable number of partners

A most common scenario for developing a partnership is for a pilot to decide that the only way he or she can continue to afford to fly is by getting together with a group of partners to share the costs. Such a pilot will often have a good idea of the equipment he or she wants and the number of hours he or she would like to fly it per year and needs to see how many partners it would take to accomplish those objectives. This process is similar to the analysis done when the model was introduced.

Table 6-1 is an example of analyzing the costs of a Skyhawk for up to six partners. Let's see what it says.

If you want to get into the Skyhawk under these assumptions, the capital you need to come up with drops off markedly as you get beyond three partners. Alone, you would need a whopping $14,000. With three other partners you each need only $3,500; a big difference.

From an operating standpoint, if you fly only 50 hours per year, you approach break-even in a three-way partnership in comparison to the rental alternative, and four partners are well ahead of the game.

Table 6-1.

Aircraft: C-172 NUMBER OF PILOTS	1	2	3	4	5	6
INVESTMENT REQUIRED	14,000.00	7,000.00	4,667.00	3,500.00	2,800.00	2,334.00
ANNUAL FIXED EXPENSES						
Tiedown/Hangar	960.00	480.00	320.00	240.00	192.00	160.00
Insurance	1,000.00	500.00	333.33	250.00	200.00	166.67
State Fees	120.00	60.00	40.00	30.00	24.00	20.00
Annual	550.00	275.00	183.33	137.50	110.00	91.67
Maintenance	1,300.00	650.00	433.33	325.00	260.00	216.67
Loan Payments	2,220.13	1,110.07	740.04	555.03	444.03	370.02
Cost of Capital non-cash	980.00	490.00	326.67	245.00	196.00	163.33
Total Fixed Expenses / yr	7,130.13	3,565.07	2,376.71	1,782.53	1,426.03	1,188.36
HOURLY OPERATING EXPENSES						
Fuel	16.00	16.00	16.00	16.00	16.00	16.00
Oil	0.31	0.31	0.31	0.31	0.31	0.31
Engine Reserve	5.50	5.50	5.50	5.50	5.50	5.50
General Maint Res	2.50	2.50	2.50	2.50	2.50	2.50
Total Op Exp / hr	24.31	24.31	24.31	24.31	24.31	24.31
TOTAL HOURLY EXPENSES						
50 Hours	166.92	95.61	71.85	59.96	52.83	48.08
100 Hours	95.61	59.96	48.08	42.14	38.57	36.20
150 Hours	71.85	48.08	40.16	36.20	33.82	32.23
Hourly Commercial Rental	65.00	65.00	65.00	65.00	65.00	65.00

ASSUMPTIONS:	C-172
Aircraft Value:	28,000
Loan Amount	14,000
Insurance/yr:	1,000
Annual:	550
Maintenance/yr:	1300
Fuel Cons gal/hr :	8.0
Oil Cons qt/hr :	0.13
Engine Reserve/hr:	5.50
Gen Maint Res/hr:	2.50
Time Before OH hrs :	2,000
Engine MOH Cost:	11,000

How about getting more partners into the group, and further cutting expenses? With six partners you each save only $1,166 on the amount of capital investment necessary, and on 50 hours of annual flying time the hourly rate drops by approximately $12, or $600 per year. So, for $1,766 the first year and

The classic Cessna 150/152 will remain the ideal low-cost trainer for years to come.

Enough partners would make this F-33 Bonanza affordable for you on a budget that you thought would buy much less.

$600 per year in subsequent years, you face the trade-off of competing for airplane availability with five other pilots instead of only three. This might be worth it to you, but the savings are diminishing in comparison to going from sole owner to three or four partners. It might be worth dredging up the extra money instead.

Given number of partners
Given number of hours flown per partner
Several types of aircraft

This scenario is another typical way in which partnerships are created. A number of pilots know they want to be partners and want to see what would be the hottest airplane they could afford (Table 6-2).

This scenario is also quite straightforward. For a given number of partners and flying hours, the more airplane you want to fly, the more it will cost. It doesn't take that much more to get into the Skyhawk instead of the Skipper, but quite a bit more to jump up to an Arrow and a lot more to get into the Mooney. On an operating basis, in comparison to the equivalent rental alternative, you have to fly at least 50 hours in each case to approach break even in this case.

So, what if you hanker for something this combination just doesn't do for you. Keep analyzing alternatives.

Several types of aircraft
Variable number of partners
Similar number of hours flown per type

Let's say you can afford a Skyhawk in a two-way partnership, but would like something more. As could be seen from the example above, stepping up in equipment with the same number of partners is expensive. The key is increasing the number of partners as well as stepping up in equipment (Table 6-3).

Now we are getting somewhere. Four partners can acquire an Arrow for a capital investment $1,375 less per partner than two partners need for a Skyhawk. If you are willing to increase the number of partners in your group to six, you can get a Bonanza for the same amount of capital needed for an Arrow, and less than you need for the Skyhawk.

Operationally, you are also better off in the Arrow in a four-pilot partnership than in the Skyhawk with one other partner; however, the more expensive Bonanza will eat approximately $30 per hour more of each partner's money than the other alternatives. At 50 hours per year, this means an additional $1,500. That extra expense might be worth it to fly a Bonanza instead of a Skyhawk.

Table 6-2.

	Skipper	Skyhawk	Arrow	Mooney
NUMBER OF PILOTS	3	3	3	3
INVESTMENT REQUIRED	2,500.00	4,667.00	7,500.00	10,833.00
ANNUAL FIXED EXPENSES				
Tiedown/Hangar	320.00	320.00	320.00	320.00
Insurance	250.00	333.33	500.00	666.67
State Fees	40.00	40.00	40.00	40.00
Annual	150.00	183.33	250.00	333.33
Maintenance	300.00	433.33	500.00	666.67
Loan Payments	396.45	740.04	1,189.36	1,717.96
Cost of Capital non-cash	175.00	326.67	525.00	758.33
Total Fixed Expenses / yr	1,631.45	2,376.71	3,324.36	4,502.96
HOURLY OPERATING EXPENSES				
Fuel	13.00	16.00	21.00	21.00
Oil	0.31	0.31	0.33	0.33
Engine Reserve	5.00	5.50	7.50	10.00
General Maint Res	2.00	2.50	3.00	4.50
Total Op Exp / hr	20.31	24.31	31.83	35.83
TOTAL HOURLY EXPENSES				
50 Hours	52.94	71.85	98.31	125.88
100 Hours	36.63	48.08	65.07	80.85
150 Hours	31.19	40.16	53.99	65.84
Hourly Commercial Rental	50.00	65.00	95.00	120.00

ASSUMPTIONS:	Skipper	Skyhawk	Arrow	Mooney
Aircraft Value:	15,000	28,000	45,000	65,000
Loan Amount	7,500	14,000	22,500	32,500
Insurance/yr:	750	1,000	1,500	2,000
Annual:	450	550	750	1,000
Maintenance/yr:	900	1300	1,500	2,000
Fuel Cons gal/hr :	6.5	8.0	10.5	10.5
Oil Cons qt/hr :	0.13	0.13	0.13	0.13
Engine Reserve/hr:	5.00	5.50	7.50	10.00
Gen Maint Res/hr:	2.00	2.50	3.00	4,50
Time Before OH hrs :	2,000	2,000	2,000	1,800
Engine MOH Cost:	10,000	11,000	15,000	18,000

Table 6-3.

	Skyhawk	Arrow	Bonanza
NUMBER OF PILOTS	2	4	6
INVESTMENT REQUIRED	7,000.00	5,625.00	5,416.00
ANNUAL FIXED EXPENSES			
Tiedown/Hangar	480.00	240.00	160.00
Insurance	500.00	375.00	366.67
State Fees	60.00	30.00	20.00
Annual	275.00	187.50	166.67
Maintenance	650.00	375.00	500.00
Loan Payments	1,110.07	892.02	1,321.51
Cost of Capital non-cash	490.00	393.75	583.33
Total Fixed Expenses / yr	3,565.07	2,493.27	3,118.17
HOURLY OPERATING EXPENSES			
Fuel	16.00	21.00	30.00
Oil	0.31	0.33	0.63
Engine Reserve	5.50	7.50	13.13
General Maint Res	2.50	3.00	6.00
Total Op Exp / hr	24.31	31.83	49.75
TOTAL HOURLY EXPENSES			
50 Hours	95.61	81.69	112.11
100 Hours	59.96	56.76	80.93
150 Hours	48.08	48.45	70.54
Hourly Commercial Rental	65.00	95.00	145.00

ASSUMPTIONS:	Skyhawk	Arrow	Bonanza
Aircraft Value:	28,000	45,000	100,000
Loan Amount	14,000	22,500	50,000
Insurance/yr:	1,000	1,500	2,200
Annual:	550	750	1,000
Maintenance/yr:	1300	1,500	3,000
Fuel Cons gal/hr :	8.0	10.5	15.0
Oil Cons qt/hr :	0.13	0.13	0.25
Engine Reserve/hr:	5.50	7.50	13.13
Gen Maint Res/hr:	2.50	3.00	6.0
Time Before OH hrs :	2,000	2,000	1,600
Engine MOH Cost:	11,000	15,000	21,000

Several types of aircraft
Variable number of partners
Different number of hours flown per type

Let's say your analysis shows that you have the financial resources to fly the Skyhawk in the preceding example (Table 6-3) for 100 hours, but you really hanker for the Bonanza; however, you do not have the extra $2,000 to fly the Bonanza in the six-pilot partnership for 100 hours. Well, if you are willing to fly the Bonanza only 50 hours, you can do it for about as much as it costs to fly the Skyhawk for 100 hours (50×$112 vs. 100×$60). The same is true if you have the money to fly 100 hours in the four-pilot Arrow partnership, but would rather fly the Bonanza for the same amount of money. Many pilots will find the tradeoff worth it.

Different aircraft types of similar performance

Budget fliers should bear in mind a very important fact. Airplane technology has changed little in the last 25 years. It is generally fair to say that an airplane with the same number of seats and the same horsepower engine built in the last few years will go no faster and fly no more economically than its equivalent built more than two decades ago. Well maintained and periodically refurbished airframes last forever, and they fly with the same overhauled engines bolted to the nose of younger airplanes. Yet, the older airplanes' purchase price is practically always considerably less. If you are interested only in the number of seats and performance, scour the airplane ads for well maintained older models with fresh engines.

Consider a Skylane built in the 1960s, an Archer built in the 1970s and a Tobago made in the 1980s. All three aircraft will take four of you the same distance at the same speed burning the same amount of fuel. Yet as Table 6-4 illustrates, depending upon your choice, you might save a bundle.

The big saving is realized in the lower price you pay for the older aircraft. But there are additional savings to be had after you buy the airplane, primarily because of reduced insurance costs.

The examples presented in this chapter are but a taste of all the permutations and possibilities out there. Be sure to get accurate data for your assumptions and then let your imagination race. Sooner or later you, too, might be flying a 300 horsepower six-seater or a prized antique on what you thought was a trainer budget.

Table 6-4.

	60's Skylane	70's Archer	80's Tobago
NUMBER OF PILOTS	3	3	3
INVESTMENT REQUIRED	4,166.00	5,833.00	10,000.00
ANNUAL FIXED EXPENSES			
Tiedown/Hangar	320.00	320.00	320.00
Insurance	400.00	400.00	400.00
State Fees	40.00	40.00	40.00
Annual	216.67	216.67	216.67
Maintenance	433.33	433.33	433.33
Loan Payments	660.75	925.06	1,585.81
Cost of Capital non-cash	291.67	408.33	700.00
Total Fixed Expenses / yr	2,362.42	2,743.39	3,695.81
HOURLY OPERATING EXPENSES			
Fuel	19.00	19.00	19.00
Oil	0.31	0.31	0.31
Engine Reserve	6.00	6.00	6.00
General Maint Res	2.50	2.50	2.50
Total Op Exp / hr	27.81	27.81	27.81
TOTAL HOURLY EXPENSES			
50 Hours	75.06	82.68	101.73
100 Hours	51.44	55.25	64.77
150 Hours	43.56	46.10	52.45
Hourly Commercial Rental	75.00	75.00	75.00

ASSUMPTIONS:	60's Skylane	70's Archer	80's Tobago
Aircraft Value:	25,000	35,000	60,000
Loan Amount	12,500	17,500	30,000
Insurance/yr:	1,100	1,200	1,600
Annual:	650	650	650
Maintenance/yr:	1,300	1,300	1,300
Fuel Cons gal/hr :	9.5	9.5	9.5
Oil Cons qt/hr :	0.13	0.13	0.13
Engine Reserve/hr:	6.00	6.00	6.00
Gen Maint Res/hr:	2.50	2.50	2.50
Time Before OH hrs :	2,000	2,000	2,000
Engine MOH Cost:	12,000	12,000	12,000

Engine hours for all aircraft assumed to be midrange, with appropriate reserves set aside.

7

The partnership agreement

THE PARTNERSHIP AGREEMENT IS THE PARTNERSHIP'S FOUNDATION. It is a vital document that spells out the rights and obligations of each partner. It sets the rules by which the partnership is established, operated, and dissolved. A good partnership agreement clearly defines how to handle the day-to-day issues of a partnership, such as scheduling, insurance, pilot qualifications, expenses, and decisions. It also guides the partners through dealing with less common events, such as disputes or the departure of a partner.

An astonishing number of pilots about to enter into partnerships see no need for a partnership agreement. Are they not joining forces, they ask, in a common cause with like-minded fliers, often best friends, among whom never a harsh word has been spoken? What could possibly go wrong? Plenty.

The mistake these pilots make is that they fail to consider the unexpected, the unpredictable. Partnerships with no written rules can quickly experience internal friction once the initial euphoria of owning an airplane wears off. An idyllic first flight with another partner on that silky summer morning is fast forgotten when you are freezing your wheelpants off in the dead of winter, staring at that same partner's parked car on the ramp where you expected to find the airplane.

The partnership can also be threatened from the outside. Your partner might, indeed, be the nicest, most understanding and generous person; so nice, in fact, that on a whim he lent the airplane to his Uncle Harry, who decided to land on the grass, stuck a wheel in the mud, and took out a Tiger Moth, a Glasair, and a brand new Bonanza as he veered off the runway. Who do you think the mob will be after? Not just Uncle Harry. You need a good partnership agreement.

SHOULD YOU GET A LAWYER?

A lawyer's advice in putting together a partnership agreement is highly recommended. Well established legal conventions help formulate the rules that make partnerships work. Lawyers get paid for bringing to your attention all the items that should be covered in a partnership agreement and advising you on how to

Cessna Aircraft Company

The partnership should carefully define pilot flying experience and pilot/aircraft checkout requirements for its aircraft.

A partnership can also mean sharing the flying.

handle them. A lawyer can suggest easy solutions for scenarios you never even envisioned. In a worst case dispute, their carefully crafted partnership agreements might well shed enough light on the problem to resolve it amicably, without having to resort to the legal system.

Questions regarding possible incorporation of the partnership should be answered with the help of a lawyer. A lawyer would be in a better position to review intentions of the partnership and a lawyer would understand state laws and their impact on the partnership and possible incorporation. In case of incorporation, the partnership agreement in this chapter will still be necessary to effectively run the partnership, but will be incorporated into the bylaws of the corporation.

The trouble with lawyers is that they are expensive and they might overstep their traditional advisory role. Before you know it they are making your decisions for you and charging by the minute for voluminous legal tomes that go way beyond your simple requirements; however, this should not deter you from using the services of a lawyer for your partnership agreement. Just do your homework and keep the leash short. Know exactly what you want, spell it out to your lawyer clearly, and accept or reject suggestions decisively. One reason why lawyers so often put on a dog and pony show is because they are searching in good faith for what an ill informed, wishy-washy client really wants.

The best way to keep legal costs down, yet benefit from a lawyer's advice, is to first draft a partnership agreement with your partners in layman's language. Have the lawyer review your draft and put it in final form for your approval. If you and your partners are well prepared, the lawyer's time spent on your partnership agreement should rarely exceed an hour or two. And remember, the agreement you get for your share of a rather modest one-time fee (less than your share of a year's worth of airplane insurance) protects an investment worth thousands of dollars.

THE TYPICAL PARTNERSHIP AGREEMENT

All partnership agreements should cover certain essential points. Where you have some flexibility is the degree of detail in which you decide to address some of the issues. You can be quite vague, or very specific, depending upon the issue, your partnership's circumstances, and legal considerations. Here is where a well managed lawyer can be very helpful.

At a minimum, cover each point in sufficient detail to leave no ambiguity about factual information, and provide a clear mechanism for resolving any conflicts that might arise.

The basic issues that the average partnership agreement should address are discussed in this chapter. Use this information as a set of guidelines, a point of departure for formulating your own partnership agreement, tailored to suit your specific circumstances. Examples of partnership agreements are in the appendices.

The asset, the partners, ownership, and financial responsibilities

This is the opening statement of the partnership. It identifies the partnership's asset (the airplane) in as much detail as possible. Make and model according to the manufacturer's official designation should be identified, the manufacturer's serial number should be included, and the FAA registration number (N-number) should be listed.

This section also identifies all partners by legal name, and records the ownership share of each partner (usually by percentage). If you decide to own the airplane under a partnership name instead of the individual partners' names, identify the partnership name and the shares it represents (more on this later).

It is important to state that ownership is *undivided*, expressing each partner's share as a percentage of the total aircraft. This means that all partners own a percentage of the entire airplane; the airplane is not divided into identifiable pieces among the partners. One partner does not own the propeller, another the fuselage, and another the engine and the instruments. This might seem like legal nit picking, but it eliminates exploiting legal technicalities, should a partnership dispute get out of hand—"I'm taking the wings home, they are mine. . . ."

The partnership's legal form must also be defined in this section. The two usual choices are *partnership* and *co-ownership*. The legal term for the form of ownership chosen must also appear on the title document filed with the FAA and should be the same as it is in the partnership agreement. The most commonly selected form of ownership is co-ownership, the term commonly used for nonprofit partnerships and also because in certain jurisdictions it might limit in comparison to a legal partnership each co-owner's legal liabilities for liabilities incurred by other co-owners. A lawyer's advice in this regard is highly recommended.

A common question asked about partnerships is what happens to the partnership paperwork and title document filed with the FAA when one partner sells his or her share to someone outside the partnership. One option is to list all partners individually in both the agreement and the FAA title document. In this case, the agreement must be amended when a partner's share is sold, and the FAA title must be refiled listing the new partner.

Another choice is to hold title under a partnership name via transferable shares so that the FAA title does not have to be refiled when a share is sold. The shareholders are specifically listed by name in the agreement. This scenario would require the amendment of the agreement when a share is sold, to replace the seller's name with the buyer's name.

If you do not anticipate frequent turnover in partners, perhaps the most simple solution is to name each partner in both the agreement and the FAA title document, and make amendments and title refilings as and when appropriate.

What you should be particularly careful to do in all cases is devise some form of consent by all partners to the sale of any partner's share, which is better explained elsewhere in this chapter. This is another area where a lawyer can be most helpful in devising a solution to best suit your particular needs and ensuring that all the documentation is in the proper legal form.

Use of the aircraft

This section lays out who can use the airplane, according to what schedule, and under what conditions. It can also explicitly forbid illegal uses. The section can be as specific or as general as the partners prefer. All issues may be handled under one clause, or you may have separate clauses such as "Scheduling" and "Persons Authorized to Fly."

You can start by specifying who is allowed to fly the airplane as pilot in command. This is the time to decide if you will allow any nonpartners to fly under any conditions. Most partnerships allow flight instructors to fly the airplane when giving instructions to partners, but there might be other good reasons for allowing nonpartners to fly. If you are going to allow nonpartners to fly the airplane in addition to flight instructors giving instruction to partners, you are best off covering the issue in a separate clause. Elsewhere in this chapter, a section on persons authorized to fly the airplane has additional information.

Scheduling can be addressed in varying degrees of detail depending upon the partnership's needs and circumstances. For small, flexible partnerships the wording "a schedule mutually agreed upon" will usually suffice. For larger partnerships with periods of peak demand for the airplane (mostly on weekends), more explicit scheduling rules might be required.

Expenses

Expenses should be addressed in great detail. The handling of expenses can be a big source of friction for a partnership. A thoughtful agreement will go a long way to forestall later headaches. The two main points you need to address are how to divide expenses among the partners in principle and how the physical payment of expenses should be handled and recorded.

The first step is to state what items the partnership considers to be expenses by simply listing them. Also include the "including but not limited to" escape language, in case you face an expense at a later date that you did not list.

Next you need to spell out each partner's share of expenses. In deciding how to determine share of expenses, it is helpful to think in terms of fixed and operating expenses. To recap, fixed expenses are expenses you have to pay regardless of the amount of time the airplane is flown, such as tiedown fees, the annual inspection fee (excluding maintenance requirements uncovered by the inspection), and any taxes and fees; operating expenses are the expenses directly associated with flying the airplane, such as fuel, oil, and the amount you decide to charge per hour to build an engine and maintenance reserve.

How to share these expenses? Two schools of thought: One holds that fixed expenses should be shared equally by all partners, regardless of the amount of flying each partner does, because these expenses are the cost of owning and preserving the investment; operating expenses should be paid individually by each partner per flying hour, because this represents a benefit only to the partner using the airplane, in exchange for the wear and tear put on the airplane by the partner.

The second school of thought takes issue with the arrangement regarding fixed expenses. It holds that if there is a substantial difference in the amount of hours flown by the partners, fixed expenses should also be divided according to hours flown because the partners flying more get more "use" out of the fixed expenses and should pay for it. We disagree with this logic because these expenses do not vary with "use," the number of hours flown. The amount to be paid by the partnership is the same regardless of how little or how much any partner flies, and should therefore be shared equally by all partners. Any use or wear and tear causing expense proportional to the number of hours flown, is taken care of by the hourly engine and maintenance reserve charge, paid separately by each partner per hour flown. In spite of our disagreement with the logic of proportionally sharing fixed expenses, review both arguments carefully and make up your own mind. What is more important is that your partners reach the same conclusion.

A fixed expense where an argument might be made for proportional sharing is insurance in cases where there is a big difference in flight experience levels among partners. Insurance premiums vary greatly with levels of flight experience. A private VFR pilot with 250 hours will usually have to pay a much bigger premium than a commercial pilot with an instrument rating and 1,500 hours. If the two are partners in an airplane, their insurance premium will be set at the rate applicable to the pilot with the lower level of experience. If they split the premium equally, the commercial pilot will subsidize the insurance expense of the private pilot. The way to determine the fair share of each pilot is to get two quotes, one based on the real experience levels of both pilots, and one assuming that both pilots have the experience level of the more experienced pilot. The proportional share of each pilot is then adjusted in favor of the more experienced pilot by the difference in the two quotes.

Having defined how to allocate expenses within the partnership, you have to devise a system for making payments and keeping accounts. Depending on the number of partners and the relationship between them, these arrangements can range from informal occasional settlement between the partners to a system of accounts and comprehensive payment rules controlled by one of the partners acting as treasurer. Whatever your choice, the issues you need to deal with are how payments will be made for bills presented to the partnership, how hourly operating expenses, such as fuel, will be handled, how engine and maintenance reserves will be collected, how late payments by a partner will be handled, how unforeseen big expenses will be paid, and how often and in what form statements will be provided to the partners.

Partners have owned airplanes together for years and restricted the tracking of expenses to the back of an envelope, but this method is not recommended. In simple partnerships where two partners each fly approximately the same amount of hours and have agreed to split all expenses except fuel down the middle, the system of payments and accounts can be quite simple; there is no need to maintain a separate bank account for the partnership because the partners can informally agree which of them will deal with the bills streaming in from the outside world (mechanics, avionics technicians, airport management).

This partner can then write and send out all the checks, and can be reimbursed by the other partner simultaneously or just before the bill is paid. The partner sending out the bills may keep a simple log of payments made and should send copies to the other partner from time to time. Fuel is most simply handled by the requirement that after each flight each partner top off the tanks and pay the refueler directly. Engine and maintenance reserve accounts need not be kept if both partners feel comfortable with the other's ability to come up with the money when needed.

Even this most simple arrangement should spell out certain requirements designed to handle any unforeseen friction that might arise. At a minimum, the agreement should be worded to set time limits for payment of a partner's share of a bill, and for the reimbursement of a partner who has made payments on behalf of other partners (30 to 60 days is a good range). It should set a low maximum dollar limit on partnership expenses that a partner might incur on behalf of the partnership without consulting the other partner, $30–50 is usually a good amount. The agreement should also require partners to meet periodically, quarterly or at least semiannually, to reconcile accounts. These meetings need not take place by mutual consent, but the mechanism to call one should be in place.

Larger, more formal partnerships or partnerships with especially exacting personalities should build on this simple structure to create a system for making payments and keeping accounts tailored to specific needs and circumstances. Two bank accounts should be established for such partnerships, one to build the engine reserve, and one to serve as the operating account. A per flying hour general maintenance reserve independent of the engine reserve can be paid into the operating account. A partner should be appointed as treasurer. He or she should be sent all the payments by the other partners for deposit into the partnership accounts as appropriate (the accounts should be managed by the treasurer, but all partners should have signing authority and expenditures or withdrawals above a certain amount should require two signatures).

In turn, the treasurer should be required to send quarterly statements to all partners; copies of the bank statements for the period and the partnership's income and expense log clearly identifying each item should suffice. The partners should have the right to inspect the books at any time, and a CPA may be retained once a year for a modest fee to independently review the records. The annual CPA review is an especially recommended sanity check for partnerships in which no partner has much financial experience.

Fuel might still be most simply handled by requiring that the tanks be topped off after each flight. Some partnerships devise a system of fuel credits and debits based on hours flown, on the theory that it is not efficient to refuel every time you just ran around the patch for 30 minutes. Tracking such fuel debits and credits may prove to be more trouble than it is worth, so consider it carefully before committing to such a system.

For expenditures beyond a certain amount, approval of the entire partnership should be required.

It might be worth recognizing in the agreement a partner's right to install equipment entirely at his or her own expense upon approval by the other partners. Occasionally, a well-to-do partner is willing to spring for, say, a loran receiver when the others simply don't have the money.

Unforeseen big expenses might require an assessment. A mechanism for making assessments should be defined.

Time limits for prompt payment become more pressing in a bigger partnership; consequences for late payment, such as loss of flying privileges should be spelled out.

Decisions

Decisions, decisions. How will the partnership make them to keep all the partners happy all the time? The key question is whether unanimous agreement should be required, or if some form of majority should suffice. Lawyers will often favor a two-third majority vote to make a decision binding, but they tend to forget that a partnership for private flying is not business or politics, but fun, and should strive to minimize the chance for hard feelings; therefore, unanimous agreement to make a decision binding is highly recommended.

Loss or damage of the aircraft

This is an important technical section spelling out the financial responsibilities of the partners in case of loss or damage of the aircraft. It usually treats three scenarios: loss or damage when not in use, as a result of legal use, and as a result of illegal use.

When illegality is not an issue, the question of financial responsibility for the loss or damage of an insured aircraft is reduced in practical terms to whom will pay the deductible. When a properly parked and tied down aircraft is lost or damaged when not in motion, no one partner is responsible, so all should bear equal responsibility and pay an equal share of the deductible. When an aircraft is damaged while in motion (in use by a partner), the partner in command should be liable for the deductible. In case of illegal use that negates insurance coverage, the partner in command should be financially liable for the entire value of the aircraft (value is defined in next section of this chapter). If the partner is lost with the aircraft during illegal use that negates insurance coverage, the surviving partners may collect from the estate, if there is anything to collect.

The rules for financial responsibility by nonowners for loss or damage of the partnership's aircraft while in use by a nonowner, should the partnership allow such use, are similar to the rules applied to partners; however, nonpartners might have very few assets from which to make restitution in case of loss or damage as a result of illegal use. Collecting from the estate of a nonowner might be even more unlikely if the value of the estate is low.

Nonowners who have renter's insurance might be out of luck because unless a partnership is commercially insured it is not allowed to rent its airplane.

Annual statement of value

Airplane values fluctuate over time, and the value of a particular airplane might be increased by improvements, such as new avionics, or an overhauled engine. It is important for the partnership to periodically establish the current market value of the airplane for a variety of reasons. Establishing the current value will determine the amount to insure the airplane. If a partner decides to leave, the current value will give the remaining partners an idea of what to reasonably offer for the departing partner's share.

This clause should define how fair market value is established and how often it is to be determined. A common and perhaps the best way to assess market value is to simply take the retail blue book value. AOPA will provide this value to association members.

An appraisal by an outside appraiser, usually an aircraft dealer, is an option, but appraisals cost money and can be manipulated, so they are not particularly attractive for most partnerships. Should you decide on an outside appraisal, make it a requirement that the appraiser be unanimously acceptable to the partners.

Partners should be required to sign the annual statement of value to signify agreement.

Insurance

This clause specifies how the partners are to determine what type of insurance coverage to get and the amounts of hull and liability coverage. The clause can be as broad or as specific as the partners would like. "A level of coverage mutually agreed upon" will keep things simple. Alternatively, for hull insurance coverage, an option is to specify current market value as defined above. For liability insurance, specific levels of coverage may be listed based upon the partners' levels of net worth threatened by potential liability suits.

Death of a partner

In the sad case of a partner's death or disability, it is important for the partnership to protect itself as much as possible from disposal of the deceased or disabled partner's shares by the estate or guardian on terms unfavorable to the partnership. In case of death, the partnership is automatically dissolved under common law and orderly dissolution follows certain well established legal steps not entirely under the control of the partnership; however, it is important for the partners to have a contingency plan presentable to the estate because if it is reasonable, there is a good chance the estate might accept it to everyone's benefit.

The first order of business is to establish the partnership's right of first refusal at a fair price. This price can be established according to the method used in the annual statement of value, an important reason for choosing a credible method. If this is acceptable to the estate or guardian, all the partners have to do to reestablish the partnership is come up with the money or find an acceptable replacement partner. The partners should specify a reasonable time, for instance 60 days, to come up with a replacement partner.

A second line of reasoning that might prove helpful is to specify that whomever the estate sells to must be acceptable to the partnership, and that the value of the buyer's share will not be worth more than the current market value (as defined in the annual statement of value) of the share of the partner being replaced.

If no solution can be found, the aircraft must be sold.

Departure of a partner or termination of the partnership

A partner wishing to leave the partnership should be required to give written notice. The departing partner should expect fair value for his or her share, and in turn should cooperate to the extent possible with the remaining partners to preserve the partnership on the most desirable terms.

The remaining partners should have the right of first refusal for a reasonable period (30 to 60 days) at the current market value. They should also be given the option of finding a replacement partner during this period.

The seller should simultaneously have the right to propose replacement partners for the unanimous approval of the remaining partners. If a buyer is found, the remaining partners should have the option of matching the offer in lieu of accepting the buyer.

The share of the joining partner should equal in percentage the departing partner's share of the partnership regardless of the dollar amount for which it was sold. The seller might have decided to sell at a discount to current market value, or might have been lucky enough to sell at a premium, but for the partnership to remain intact on equal terms, the only figure that counts is percentage share, and this should be acceptable to the buyer.

If the partners cannot reach agreement, the partnership should be dissolved and the aircraft sold to the highest bidder following exposure to the market for a reasonable length of time.

If more than one partner wishes to buy the airplane in its entirety for his or her own account, the highest bidder wins on a sealed bid. In such an eventuality, the partnership should agree on a minimum acceptable bid.

Arbitration

All partnerships might encounter seemingly irreconcilable differences; however, life must go on and arbitration is the legal profession's well established way of breaking the impasse. The partners agree to submit their dispute to a mutually acceptable lawyer for arbitration, and agree to accept the arbitrator's judgment. To ensure impartiality, the lawyer should be required to conduct the arbitration according to the rules of the American Arbitration Association (a standard and well proven procedure). Arbitration is a good way to keep all but the nastiest disputes out of the courts.

Legality clause

This clause requires all persons authorized to fly the airplane to agree to fly it only in compliance with all legal requirements and within the limitations of the insurance policy. This section may be a subclause of the use of aircraft clause, but should be explicitly stated.

Nonpartner operating authorization

In general, you might want only the partners to fly the airplane, with the exception of certified flight instructors giving instruction to partners; however, there might be other occasions when a partner might benefit from a nonpartner acting as pilot in command. Examples are an airframe and powerplant mechanic who works on the aircraft, a partner whose spouse is a pilot but for whatever reason not a member of the partnership, or a partner who does aerial photography from time to time and needs a qualified photo pilot.

Be sure to explicitly state the qualifications and experience required of nonpartners allowed to fly the partnership's airplane. Be sure to include the certificate held and any ratings, such as a flight instructor or commercial pilot with instrument rating, as well as general flight experience, experience in type, and checkride requirements. To minimize the chance of misadventure, you might want to set considerably higher standards for nonpartners compared to partners.

It is extremely important to check your insurance policy, as well as every policy renewal, for information regarding nonpartners operating the partnership's airplane. Watch for severe insurance restrictions on such flying; nonpartners might be completely forbidden from flying the airplane; they might have to be specifically named on the policy, and there might be additional qualifications and experience requirements. Permitting nonpartners to fly the airplane on the partnership's insurance policy might mean incurring significant additional insurance expense.

Financing

This section describes any financing incurred by the partnership and spells out the obligations of partners with respect to such financing. Usually, a financial institution, such as a bank, will want one monthly payment check from the partnership. This arrangement requires that one partner handle the payment book and send in the periodic payments (usually monthly). In turn, this partner has to receive the other partners' share of the monthly payments on time to make the payment to the bank. This clause describes the payment arrangements. It requires payments by all partners to be made on time. It establishes a partner's reimbursement obligations to other partners, of any penalties incurred by the partnership, due to a late payment or payment default by the partner.

Collateralization exclusion

This clause states that no partner may pledge his or her share of the airplane as collateral for obligations outside the partnership. Such a pledge without the explicit written approval of the other partners would not stand up in court anyway, but the exclusion clause might short-circuit a messy legal skirmish.

Amendments

As circumstances change, it might become necessary to make changes to the partnership agreement. This section states the procedures for making such amendments and also calls for the review of the agreement annually to determine if amendments are in order.

Communications

This clause describes how partners are to communicate in matters that might require proof of communications in case of a dispute. It is a standard legal clause used mostly when the partnership has already taken a turn for the worse. It usually calls for communications in writing by registered mail, unless otherwise stated.

8

Financing the partnership

BUSINESS PEOPLE WILL SOMETIMES TELL YOU that a cardinal rule of business is to do it with someone else's money. Many of us have also taken this point to heart in our private lives. We borrow to buy our houses, cars, furniture, vacations, fancy meals at restaurants, and educations. So why not borrow to buy an airplane? Under the right circumstances, borrowing is a perfectly sound means of gaining access to an airplane you otherwise could not afford.

Borrowing is really like renting something. You are paying a rental charge (interest) for the use of someone else's money (principal) for a period of time.

You are expected to have a sufficient flow of income to repay the loan in addition to paying obligations you already had when you got the loan. As a fallback source of repayment, you are usually expected to pledge to the lender the airplane as collateral—other forms of collateral may be pledged under certain circumstances—for the life of the loan. If you stop making your loan payments, the lender will want to collect the remaining amount you owe by repossessing and selling the collateral. In addition to paying interest monthly, most lenders will also want you to start repaying the principal monthly throughout the period for which you borrowed. They don't want to put faith in your ability to come up with a big lump sum at the end. Also, as you use the airplane (the collateral), its value declines. So, in order to maintain the original ratio of the loan to the airplane's value, the outstanding principal has to decline too.

The problem with borrowing is that it is very expensive. The interest (the rental charge for using the money) comes out of your pocket. Like the rental charge for a car or an airplane at the FBO, it is gone forever. For paying back the principal, you at least get to call more and more of the airplane truly your own, but this amount, too, is cash which you have to come up with every month. You must be sure that you can afford to borrow.

Many borrowers have difficulty with realistically assessing how much credit they can pay back comfortably and over what period of time. And don't always believe what your friendly banker says you are able to pay either. (The United States' financial industry's ability to analyze the paying capacity of its borrowers should be suspect to say the least, given the recent track record of hundreds of billions of dollars in bad loans that will never be repaid.)

For a partnership, a loan might pose additional problems. If the partnership is the borrower, most lenders will want each partner to be responsible for the entire amount of a loan to the partnership. In effect, the lender will want each partner to guarantee that the others will perform; thus, each partner must be satisfied that each of the other partners has the financial capacity to reliably make his or her share of the loan payments. Should a partner fail to pay, the others will be liable to the lender for the unpaid amount. Should they not be able to make the payment, the lender will be entitled to repossess the airplane, and the credit ratings of all the partners will be affected because one let the others down.

Ultimately, you should analyze the option to borrow just as carefully as you weigh the pros and cons of all the other options that go into making the decisions about your partnership. The remainder of this chapter examines how to figure out what it costs to borrow, and where and how to seek financing.

BORROWING IS EXPENSIVE

Lenders are rarely willing to finance 100 percent of an asset, in this case the airplane. They want to see some of the borrower's own money in the asset financed. Banks are willing to lend at most up to 80 percent of the fair market value of an airplane to credit worthy borrowers. Fair market value is often determined as the *retail blue book value*. In the examples below, let's consider a typical bank loan for a single-engine 200 horsepower complex airplane. The fair market value, which should also be the purchase price, of the airplane is $45,000. The bank loan is $36,000, or 80 percent of the purchase price. The loan is for 10 years at an annual interest rate of 12 percent. Table 8-1 compares annual costs without any financing and with 80 percent financing for two, three, and four partners. What do the numbers say?

The main point is made by the first line of numbers. For two partners, the additional cash expense is a whopping $2,610 more per partner per year with the loan. For four partners, the figure is halved but is still a hefty extra annual cash expense.

Another way of looking at the extra cost of borrowing is calculating how much you will spend on interest during the life of the loan. The amounts can be surprisingly large. For the $36,000 loan for 10 years at 12 percent, the interest cost is $25,979. This translates to $12,989 per partner in a two-person partnership; $8,660 among three partners; $6,494 among four partners. Any way you look at it, that is a lot of money that would have stayed in your pocket.

The bottom line is that in order to minimize the cost of flying it is in your interest to borrow as little as possible. Excessive borrowing might even increase the cost of your flying above the rental option; however, if it takes some borrowing to get you into the airplane you have always wanted, at an all-in cost that beats rentals, and you can make the monthly payments, head for the cheapest source of a loan immediately. Just make sure that your partners can also afford their share of the payments.

Table 8-1.

NUMBER OF PILOTS	2	2	3	3	4	4
	NO LOAN	20% DOWN	NO LOAN	20% DOWN	NO LOAN	20% DOWN
ANNUAL FIXED EXPENSES, Non-fin. expenses not shown						
Loan Payments	0.00	2,610.00	0.00	1,740.00	0.00	1,305.00
Cost of Capital (non-cash)	1,800.00	360.00	1,200.00	240.00	900.00	180.00
Total Fixed Expenses / yr	3,935.00	5,105.00	2,623.33	3,403.33	1,967.50	2,552.50
Total Op Exp / hr	27.25	27.25	27.25	27.25	27.25	27.25
TOTAL HOURLY EXPENSES						
50 Hours	105.95	129.35	79.72	95.32	66.60	78.30
100 Hours	66.60	78.30	53.48	61.28	46.93	52.78
150 Hours	53.48	61.28	44.74	49.94	40.37	44.27
Hourly Commercial Rental	90.00	90.00	90.00	90.00	90.00	90.00

BANK FINANCING FOR THE PARTNERSHIP

Most banks think that financing small airplanes flown for fun is more trouble than it is worth. To be done right, it requires developing a considerable amount of specialized industry knowledge in a market that is fairly small. The chances that someone is going to walk through the door asking for a home improvement loan are far greater than a rush of customers demanding aircraft financing. And home improvement loans are oh so much more comprehensible to bankers than those dangerous little airplanes. Fortunately, one bank's lack of interest is another bank's niche, and there are a handful of banks nationwide willing to finance airplanes. Good sources for finding out about them are aviation trade publications, such as *Trade-A-Plane*, where the banks advertise their services.

Services offered by these banks vary, so shop around (Table 8-2). Banks might have different minimum amounts for a loan, different lengths of time for which they are willing to lend, different rates of interest (high, low, fixed, variable), and different maximum percentages of an airplane's value up to which they will make a loan.

Bank lending standards

When a bank lends money for anything, its main concern is how it will get repaid. Some bankers claim that owner pilots are the best credit risk because they will sell the house, the dog, and the kids before missing an airplane payment. A good banker will want the borrower to have reliable sources of cash income as a primary means of repayment, and will want a fallback source if the cash flow dries up. The bank will also want to check if the borrower has a good credit record, a history of paying obligations promptly.

In the case of individual borrowers (as opposed to businesses), typical sources of cash income are regular paychecks, investment income, rental income,

Table 8-2.

LOAN TERMS	BANK:	BANK:	BANK:
Have ready for bankers: Aircraft make, model, year, total time , time since major overhaul, detailed equipment list, damage history, annual date, hours per year to be flown. If specific aircraft is not yet located, define the specs you are looking for.			
Minimum loan amount			
Max % of value financed, new a/c			
Max % of value financed, used a/c			
How value determined?			
Min downpayment requirements			
Max loan maturity, new a/c			
Max loan maturity, used a/c			
Fixed or variable interest rate?			
Annual Percentage Rate (APR)			
Must all partners co-sign for full amount?			
Closing and other fees			
Preapproval available?			
LOAN AMOUNT REQUESTED:			
MATURITY REQUESTED			
MONTHLY PAYMENT			
COLLATERAL REQUIREMENTS			
First lien on aircraft			
Additional collateral requirements			
BORROWER STRENGTH, INFO			
Should each partner be able to carry total loan?			
Application form is sufficient information			
Tax returns also required (how many years?)			
Other evidence of income (W 2, paystubs, etc)			
INSURANCE REQUIREMENTS			
All risk?			
Bank named as loss payee?			
Market value or stated value?			
Maximum deductible			
Waiver of subrogation?			

Prudent financing will reduce your need for capital in a partnership to a level that is below what you would spend to buy a new car.

royalties, and the like. To assess a borrower's ability to repay the loan, a banker must see tangible proof of these sources and amounts and must examine where the money goes, including what loans or other liabilities the borrower is already obligated to pay. If, after meeting existing obligations, there is a sufficient amount of cash left over to support the proposed loan, the borrower is in business. Well, almost. As soon as the banker establishes a fallback source of repayment and checks out the borrower's credit history.

The fallback source of repayment is necessary because there is always the chance that the financial statements do not represent a full picture of the borrower's financial condition, and because sources of cash might dry up. You might get laid off. The fallback source is inevitably the asset being financed, the airplane. The banker will file a lien on the airplane with the FAA. This filing establishes the bank's security interest in the airplane and the right to repossess the airplane and sell it to repay the loan, if you stop making payments (default).

Financial information requirements

Proof of sources and uses of cash is the financial information you will be asked to submit in the form of income tax returns and signed personal financial statements. For smaller loan amounts, the financial information on the bank's standard application form will suffice. For larger amounts, greater detail might be required. Below are typical minimum information requirements, depending upon the size of the loan:

$10,000 to $50,000
- Completed application, dated and signed.
- Most current personal tax return (1040) or W-2 form.

It might take some effort to convince your banker that this German Speedcanard is a production airplane worthy of an aircraft loan.

$50,000 to $100,000
- Completed application, dated and signed.
- Two most recent years of personal tax returns (1040).

$100,000 and up
- Detailed personal financial statement, dated and signed.
- Three most recent years of personal tax returns (1040).

The bank's view of partnerships

These requirements seem straightforward for one borrower. But what if a partnership wants to borrow? What information will the bank want, and what obligations does it expect the individual partners to assume? The answer is simple. To the bank, a partnership is the sum of its partners; thus, all partners will have to provide the information required of a single borrower. The bank will determine the partnership's ability to pay by combining the individual partners' ability to pay. In turn, the bank will want all partners to be responsible for the loan *jointly and severally*. In English, that means all partners are on the hook for the entire amount. Everybody signs the whole note. The bank doesn't want to be in the business of chasing partners individually. It wants to deal with the partnership as a whole and wants all partners to be financially and morally committed to the partnership's obligations. Let the partners chase each other if necessary.

Credit and employment checks

Your credit history will be checked out through the usual credit bureau reports to which all banks subscribe. These reports will also be used to verify the statements you made about your existing debts on your personal financial statement. Most banks will also want to verify your employment.

Loan amount vs aircraft value

Before you approach a bank for a loan, it is worth having a good idea of the maximum amount you can reasonably expect based on the airplane's value. As stated earlier, the most a bank is typically willing to finance is 80 percent of the fair market value, usually the retail blue book value. To be able to determine this amount, the bank will want a very detailed description of the airplane, including number of hours on the airframe and engine, avionics, options, and damage history.

If you are not sure of how reasonable the asking price is of the airplane you are considering buying, you can get some good information from your banker indirectly. The price is between you and the seller, so your banker can't explicitly tell you that you are overpaying. But what he or she can tell you (following a detailed description of the airplane), is what the maximum amount is that the bank is willing to finance. That figure will be 80 percent of the fair market value. You can figure out the rest.

The bank's insurance requirements

If a bank decides to make a loan to the partnership, the bank will want to protect its interest in the financed airplane with stringent insurance requirements. These requirements might exceed the partnership's planned levels of coverage, and might mean additional expense, so they are worth knowing in advance. Insurance requirements demanded are similar among banks:

- The policy must include the name of the registered owner as primary insured.
- The aircraft must be identified by year, make, model, and FAA registration number.
- Coverage must include all risk of physical damage, in flight or on the ground.
- Coverage should be for the full purchase price.
- Deductibles should not exceed 10 percent of insured value.
- The policy must name the bank as loss payee.
- The policy must include a breach of warranty endorsement to the bank for the amount financed.
- The policy must contain 30 days cancellation notice to the bank.

Before a bank disburses a loan, it has to receive proof that the borrower has acquired insurance for the airplane to be financed. Such proof is evidenced by the insurance binder sent by the insurance company to the bank. (Chapter 9 has more details regarding insurance.)

Loan closing and documentation

When the bank approves your loan, it will do a title search (for which you pay a fee) and it will ask you to arrange insurance for the airplane you are about to buy and have the binder sent directly to the bank. When these essential pieces of bureaucracy are in hand, and all that remains is to actually buy the airplane, you will have to go to a loan closing to sign the loan documents and get the money. You should fully understand these documents; unless you are a lawyer or an experienced borrower, the information can be overbearing when first seen at a closing. These documents are standard forms, and it is an excellent idea to ask the lender for blank examples well in advance of the signing, so that you can take your time to fully understand them. Do not hesitate to call your banker or your lawyer with questions as you study the documentation.

Documentation of the loan usually consists of three sections: the promissory note, the consumer credit disclosure statement, and the security agreement. All three items may be combined into one document, but often the security agreement is separate. Sample aircraft loan documents are in appendix C.

The *promissory note* is evidence of your borrowing. It is the loan agreement. It lists the total amount you promise to pay (principal and interest), the terms of repayment, and all other obligations to which you agree during the life of the loan, such as prompt payment, late charges, events of default, conditions of prepayment, and the like.

The *disclosure statement* is a statement of the costs and duration of your loan. The statement lists the amount financed, the total dollar amount of the finance charge, the total dollar amount you will have paid when all scheduled payments have been made, the cost of borrowing expressed in an annual percentage (the annual percentage rate (APR)), the number of monthly payments and the amount of each payment, and any additional fees and closing costs. It is a statement required by consumer protection laws to ensure that you are not tricked into inadvertently accepting any hidden charges and fully understand the amount of interest you are required to pay. Most agreements have made the disclosure statement an integral part of the promissory note, rather than separately restating this information.

The *security agreement* gives the bank ownership of the airplane up to the financed amount. It is the document giving the bank the right to file a lien on the airplane. It spells out the conditions under which the bank may take possession and dispose of the airplane, and it lays out the obligations of the borrower to insure and maintain the airplane. It also explicitly states the bank's obligation to release its security interest when the loan is paid in full.

Payment problems

If the partnership gets into trouble making payments on the loan for whatever reason, it is extremely important to let the lender know sooner rather than later. Prompt notification will result in a much more cooperative banker who might be very helpful in working out an alternative solution that might keep the partnership intact. Whatever the outcome, the banker will be in a good position to preserve your credit rating by an orderly dissolution of the partnership before a serious default. If you are elusive or pigheaded, the bank will repossess the airplane anyway, and nobody will lend you money to bore holes in the sky for a long time to come.

Denied loan applications

There is always the chance that the bank will deny your loan. In this case, you have a legal right to receive a written statement of the specific reasons for denial. Treat a denial constructively. Selected reasons might be ironed out easily. Perhaps a credit report erroneously contained negative information. Maybe the title on the airplane had a problem from preceding ownership that can be removed with a few phone calls.

Other reasons might be more difficult to counter. You might already have too much credit compared to your income. You might be paying too much for the airplane and the amount you want financed is too high a percentage of what the bank thinks the airplane is worth. Perhaps a bigger down payment would help, if you can afford it, or an additional partner. Whatever the reason for the denial, ask what is necessary to overcome the denial and get approval the second time around. Never stop trying.

ALTERNATE SOURCES OF FINANCING

Bank financing is a nice option to have, but it might not suit your partnership's particular needs. Not all partners might want to borrow. Partners might not want to sign for each other. Some partners might not want to disclose financial information about themselves. You might think bank financing is too expensive, or there might not be a bank in the airplane loan business nearby. So what are the alternatives? Two popular options keep the partnership free of debt as an entity and have the added benefit of somewhat reducing the cost of borrowing. One is a personal bank loan taken out independent of the partnership and the airplane, and the other is financing from one of the partners.

Personal bank loans

The option of a personal loan works best when, for whatever reason, the partners don't want the partnership to borrow. In that case, the partners who need to borrow should consider taking out a personal loan that is granted to them alone, outside the partnership, for general purposes.

The most popular form of such a loan is the home equity loan. If you have a house on which the mortgage is substantially paid down, you have a good chance of borrowing against the house. As a condition, the lender will take a second mortgage on the house, behind the institution to whom you owe the remainder of the original mortgage. An added advantage of this type of loan, besides keeping the partnership free of debt, is that the interest is tax deductible, which could mean substantial savings depending upon your tax situation. Home equity lines are also likely to be less expensive than other forms of consumer debt, and might be more readily available at fixed rates.

Other options for obtaining personal loans are to take them out against other forms of security that you might be fortunate enough to have available, such as stocks or bonds that you do not wish to sell, or long-term deposits that you do not wish to break, or the cash value of life insurance.

Partner financing

In certain instances, when a partnership as an entity does not want to borrow, the partner in need of financing does not have a personal bank loan available as an option, but another partner is willing to finance the partner in need. Whether or not such an arrangement is desirable is a matter of personal opinion and circumstance; however, it is fair to say that it generally carries a higher risk of friction than a partnership in which partners do not finance one another.

In spite of the potential for friction, there is something to be gained from financing a partner besides making the partnership possible. The lending partner might be able to realize higher income on a loan to another partner at fair commercial rates than on alternative forms of investment. Think about it. When bank deposits yield 5 percent, conservative mutual funds yield 10 percent, and consumer loans go for anywhere from 13 to 19 percent, a loan at 12 percent to a partner you know, secured by an airplane with a value far in excess of the loan amount is not such a bad deal.

The key to minimizing the possibility of friction when financing another partner is to make the loan a completely arm's length business transaction as if it were done between two businessmen who, but for the situation, don't even know each other. The loan should be documented in a promissory note just as a loan from a financial institution, and the lending partner should take a security interest in the airplane, and file a lien on it. It is imperative that you get a lawyer to draft the note and security interest. From a legal standpoint, this is a very simple procedure and should not require more than an hour or two of the lawyer's time.

If there are more than two partners, a loan from one to another should not affect the rest, except perhaps by forming entangling alliances if decisions do not have to be unanimous. It is true that the lending partner has a lien on the airplane, but by virtue of the partnership agreement that has no effect on the other partners because their percentage share is recognized in any sale of the airplane. The lien only gives the lending partner a right to the share of the borrowing partner up to the amount of the loan. If the lending partner follows prudent banking practice and lends only a percentage of the value of the borrowing partner's share, there should be adequate cushion to cover any decline in aircraft value, provided orderly principal reductions are made during the life of the loan.

And when all the clouds are dark, and your dream machine seems far out of reach for the want of financing, don't despair. A penniless guy just out of school acquired two credit cards one month after landing his first job. Instantly he drew both in-full for down payments on two airplanes, one in a three-way partnership. A friendly banker who asked no questions about credit card use gave him airplane loans for the rest of the money. Many airplanes have followed those, all of them financed and he has never missed a payment. That last bit is important, it will do the trick.

9

Insuring
the partnership

INSURANCE IS ONE OF THE MOST IMPORTANT CONSIDERATIONS of owning an airplane. It protects your investment if your airplane is damaged, destroyed, or otherwise lost. It also protects your other assets from any claims arising out of damage or loss caused by your airplane. Insurance is expensive and, for most pilots, confusing at best. It is not inherently complicated, but is sufficiently specialized to require careful study to be fully understood. The insurance question is further compounded by the wide range of available options offered by an industry with motives that are traditionally viewed with suspicion and mistrust by the consumer.

This chapter outlines insurance basics, walks you through a typical insurance policy, gives you advice on insurance considerations specific to partnerships, and offers advice on where to get insurance.

INSURANCE BASICS

Insurance is protection against the risk of financial loss related to the asset insured. Aircraft insurance coverage has two basic elements: hull and liability.

Hull insurance, as the name implies, is insurance against damage to the airplane. If the airplane suffers any damage, the insurance company pays to fix it. If the damage results in the total loss of the airplane, the insurance company forks over to the owners an amount of money equal to the value of the airplane as defined by the insurance policy.

Liability insurance is protection of the airplane's owners against claims by others who have suffered some form of injury or property damage as a result of damage caused by the owners' airplane. This is the big bucks world of the dreaded liability lawsuits in which everything you own and in some cases even your future salary is fair game as compensation to the victims and their lawyers. A liability suit can ruin you and your family financially, so you must carefully consider the level of coverage you feel is appropriate for your situation.

Other forms of coverage usually included in aircraft owners' insurance policies are some amount of medical coverage for the aircraft's occupants and insurance covering you while you fly an aircraft you don't own. As we walk through an insurance policy, we will examine both forms of insurance and the way to assess appropriate levels of coverage in much greater detail.

Deductibles

An important feature of insurance policies is the deductible. It is the amount you are required to pay toward hull damages when you make an insurance claim. In-flight and not-in-flight damage have different deductibles. The amounts depend upon the size of the insurance policy, but are usually modest amounts, low to middle hundreds.

Do you need insurance?

Hull insurance is entirely at the owner's option, and liability insurance is a legal requirement only in a handful of states. So with annual insurance costs (premiums) commonly running in excess of $1,000, who needs insurance? You do. Flying without insurance poses risks of such high financial loss that some form of protection is practically mandatory and doing without is downright stupid. The real question is what type of insurance do you need and how much coverage should you obtain.

Hull insurance needs are relatively easy to assess because you can accurately estimate your maximum loss. If you fly without hull insurance, the most you stand to lose is your investment in the airplane. Many pilots claim that they are too good to bend an airplane or, if they do, it is their own fault, so they forego or minimize hull insurance coverage. They find out too late that hull damage can easily occur due to circumstances beyond their control even when the airplane is under their command. Various hull insurance options cover air and ground operations at a variety of prices. Analyze them carefully as you go through the process of obtaining insurance quotes and decide what option best suits you. Just bear in mind that if you decide to forego hull insurance or limit coverage, you are gambling with the amount of your uncovered investment.

The appropriate level of liability insurance coverage is harder to assess. In a worst-case scenario, there is no way to estimate the maximum amount of a liability award against you. It can run into the millions, especially if you have millions. The courts can come after everything you have, over and above your airplane and can even attach future earnings; thus, as a rule of thumb, it is advisable to have coverage in excess of your assets. Again, it would be gambling to minimize liability coverage, and if you have a family, it would be totally irresponsible. As you assess your insurance needs, pay particular attention to the details subsequently described in this chapter regarding liability limit options before making a decision to suit your financial circumstances. Determine your needs first and then shop around. Do not compromise on needs for the sake of a few dollars.

How are insurance rates determined?

Setting insurance rates is a complex process of blending together a variety of risk factors based upon actuarial (statistical) records of events and losses and assigning a price to them. The industry's past loss experience with pilots and equipment fitting your profile plays a key role in establishing your insurance rates. The consistency of rates is compounded by the laws of supply and demand; how many insurers are chasing how many airplanes to be insured. Following a string of high payouts, many insurers might decide to exit aviation underwriting. Rates skyrocket. In times of a steadily improving general aviation safety record, evidenced by decreasing payouts, insurers might flock back into the business. Rates plummet. At the end of the 1980s the cost of insuring a Piper Arrow III flown by two relatively experienced private pilots under a fairly typical insurance policy declined in one year from $2,250 to $1,100 merely because a much larger number of insurers were offering insurance.

Common determinants are applied to specific policy costs:

- Experience and qualifications (total flight time, recent flight time, license and ratings held, time in proposed equipment)
- Type of aircraft
- Equipment in aircraft
- Home base of aircraft
- How aircraft is stored (hangar or tiedown)
- Aircraft use (pleasure, pleasure and personal business, commercial use)
- How many hours the aircraft is likely to fly during the insured period

Make sure you and your partners meet the insurance company's experience requirements before you buy this antique Stearman.

UNDERSTANDING YOUR INSURANCE POLICY

Aviation insurance policies are generally structured in similar fashion and consist of two components: a standard format of general terms and conditions and a data sheet spelling out your coverage and terms and conditions specific to your policy. The standard section of the policy provides a set of general definitions to pin down the terms used throughout the policy and defines general terms of coverage for hull and liability insurance in separate sections. Then, in a separate and very important section usually labelled *exclusions*, the policy specifically spells out what is not covered. Additional exclusions might also be scattered throughout the policy. Another section deals with general conditions such as renewal, cancellation, and conformity to state laws.

This boilerplate policy is customized by a data sheet identifying you as the named insured, identifying the aircraft insured, spelling out the amounts and costs of your coverage, and defining who is authorized to fly the airplane in addition to you and your partners. Any special provisions tailored to your needs are attached to the policy as separate *riders*.

The policy language of each insurance underwriter is standard, but there can be substantial differences in language from underwriter to underwriter; thus, it is important to read the policy before signing on the dotted line. Standard policies should be readily provided for your review.

Let's go through the sections of a standard policy.

General definitions

Terms used in the policy are defined:

- insured aircraft
- accident
- bodily injury
- property damage
- in flight
- not in flight
- in motion
- not in motion
- geographic coverage

From the standpoint of hull insurance, it is important for you to understand the definitions of flight and motion. If you intend to fly abroad, you might want to pay particular attention to geographic coverage.

Hull insurance

Hull insurance covers your airplane against damage. The decisions you have to make are what types of activity do you want coverage for, and what value to insure the hull for. Coverage is available for a variety of aircraft operations in flight and on the ground.

All risk coverage. The most comprehensive (and most expensive) coverage is "all risk." Under the all risk option you are covered in flight and on the ground regardless of whether the airplane is tied down, taxiing, or being towed or pushed around.

All risk not in flight. This is a lower (and less expensive) form of coverage. Under this option, your aircraft is covered against damage only on the ground, regardless of whether or not it is in motion. It is important for you to understand the definition of in flight. Does it include the takeoff and landing roll? Does it cease the instant the wheels touch the ground? Many self-confident pilots choose this type of hull insurance, reasoning that they can handle a well maintained airplane once free of the earth's confines. They reason that if they fly safely for long enough, and save the hull premiums, they will be ahead financially as soon as the sum of their saved premiums exceeds the value of the aircraft. Some make it (it can take 20 years), some have to give up flying forever because of an uninsured blown landing, or the like.

Before you and your partners choose this not-in-flight option, bear in mind that in case any one of you is forced down in a forest by a mechanical failure impervious to your impeccable piloting skills, the ensuing damage to the aircraft will not be covered. Only if you and your partners are fully willing to lose your investment in the airplane should your partnership select this option.

All risk not in motion. This is the lowest form of hull insurance coverage and covers your airplane only on the ground when not in motion. It provides protection against theft, fire, and vandalism and incidents such as someone sideswiping the airplane while it is parked. This type of insurance might make sense if for some reason you have a grounded airplane (perhaps awaiting restoration) that you are not planning to move during the insurance period.

Agreed value. Hull value is determined by what is known in the trade as agreed value. Agreed value is whatever you and your insurance provider agree your aircraft is worth. Customarily the insurance company will accept your valuation if it is within ±10 percent of retail bluebook value. If your figure is outside these parameters, you might be asked to justify it. The agreed value is the amount, less deductibles, that you will receive in case of total loss. In case of partial loss, when the insurance company pays to repair your aircraft, the company has the right—often exercised—to replace the damaged part with a used part in an equivalent condition; if a propeller had 1,800 hours on it when dinged by an extremely hard landing, the insurance company is only obliged to replace it with another propeller that has 1,800 hours on it. In the case of partial loss, the replacement obligation is based upon actual cash value.

Beware of the pitfalls of overinsuring and underinsuring. If you overinsure, the insurance provider might find it less expensive to repair a badly damaged aircraft instead of writing it off and handing you over enough money to buy a new one. If you underinsure, you run the risk of having a repairable aircraft declared a total loss and not having sufficient funds from the insurance profits to purchase a replacement. The insurance company's motivation to declare a total loss is to take possession of the aircraft, repair it, and sell it at a profit.

Deductibles. Deductibles vary depending upon your preference and the phase of flight in which the damage occurred. A willingness to accept a higher deductible might result in lower premiums, but the difference is usually negligible.

The types and amount of hull insurance and the deductibles specific to your policy can usually be found on your insurance policy's data sheet.

Liability insurance

Liability insurance covers you against claims by persons to whom the operation of your airplane caused some form of loss or damage. They could be your passengers or anyone outside the airplane or their heirs and survivors. Loss or damage is separated into two categories, *bodily injury* and *property damage*. Your policy sets limits to liability coverage, with which you should be thoroughly familiar. The limits offered by different insurers might also differ significantly. The structure of liability coverage limits should be one of your top priorities when you shop around for insurance.

Most policies today have combined liability coverage and limits for bodily injury and property damage, but some might not, so be sure to check. Let's take a closer look at typical types of liability limits.

Each occurrence. This amount is the maximum amount of liability insurance coverage you will receive for each accident or incident. It is tempting to choose the lowest amount of coverage available, to save on insurance premiums. The fact is that these amounts are unlikely to be sufficient in case of any major mishap. Carefully weigh the cost of extra coverage, and don't be too tightfisted. In this era of multimillion dollar liability awards, liability coverage of at least $1 million is considered prudent.

Each person. This is a sublimit of each occurrence. It is the maximum amount that will be paid to each claimant per occurrence. Here is where a spectacular amount of total liability insurance can quickly erode. Many policies will set very low limits per person. A $1 million total liability limit is worthless when your runaway prop drilled an irreparable hole in a sole provider to a family of eight and all they will get under the policy is $100,000 because that is your per person limit. Be sure that the per person coverage is substantial. The best policies do not have a per person restriction.

The per person limit is usually also the maximum amount for which medical expenses will be paid to each occupant of your aircraft. Some policies spell out this medical coverage in a separate section to be explicitly clear.

Family member limits. This is where a number of insurance companies provide practically negligible amounts of coverage. Limits on spouses (25 percent of the per person limit) and children (12.5 percent of the per person limit) are common. The theory is that immediate family members are not likely to sue each other, nor should they be tempted to.

Exclusions

What the large print giveth, the small print taketh away. Beware of exclusions. Read them carefully and make it a top priority to understand them fully. Many exclusions are standard, for instance prohibiting commercial operations, or trafficking in narcotics. But other exclusions can slip in there that can have a much greater impact on your coverage. Let's take a look at some typical exclusions.

FAR violations. Some policies will have an FAR violation exclusion, meaning that if you violated any FARs, you are not covered. This is bad news because it is practically impossible to be involved in a major mishap without some FAR violations. Furthermore, insurance companies have used this exclusion to deny claims when the violation of the FAR had nothing to do with the cause of the accident. An example is a denied claim because the proper aircraft documents were not on board when the airplane struck a landing light and folded a gear on landing. A gross violation will always be challenged, but an FAR exclusion is a sure sign of an intent by the insurance provider to stiff you in case of trouble.

Flights on legal airworthiness certificate waivers. An exclusion of flights on an airworthiness certificate waiver excludes some perfectly routine operations, such as flights on a ferry permit. This is not a major problem, but be aware of it and be sure to get additional coverage if the need arises.

Pilot qualifications. This is an important exclusion that deals with pilots other than the owners flying the airplane. The exclusion will usually refer to the data sheet that will spell out the requirements nonowner pilots must meet. The most restrictive option requires that only pilots named in the policy can fly the airplane. The less restrictive alternative imposes conditions to be met by nonowner pilots in order to qualify to fly the airplane. Some policies might even exclude maintenance personnel conducting test flights in connection with performed maintenance. Be sure to look because most maintenance personnel simply assume they can test fly the airplane.

Instruction exclusions. Many policies will exclude the use of the aircraft for instructing nonowners. So, if you are an instructor and want to give an occasional lesson or checkride to a friend—out of the goodness of your heart because accepting payment would be a commercial operation—be sure to check the exclusions.

In-flight operation by nonowner. This exclusion states that nobody other than the people authorized by your policy may operate your airplane in flight, even if you are in it. If your policy has such an exclusion, letting a friend handle the controls in flight who does not meet your policy's pilot requirements invalidates your policy. How will they know, you ask? Maybe they won't, but sometimes they find out as evidenced by court cases over denied claims due to such circumstances.

Off airport landings. Some policies specifically exclude intentional off-airport landings. The pilot of a Piper Cub heading for a surprise visit to Uncle Harry's ranch should take note.

Normal wear and tear or mechanical failure. This exclusion states that insurance will not pay for repairs required as a result of normal operations. The insurance provider will not buy you a new engine when the old one wears out. This is clear enough, but the mechanical failure exclusion can get murky. It basically means that if you have an in-flight mechanical failure and no damage beyond this mechanical failure occurs, the insurance company will not pay; however, if as a result of the mechanical failure other damage was sustained (during a forced landing), the insurance company will pay for the damage but not the original mechanical failure. This can get especially confusing when an engine failure leads to a forced landing and the airplane is totaled. Will the insurance company fully pay out? Will it reduce payment by the estimated amount of the mechanical failure? Check with your insurer.

Military airport waivers. Military airports require civilian users to sign liability waivers. Certain insurance policies therefore exclude the use of such airports; other policies state that in spite of your signing the waiver, your insurance remains in force.

War, revolution, insurrection. This exclusion states that if you are caught in such activities don't look for an insurance check when your airplane blows up. This is a standard insurance industry exclusion and also applies to many other forms of insurance.

Let the buyer beware: Many other exclusions might be found within an insurance policy, depending upon the insurer and coverage sought. Ask every question that comes to mind and ensure that you are fully satisfied with the respective answers.

PARTNERSHIP INSURANCE CONSIDERATIONS

Insuring an aircraft partnership requires dealing with a number of issues over and above the general insurance considerations usually faced by a sole owner. When the sole owner goes flying he risks only his own investment. He has only himself and his family to answer to in making insurance decisions and living with the consequences. When a partner takes to the air, he risks the investment of all the other partners, as well as his own. Any poor insurance choice by the partnership will cause a financial loss to all partners, not only the one doing the flying when the airplane is bent. Different experience levels among the partners and different preferences in levels of coverage can be additional sources of friction in a partnership. Let's take a closer look at the most common partnership insurance issues and how to deal with them.

Partnership hull insurance

The choice faced by the partnership is what level of coverage to get. Should it be all risk, all risk not in flight, or all risk not in motion? As stated earlier, certain pilots are so confident of their flying skills that they get only all risk not in flight hull insurance. If a partnership selects all risk not in flight coverage or less, it implies that each partner has complete confidence not only in his or her own flying abilities but also those of all the other partners. It is one thing to think that you fully trust the skills of your partners when you are writing out the insurance payment check and quite another to say "Aw, forget about it" when a partner has just wiped out your $20,000 investment because he forgot to put the gear down and the partnership did not have all risk insurance.

Experience has shown that the fingers start pointing quickly at the partner in command in case of trouble in an underinsured partnership, so all risk hull insurance is strongly recommended. The good news is that the incremental increase in insurance costs for all risk coverage is spread among the partners and should not, therefore, amount to an especially large additional financial burden per partner.

The selection of actual cash value or stated value coverage is a matter of preference, as it is for the sole owner. Just remember that stated value will give you a known amount (less deductibles), and be sure that all partners are satisfied with the choice.

Who pays the deductible?

This question is simple on the face of it. If a partner was in command at the time of the accident or incident, he or she should logically pay the deductible. If the aircraft was not in motion, it is logical for all partners to pay equal shares of the deductible.

Some partnerships consider an aircraft away from home base to be under the control of the partner using it, and require that partner to pay the deductible if an away from home accident or incident occurred even if the aircraft was not in motion at the time.

Partnership liability insurance

It is the selection of the appropriate amount of liability insurance coverage that poses the greatest insurance challenge for partnerships. The reason is simple. Different partners have different ideas of how much liability protection they need. A collective decision becomes particularly difficult if there is a great difference in the amount of assets the various partners have. A partner just out of school with few assets but a good income might be paired with a partner who has been working for ages and is worth a very substantial amount but does not want the hassle of sole ownership. While $500,000 in liability coverage might be sufficient for the partner just out of school, the one with substantial assets might want at least $2 million of coverage. The partner who wants higher overall coverage might also want significantly higher per person per occurrence coverage.

The first step to sorting out levels of partnership liability coverage is for the partners to see if a coverage amount sufficient for everyone can be obtained at an acceptable price. Depending upon the number of partners, the additional cost to each partner of substantially higher liability coverage might be quite low.

If the partners can't resolve their differences regarding levels of liability coverage, the partners seeking higher coverage might be able to purchase additional liability insurance independent of the partnership under an umbrella policy covering the partners' property and possessions. Most umbrella policies exclude aviation and additional coverage might be difficult to acquire. Ask your insurance provider for assistance.

A pro rata division of liability insurance costs with the partners seeking higher coverage paying proportionally more is not an equitable option. All partners would benefit from the same level of high coverage when they fly, regardless of their share of the payment; therefore, partners paying proportionally more would be subsidizing the partners paying less. A more acceptable option might be to have the policy written to provide higher liability coverage for certain specifically named partners who would pay the higher cost.

Liability implications of the legal form of the partnership

A big concern in partnerships is the exposure to liability claims of all partners caused by the actions of one partner. The problem can be especially disastrous if the partner causing the liability claim did something that invalidated the partnership's liability insurance. An opportunity to reduce each partner's liability for the actions of other partners lies in the legal form of the partners' ownership of the aircraft. From this perspective, incorporation, even at the partnership level, might be desirable. Check with your attorney to determine the ownership structure that makes the most sense for you. The legal form of ownership appears on the registration filed with the FAA (a sample registration form can be found in the appendices) and should also be clearly defined in your partnership agreement.

Insurance cost implications of different experience levels

Generally, insurance rates will be higher for pilots with lower levels of experience. In the case of an aircraft flown by a number of pilots, an insurance company will determine the insurance rate based upon the experience level of the least experienced pilot. In partnerships where there is a wide range of experience, this will mean that if insurance expenses are shared equally, partners with higher levels of experience would be subsidizing the partners with less experience.

If this subsidy is substantial, the partners might wish to divide insurance payment shares more equitably. Get separate insurance quotes; in addition to the actual insurance quote, a hypothetical quote should be obtained assuming that only the experienced partners would fly the airplane. The payment share of the experienced pilots should then be determined by an equal distribution of the hypothetical quote. The difference between the actual quote and the hypothetical quote should be shared by the less experienced partners only.

Consider a partnership of three pilots in a Warrior. Two are VFR private pilots with 150 hours each. The other pilot holds a commercial license with an instrument rating and has 3,000 hours. The actual annual insurance quote is $1,200. This would imply that each partner's share is $400; however, if all three pilots had a commercial license with an instrument rating and 3,000 hours of flying time, the insurance premium would be $800. This amount divided three ways is $267. Any amount in excess of $267 paid by the more experienced pilot in the actual partnership would be more than required from a pilot with his level of experience, essentially a subsidy of the less experienced pilots; thus, the fair shares of the annual insurance payment would be $267 by the experienced pilot and $467 each by the two less experienced pilots ($400 plus half of $133, the extra amount to be paid because of their lower level of experience).

When obtaining differential quotes, ask for the higher experience level first. Chances are it will be more competitive than if you received a quote at the low experience level and had it adjusted for hypothetically higher experience levels.

Prorating insurance payments for amounts of time flown

Some partnerships prorate insurance payments on an hourly basis. The partners who fly more pay more of the annual insurance costs. This arrangement is most often used when there is a big difference in the amount of time the various partners fly the airplane. The validity of this rationale is a matter of opinion. On the one hand, the partners who fly the airplane more, expose it to risk more often. On the other hand, all partners are free to fly the airplane as much or as little as they care to, yet, regardless of anticipated annual flying time, the insurance expense for the year would be approximately the same and would have to be paid anyway. In our opinion, insurance is practically a fixed annual cost of getting airborne, so, except for big differences in the partners' flight experience levels as addressed above, we favor an equal sharing of insurance expenses.

The importance of a good partnership agreement

As you can see, partnership insurance arrangements can be quite involved and the consequences of a bad insurance decision might be substantial. All partners should clearly understand and fully agree to the insurance arrangements entered into by the partnership; therefore, it is imperative to spell out in writing the way the partnership handles insurance, and the place to do this is in the partnership agreement with the advice of a lawyer.

WHERE TO GET INSURANCE?

Within the insurance industry, aviation insurance is a specialized branch, offered by specialist firms. Generalist agents who insure your house and car could possibly get you a quote too, but they will have little understanding of either the industry or your needs, so go to the specialists. Aviation insurance is generally available from two sources: underwriters and brokers.

Underwriters

Underwriters are the firms that actually take the risk on you when you get insurance for your airplane. They offer insurance directly, cutting out the middleman. Some of the middleman's commission they pass on to you, most of it they keep. The benefit of insuring directly with an underwriter is some savings on the cost of your coverage. The drawback is limited flexibility. Underwriters tend to offer stock policies with little scope for tailoring them to your specific needs. They are not in the business of advising you regarding alternative options in the insurance industry. You are expected to know what you want on which they will give you a quote. Another disadvantage is that you have to do the donkey work of contacting a variety of underwriters for competing quotes. This is time consuming and you might not be aware of all the available underwriters due to your lack of experience in the industry.

Brokers

Insurance brokers are middlemen. They help you assess your needs and go out to the underwriters to get the coverage you want at the best price available. An insurance broker expects to spend a considerable amount of time with you assessing your needs, explaining to you the various options available, and tailoring a policy to best meet your requirements. A good broker is perhaps the best option for personalized service. Brokers are paid by receiving a commission from the underwriter for policies placed. The commission is usually approximately 10 or 15 percent. Going through a broker is rarely more expensive that dealing with the underwriters directly. A good broker should be able to save you the amount of his commission or more on the policy price by shopping around and customizing your coverage to get the most protection for the best price.

Competing broker quotes. You should be aware of a peculiarity of obtaining insurance quotes through a broker. Once you appoint a broker to get you a specific quote, it is industry practice to consider that broker to have an exclusive right to obtain quotes for you for a reasonable period of time; thus, if you appoint a broker and then call an underwriter directly to shop around after your broker has had contact with the underwriter, you will be told that a broker is already handling the case and you will not be given a quote. This practice protects a broker from having clients essentially stolen by competing brokers. If you don't like what your first broker is telling you, the proper way to get competing quotes is to go to other brokers consecutively.

Choosing an insurer

With the limited insurance industry experience most of us have, choosing an underwriter or broker can feel like going to a potluck dinner; however, relatively simple procedures can take the uncertainty out of choosing an insurer. For best results, make an effort to apply as many of these procedures as possible.

Talk to the insurer. There is no reason not to interview the insurer, be it an underwriter or a broker. Find out how long the insurer has been in business. Ask what professional aviation background its agents have. Are any of them pilots? Underwriters might be public companies that publish annual reports you can get. You might not have the qualifications to analyze the financials in the annual report, but it should be full of a wealth of other information that will give you some insight into the company. Chat with a broker about his or her background, training, aviation interests and qualifications, and ask for references.

Word of mouth. This is an excellent source of information if you do a good job of your homework. Talk to as many airplane owners and FBOs in your aviation community as you can. Ask them about rates and quality of service. Make every effort to talk to airplane owners who have had to collect under a policy. Were they paid what they expected? Were they given a hard time? Did the insurer try to pressure them into a settlement they considered unfair? Did the policy cover what they were led to believe, or were there surprises regarding coverage?

Aviation associations. From time to time aviation associations such as AOPA and EAA enter into agreements with insurers to provide coverage for association members. While the associations are unlikely to explicitly endorse the insurer to you personally, you can take some comfort in the link between the two institutions and might qualify for the programs being offered.

Banks and other financial institutions. Good sources of information about insurance providers are banks and other financial institutions who lend for aircraft. They require insurance for financed airplanes and they are familiar with the industry.

Regulatory and rating agencies. Call your state insurance commission to see if there have been any complaints against the insurer you are considering. Several independent insurance rating agencies in essence give grades to the insurers they cover. The A.M. Best Co. is the most widely used. Get an understanding of the grading system and see how your insurer stacks up. Sometimes the rating agencies' books are hard to decipher. Get your insurance agent to help.

BEWARE OF MULTIPLE INSURANCE

Every once in a while someone gets the bright idea of buying two separate insurance policies for one aircraft. More often, two policies end up being in place for one aircraft when the owners want to change insurers and buy the second policy without simultaneously canceling the first one.

If you change insurers, be careful because *at any time when two different policies are written for the same aircraft, both policies are invalidated and you will be without coverage.*

INSURANCE WORKSHEET

An insurance worksheet (Table 9-1) is designed to help you collect data on insurance options. Use it to talk to the partnership, a broker, or to deal directly with underwriters.

Table 9-1.

Have for insurers each partner's age, licences and ratings, total hours logged, hours in type, hours of relevant experience (R/G;tailwheel,multi, etc).

	DESIRED LIMIT	INSURER 1: COVERAGE	INSURER 1: COST	INSURER 2: COVERAGE	INSURER 2: COST	INSURER 3: COVERAGE	INSURER 3: COST
HULL							
All risk							
All risk in motion							
All risk not in motion							
Deductibles							
TOTAL HULL COST							
LIABILITY							
Per occurrence							
Per person per occurrence							
Per occupant per occurrence							
Bodily injury sublimit							
Spouse sublimit							
Child (a/c owners') sublimit							
TOTAL LIABILITY COST							
MEDICAL							
Per occurrence							
Per person per occurrence							
TOTAL INSURANCE COST							

EXCLUSIONS (use above insurer numbers for YES/NO)	YES	NO
FAR violations		
Flights on legal airworthiness cert. waivers		
Instruction for owners or non-owners		
In flight operation by non-owner		
Intentional off airport landings		
Ops under govt. liability waiver		
Other exclusions:		

Note: Only generally undesirable exclusions are listed above. Check policies carefully for other exclusions

OTHER TERMS, CONDITIONS AND ISSUES

Flights by non-owners:

Geographic coverage:

Experience needed to reduce policy cost:

Insurance provider rating:

Other:

Other:

Other:

10

The joining partner

IT IS ENOUGH OF A CHORE to form a partnership from scratch, but in some respects joining a partnership already in existence can be even trickier. When a whole new partnership is formed, everyone sets out on an equal footing. The partners might know each other quite well, but the habits and ways of the partnership are yet to be established. There is plenty of room for give and take all around; however, when you join an existing partnership, you are in a sense intruding on a relationship that has been going on for some time. Chances are it has developed little nuances and has become comfortably set in its patterns that you will have to adapt to or patterns that will have to be adjusted to accommodate you. If forming a partnership is like getting married, then joining one already in existence is like joining your in-laws in their family business.

No matter how good the intentions are of the partners taking you in, the fact remains that you will be the new kid on the block. The partners will be paying close attention to you, and on a subconscious level at least, they will be waiting for you to prove yourself, to give signs that you really deserve to be one of the group. This will certainly be the case while you are negotiating to join the partnership, and will most likely linger for some time after you join, until the partnership's patterns settle once again into a familiar groove.

It can be quite intimidating to be under a partnership's magnifying glass. Such scrutiny might cloud the joining partner's thought process in evaluating the partnership and might even pressure the joining partner into conclusions or decisions that might be discomforting. This need not be so. A little assertiveness and self-assurance backed by a good dose of quiet competence will make joining a partnership as smooth as forming one. Once you have defined your personal objectives and financial commitment, your task will be twofold. You will have to closely scrutinize the partnership's aircraft and you will have to carefully evaluate your potential partners. To some extent mutual interests will be at work because your partners will also want to make the right decision. But misperceptions can arise, even with the best of intentions. Let's take a closer look at how to go about it if you are the joining partner.

CHECKING OUT THE AIRCRAFT

The evaluation of the partnership's aircraft should be the joining partner's most straightforward task. It should be a pure business decision, deliberated in as much detail as if the aircraft were being purchased to form a new partnership. Yet it is in the evaluation of the aircraft that a joining partner is most easily badgered by the members of the partnership.

For most people, their airplane is a matter of deep personal pride. It is only natural for the members of a partnership to view a critical outsider with suspicion and to be defensive. On the other hand, a potential joining partner is reluctant to behave as if he were bargaining at the horse thieves' market. At the market and in a normal sale of an airplane, once the mutual bullying is over and the bargain is struck, buyer and seller say goodbye and might never see each other again. But should the joining partner decide to buy, he will be moving in with the sellers, the whole lot of them. So, just to get a better deal, he will be wary of loudly declaring that his potential partners' alleged cream puff is a bucket of bolts that would make the Wright brothers get back into bicycles. This wariness is misplaced. The joining partner should place personality considerations firmly behind the task of evaluating whether or not the airplane would be a good buy.

As the joining partner, your first order of business is to get all the pertinent details on the airplane and the financial terms of the sale. Evaluate this information in light of the research you have done, according to the guidelines offered in part IV, regarding buying an airplane. Does the price make ballpark sense? Does the airplane have all the features, characteristics, and equipment you set as your objective? Is the airplane in the age group you were looking for, and can you live with the number of hours on it? All routine questions, right down the list.

If the preliminary information checks out, proceed with inspecting the airplane, also described in part IV. When you are joining a partnership it is especially tempting to rely on the partners' mechanic, or even soothing statements from the partners themselves. After all, won't they continue to fly the airplane right along with you when you join the partnership? Sure they will, but if the engine is about to blow up and will require an overhaul in the next few months, their share of the bill will be that much less. Consider your share of a $15,000 overhaul in a three-way partnership before you lamely accept your future partners' assurances. The only way you will know for sure is by having the aircraft checked out by your own mechanic.

There is another reason to get your own mechanic. Inevitably, psychology is at work during the transaction. You might end up feeling pretty lonely and pressured when you show up by yourself to face two or three partners and their mechanic. Appearing with your own mechanic in tow puts you on a more equal footing. It shows that you really mean business and know how to go about it.

Because the airplane will be in your neighborhood, it should be easy to arrange for the assistance of a mechanic you know or who has been recommended by people whose opinions you trust. Conduct the prepurchase inspection just as you would if you were buying an airplane to form a brand new partnership. Follow the guidelines in part IV.

Fly the airplane. Better still, also have one or more of the partners fly it and observe their skills and habits. Use the flight to check if all systems and avionics function as advertised. When the inspection is complete and you have come up with a list of squawks, you have three options:

- Reduce the price of joining based upon your share of repair costs.
- Specify in writing that repairs shall be performed at the expense of the original partners prior to joining.
- Walk away.

A worthwhile option, if the timing is right, is to participate in or observe an annual done on the partnership's airplane just before you buy into it. Besides teaching you a lot about the airplane's mechanical condition, the annual will also tell you a lot about the partnership. Note how the partners handle problems, how much personal labor they apply, how much maintenance they defer, and most importantly, how their approach to maintenance fits in with your approach.

If the airplane checks out and the price is right, it is time for the joining partner's more challenging task, evaluating the partnership.

EVALUATING THE PARTNERSHIP

As in most situations where human emotions are a factor, the evaluation of a partnership is a subjective process. In the end, you click or you don't. It is fine for the members of the partnership to be laid-back good ol' boys if you are too; they can be walking computers if you are, too. The trick is to find the common (missing?) link.

In spite of human emotions and personalities, there are objective factors you can evaluate that will help you decide whether or not to join the partnership. A good place to begin is the partnership agreement.

Read the partnership agreement carefully and see how well it fits with your ideals. A good partnership agreement is a promising sign. Take note of any sections particularly important to you. Scheduling, the sharing of fixed expenses, fuel purchases, decisions, and the sale of partnership shares come to mind. If something is not to your liking, see how willing the partners are to make amendments.

Next, evaluate how the partnership practices what it has set for itself in the partnership agreement. The greatest agreement is worthless if not put into practice. During your checkout of the airplane, you will have had a chance to observe the partners in action, especially if you flew with one or more of them, or participated with them in an annual.

Try to get a handle on how orderly or casual they are around the airplane. What preflight habits do they have and expect from you? Do they insist on checklists or do they rely on memory? If the latter is the case, how good is their memory? Do they consistently practice particular operating procedures in flight? Do they show a tendency to believe in an exclusive procedure, or are they keen to

The classic Globe Swift is a joy to fly, but might be a handful for the inexperienced pilot.

explore and allow the practice of legitimate alternatives? What postflight procedures do they follow? How do they expect to find the aircraft every time they come out to fly?

Discuss with them at length their use of the aircraft. Do they really take turns flying it away for days on end, or do they all fly to the coffee shop 50 miles down the 233 radial every single weekend?

Examine carefully how they keep track of flight time and expenses. Review all the flight records. The partnership flight log is an excellent insight into the group's flying activity. Ask to see the partnership financial records and review them closely. Does the checkbook balance? Are the records accurate? Are all the partners regularly informed of the partnership's financial transactions? Do all partners appear to pay their share of expenses in a timely fashion? Does the partnership have a separate engine reserve account? Is enough being reserved per hour?

As long as regulations and safety margins are observed, there is really no right or wrong way to run a partnership, and that is not the question to ask when evaluating one. What ultimately makes any partnership work is that all of its members are comfortable with the style in which it is organized and run. As a joining partner, your big concern besides the airplane should be how well you fit in.

Beyond checking out the facts, the best way to get to know your potential partners is to hang out with them for a while before you make a final decision. And remember, they will be as keen to make the right move as you are.

11

Keeping the records

MAINTAINING ACCURATE INFORMATION about a partnership's operations, finances, and obligations is one secret of ensuring a smooth and trouble-free partnership. The extent to which you and your partners keep records will depend upon the partnership's size, its level of activity, and the personal inclination of the partners to be meticulous and well informed. It is fine to get by with minimal recordkeeping as long as all partners recognize the limitations of such an approach and nobody pretends to be surprised when the muddled scribbling on the back of envelopes causes great confusion and disagreement.

Recordkeeping can be loosely grouped in three broad categories: aircraft operations, financial records, and partnership documents.

AIRCRAFT OPERATIONS

Certain recordkeeping is mandated by the FAA. Engine and airframe logs must be kept; aircraft operating manual (including current weight and balance), airworthiness certificate, and registration must be onboard the airplane. But for a well organized partnership, there is far more to operations recordkeeping than regulatory requirements. Scheduling, keeping track of hours flown, logging maintenance squawks, and monitoring aircraft performance all require some form of recordkeeping.

Scheduling

Many partnerships do the scheduling by word of mouth, but if there are more than two partners it is a good idea to take turns being the scheduling coordinator and keeping some form of written schedule. The schedule you design will depend upon the arrangements you and your partners have for using the airplane. Most partnerships have some priority system where one partner has the airplane for a day, a weekend, or a whole week, and the other partners have access to the airplane only if the partner with priority decides not to fly. This system is usually on a set rotation; therefore, it can be published far in advance and sent to all the partners. The scheduling partner is then responsible for coordinating the use of the aircraft over and above the needs of the priority pilot. It is the responsibility of the pilot with priority to let the scheduler know when and if the airplane will be available during the priority slot. The scheduler can then allocate the airplane among the nonpriority partners on a first come first serve basis. For partners without priority, and if there are periods during the week when nobody has priority (Monday through Thursday), it is advisable to block out some comfortable window of time that will allow leisurely use of the airplane, but will also make it available for others on a reasonable timeframe. Dividing the day for nonpriority partners between morning use and afternoon use usually works quite well.

It is a good idea to provide the scheduler with a scheduling calendar used exclusively for the airplane to avoid confusion and to maintain a booking record. If your partnership is on a priority system, the priority information should be entered in the calendar in advance. It is also strongly recommended that the scheduler have an answering machine and be committed to returning phone calls within a specified period of time. Few things are more frustrating in an aircraft partnership than an unreachable scheduler.

If your partnership does not have a priority system, it is still advisable to agree on standard time slots of generous duration, depending upon the type of flying you and your partners generally do. If your flying is mainly local or instructional, half-day limits are convenient. If you all take day-trips frequently, full-day availability should be your standard. If there is frequent demand for the airplane for longer periods of time, you should be on some form of priority system instead of an ad hoc arrangement.

Trial and error will prove what works best for your partnership, but it is important to have a good scheduling system to keep everyone happy and maximize the use of the airplane.

Flight log

The next important item after scheduling is keeping an accurate log of when the airplane was used and by whom (Table 11-1). The best solution is a flight log kept in the airplane to be filled out by the pilot immediately after every flight. This log can be used to record a variety of information, but at a minimum should include the following:

- Date of flight
- Route of flight
- Pilot's name
- Beginning tach or Hobbs time
- Ending tach or Hobbs time
- Total duration of flight
- Remarks

Table 11-1.

DATE	PILOT	TACH 940.6	FLT TIME	ROUTE
6/15	SANDERS	942.5	1.9	BED - EEN - HVN - BED
6/18	BROWN	943.6	1.1	BED - LOC
6/18	SANDERS	944.8	1.2	BED - BLD - BED
6/20	BROWN	948.0	3.2	BED - FDK
6/21	BROWN	949.5	1.5	FDK - TEB
6/23	BROWN	951.5	2.0	TEB - BED
6/24	SANDERS	954.6	3.1	BED - IAG

This log should be the basis for charging partners for the hourly use of the airplane. The partner that maintains the financial records should frequently proof the hours logged by partners against payments received from pilots flying the airplane. It should be a standard procedure for partners to know the hourly rate to be paid for the airplane and to send the partner handling the finances a check for the appropriate amount immediately after each flight with an appropriate notation: N37RW, 1.7 hours, 5/15/92, $58.

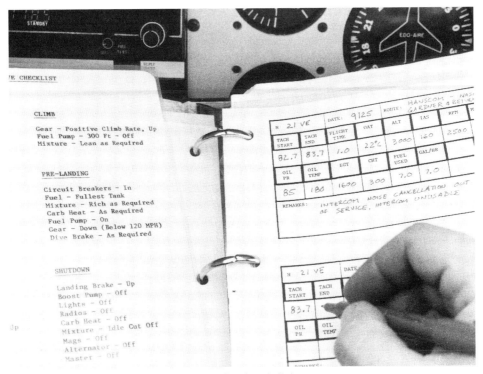

It takes only a few minutes to record the details of each flight.

Invoice and check box

Some partners are notorious for slovenly administrative habits, including being chronically late sending in the checks they owe. Others are frugal, and hate to waste a postage stamp every time they have to make a payment for a few hours of flying. For them, there is a convenient solution in the form of an invoice strongbox that normally might be stored in the airplane or, if possible, in a secured hangar accessible only to the partnership. It is a metal box available in most stationery stores. Its top surface contains blank invoice forms. It also has a slot on the side and room for lots of invoices and checks inside, and it can be kept locked. The partnership can get such a box into which every partner could slip his or her check along with a completed invoice immediately after a flight. The partner handling the finances could clear out the box periodically, allowing plenty of time for checks to clear prior to a loan payment or other billing. Nobody would have an excuse for not making a payment, and no postage would be wasted. Some people dislike the idea of leaving uncashed checks in the airplane, but if the box is kept discreetly away from prying eyes, strictly no cash is put in it, and it is frequently emptied, the convenience might be worth the minimal risk of having to stop payment of a few checks.

Maintenance squawks

It is important for partnerships to keep a record of maintenance squawks on some standard form (Table 11-2). The sole owner knows if there is a problem and whether or not he or she has had it fixed, making a squawk record an unnecessary burden. But for partners who might not always see each other and don't keep close tabs on each other's flying, a record of mechanical squawks and subsequent resolution can be invaluable. Examples in this chapter provide the basis for a customized squawk sheet. Bear in mind that a good squawk sheet has a dated column not only for noting the problem, but another one for noting the resolution. Any mechanical glitch that makes the aircraft unairworthy should be considered an emergency to be immediately reported to all partners in addition to being entered on the squawk sheet. A note declaring the aircraft unairworthy should also be prominently displayed in the cockpit.

Table 11-2.

AIRCRAFT SQUAWK REPORT		N: 692 W	TACH: 1161.3
DATE NOTED: 8/17	PILOT: SANDERS	DATE RESOLVED: 8/19	BY: SMITH ; PGAIR
SQUAWK:		RESOLUTION:	
GEAR WARNING LIGHT ILLUMINATES INTERMITTENTLY IN FLIGHT WHEN GEAR IS IN THE "UP" POSITION IN CRUISE.		Faulty microswitch. Installed new microswitch. Performed retraction test; Flight tested in moderate turbulence. Works ok.	
SIGNATURE: J. Sanders		SIGNATURE: Hop Smith	

Aircraft performance records

Professional flyers have long made it a practice to keep records of in-flight aircraft and engine performance parameters. For the pilots of small airplanes on pleasure flights, this is an option but a useful one. It will teach users a lot about the performance of their airplanes, it can provide early warning of mechanical problems, and it can clear up uncertainties about performance by providing historic references.

Items most commonly logged are power settings, fuel consumption, engine pressures and temperatures, altitude, outside air temperature, and indicated airspeed (Table 11-3).

Table 11-3.

TACH END:	DATE: 7/26		N: 949X		PILOT: EVANS		
653.6	ROUTE: 6B6 - MHT - 9D7 - 6B6						
(-) TACH START:	OAT	ALTITUDE	IAS	MP	RPM	MIXTURE	
651.2	+15°C	6000	125	24.7	2400	+50° PEAK	
= FLIGHT TIME:	OIL PRESS	OIL TEMP	EGT	CHT	GAL/HR	TAS	
2.4	85	180	1260	307	10	139	
REMARKS ✱ 1.5 HR IFR (HOOD) 3 ILS MHT; BROWN SAFETY PILOT ✱ ADDED 1 QT OIL ON LANDING							

Inspections due date chart

A very useful chart, prominently displayed in the cockpit for best effect or available with the flight logs, is a record of the due dates of the next required inspections such as the annual or 100-hour inspection, transponder and altimeter checks, and VOR checks as applicable (Table 11-4). It is important for someone to take charge of keeping the chart current, but if a recent inspection is inadvertently not recorded, the error, while annoying, is on the conservative side and will not compromise flying safety.

Flight planning and briefing forms

A partnership might find it convenient to have an indexed binder of pre-printed blank flight planning forms, weight and balance forms, weather briefing

Table 11-4.

RECURRENT CHECKS DUE	N: *106 PE*	
Enter date or Tach hours when **next** check due. Cross out superseded date.		
ANNUAL INSPECTION:	~~4/30/91~~	4/30/92
100 HOUR INSPECTION:	N/A	N/A
TRANSPONDER CHECK:	3/31/92	
STATIC/ALTIMETER CHECK:	3/31/92	
FCC RADIO LICENSE (renewal):	7/31/93	

VOR CHECKS:	~~4/30/91~~	~~5/30/91~~	~~6/29/91~~	~~7/29/91~~
	~~8/28/91~~	~~9/27/91~~	~~10/27/91~~	~~11/26/91~~
	~~12/26/91~~	~~1/25/92~~	2/24/92	

forms, and flight plans. It might even be worth keeping the used forms in the binder for reference and as a record of the airplane's activities.

FINANCIAL RECORDKEEPING

Keeping the financial records, collecting payments due from partners, and making payments on behalf of the group is one of the more thankless tasks of an airplane partnership. It requires a lot of administrative discipline, it can be somewhat time consuming, and if it gets messed up, it can be a big source of friction among the partners and might even cause the partnership to break up.

The partner "volunteered" to handle the finances should have the requisite skills and the discipline, and should be aided by the other partners in every way possible. Think long and hard before you make the financial recordkeeping task a rotating responsibility among partners. If one partner is especially good at it, you might all be better off by allowing him or her to permanently handle the finances and find other ways for the rest of the partners to make a contribution.

The basic task

The financial management of the partnership consists of basic responsibilities:

- Collecting money owed the partnership from the partners in a timely fashion
- Paying the partnership's bills in a timely fashion
- Keeping accurate records of the partnership's financial transactions
- Providing an accurate periodic accounting to all partners of the partnership's financial transactions

You might set up a Fouga Magister partnership for the price of a Bonanza, but you better have a huge limit on your avgas credit card.

A big part of the job is keeping after the partners to send in their share of imminent expenses. It is not advisable to cover for a partner and pay any bills prior to receiving each partner's share of the payment. Practically all bills are presented with sufficient lead time to allow all partners to forward their share of the money before the bill needs to be paid. If a partner lacks the discipline to make timely payments, an arrangement should be made with him to put an advance into the partnership for upcoming bills.

Checkbook accounting and partnership accounts

In spite of the dreary administrative responsibility, keeping the partnership's books is a fairly simple financial task. It is best tracked on a cash basis. It is a record of the movements of cash into and cash out of the partnership. Actually, accounting for the partnership is like keeping a checkbook. The partners' payments into the partnership are the deposits. The payments are the expenses for which the checks are written.

The tool for a good partnership's financial transactions is the partnership checking account. It is usually opened in the name of the partnership. All partners should have signing power on the account, and withdrawals above a certain amount should require the signature of two partners. Many easygoing small partnerships open a partnership checking account and simply use the checkbook as the record of financial transactions. This is certainly a viable form of minimum financial recordkeeping from which periodic summary reports of the partnership's financial activities and condition can be extracted.

The checkbook is the original financial record of the partnership account, and more detailed financial reports must reconcile to it. For partners interested in more closely tracking partnership financial transactions and their own shares of it, a more detailed yet still simple form of recordkeeping might be a worthwhile effort. If diligently kept current, it will always provide accurate up-to-the-minute financial information broken down by partner.

Examine the partnership financial statement in Table 11-5. It is a financial reporting sheet for a partnership of three pilots. The income side is simply a breakdown by partner of the deposits made into the checking account for all the expenses of the partnership, tiedown, insurance, loan payments, plus a payment per flying hour that includes the engine and airframe reserve (but does not include fuel if in your partnership each partner pays fuel individually and leaves the airplane topped off after every flight). The expense side is the record of payments transposed from the checking account. Ideally each partner would pay his share of each expense item with a separate check that would make things very clear; however, in practice, partners may send one combined check from time to time to cover a variety of expenses that are due at the same time. The partner keeping the books can get around this problem by entering in the description column an accurate dollar breakdown of what each check was for.

On a periodic basis, at least annually, all partners should be provided with a summary table (Table 11-6) that formally reflects cash flow: a total of cash paid into the partnership by each partner for the year, the cost of capital for the year (determined according to the definition in part I), and the per hour costs of flying for each partner for the year (the sum of cash expense and cost of capital divided by hours flown). If each partner pays for fuel out of pocket, each partner must add this figure to his expenses run through the partnership account.

The table ties back into the financial model used to estimate the partnership's annual cost of flying. In fact, it is proof of the accuracy of your assumptions or the need for their revision. It shows how close you came to where you thought you should be financially at the end of the year. If you want to only see what the per hour outlay of cash was from your pocket for the year, you can simply ignore the cost of capital.

The engine and airframe reserve is equal to whatever reserve money was paid into the partnership account as part of the hourly payments made during the life of the partnership. Reserves contributed during the year should equal the total hours flown during the year multiplied by the per hour reserve charge (you can calculate this amount and proof it toward payments received during the year for hours flown). This amount is added to reserves already accumulated, and any assessments during the year are also added, to arrive at total reserves.

Note that because the partnership pays all of its expenses as they arise and the only additional money put into the account is reserve money, the balance in the account at any time should be very close to the reserve amount, except for timing differences in checks issued by the partnership but not yet cashed.

Table 11-5.

N1786L PARTNERSHIP FINANCIAL STATEMENT 1990

HOURLY RATE: 27.00

BEGINNING BALANCE: 4568.00

CURRENT BALANCE: 5790.00

INCOME

SZUROVY

Date	Amount	Description	Chk#
12/31/90	1795.00	Annual	245

SCHUETTE

Date	Amount	Description	Chk#

HOWARD

Date	Amount	Description	Chk#

EXPENSE

Date	Amount	Payee	Chk#

Table 11-6.

FINANCIAL SUMMARY 1990

	SZUROVY	SCHUETTE	HOWARD	TOTAL
HOURS				
CASH EXPENSES ($)				
COST OF CAPITAL ($)				
$ PER HOUR				

ENGINE AND AIRFRAME RESERVE

BEGINNING HOURS	
ENDING HOURS	
BEGINNING E & A RESERVE ($)	
ADDITIONAL E & A RESERVE ($)	
ASSESSMENTS	
ENDING E & A RESERVE ($)	

A more informative financial statement

If you really are in the mood to track the actual costs of your flying compared to what you projected with this book's financial model, you may get a lot fancier in your financial recordkeeping. Examine another set of partnership financial statements in Tables 11-7 and 11-8. The income side differs from the simpler statement discussed above in that it lists hours flown and breaks out operating income separately. This is the per hourly payment of each partner for hours flown and includes the reserves (not including fuel if paid individually); thus, you have up-to-date information on how many hours each partner has flown

Table 11-7.

N1786L PARTNERSHIP FINANCIAL STATEMENT 1990

HOURLY RATE 27.00

BEGINNING BALANCE 4568.00

CURRENT BALANCE 5790.00

INCOME

SZUROVY

Date	Hrs	Op Inc	Oth Inc	Description	Chk#
12/31/90	2.7	57.60		Local instruction	245
1/11/91			1367.00	Annual	246

SCHUETTE

Date	Hrs	Op Inc	Oth Inc	Description	Chk#

HOWARD

Date	Hrs	Op Inc	Oth Inc	Description	Chk#

Table 11-8.

N1786L PARTNERSHIP FINANCIAL STATEMENT 1990

FINANCIAL SUMMARY 1990 ($)

	SZUROVY	SCHUETTE	HOWARD	TOTAL
FLIGHT HOURS				
HANGAR				
INSURANCE				
FEES				
ANNUAL				
MAINTENANCE				
OP/RES				
OTHER				
TOTAL CASH				
COST OF CAPITAL				
TOTAL EXPENSES				
$/HOUR				

ENGINE AND AIRFRAME RESERVE

BEGINNING HOURS	
ENDING HOURS	
BEGINNING E & A RESERVE ($)	
ADDITIONAL E & A RESREVE ($)	
ASSESSMENTS	
ENDING E & A RESERVE ($)	

Account Types: Hangar, Insurance, Fees, Annual
Maintenance, Op/Res, Other

EXPENSE

Date	Amount	Payee	Chk#	Account
				Hangar
				Insurance
				Maintenance
				Fees
				Op/Res
				Annual
				Other

since the beginning of the year (cross-checked to the logs), and how much each partner has spent on operating and fixed expenses.

On the expense side, the keeper of the books assigns the appropriate expense category to each expense. At the end of the year, each category is summed and each partner is assigned his or her share. The categories tie in with the book's financial model. Assumptions can be compared to results in great detail, and the costs of flying can be better understood as a result of experience.

A separate engine reserve account

Engine reserves may be kept as surplus cash in the regular partnership checking account, but it is a nice refinement of partnership accounting to keep a second, separate account strictly for the accumulation of the engine reserve (Table 11-8). As payments are received for hourly flying charges, the partner keeping the books transfers the reserve amount of each hourly charge into the reserve account. A separate reserve account is a good idea because it protects the engine reserve from the temptation of alternate use. It can be a savings account earning a higher rate of interest than a checking account, and partners can tell at a glance how well their engine reserve is doing in comparison to the amount of hours the airplane is flying. They can more accurately evaluate whether or not they are reserving at a sufficiently high rate or if they are facing a potential special assessment at overhaul time.

Periodic financial reporting to the partners

It is important for the partners to be well informed about the financial affairs of the partnership. The partners need to know how much they have been putting into the pot and what expenses have been paid on behalf of the partnership. To this end, the partners must be sent periodic financial statements, as well as proof that payments made by the partnership were for legitimate invoices. Monthly statements come to most partners' minds when the partnership is initially formed, but, frankly, in most cases this would be too time consuming. For the majority of partnerships, quarterly statements will be sufficient, perhaps sent just before quarterly meetings. For proof of payment of legitimate bills, copies of invoices over a certain amount, perhaps $50, should be attached.

If the financial statements such as the ones presented above are diligently kept up-to-date, the checkbook is regularly balanced, and invoices are carefully filed, the quarterly financial record mailing to the partners should be a nonevent.

Automate the partnership's financial statements

You can further simplify maintaining financial statements by programming them on your personal computer and practically eliminating the time-consuming task of hand calculations. The statements presented are easily automated by anyone with basic spreadsheet skills.

KEEPING ESSENTIAL PARTNERSHIP DOCUMENTS

Partnerships will accumulate a fair number of essential documents: partnership's founding document, partnership agreement, aircraft bill of sale, title search results, title insurance, annual insurance policy, loan agreement if financed. While legally acceptable duplicates of these documents could be obtained from the issuing entity in case of loss, it is best to take good care of the originals in your possession. The best place for them is a fireproof safe. Make sure that all the partners have a set of copies of all documents but put the originals away in a secure place.

12

Partnership choices

NOW YOU SHOULD BE IN A GOOD POSITION to establish a partnership of your own. The degree to which you want to make use of the guidelines presented so far is largely a function of partnership size and the nature of the partners. You are likely to find the potential for greatest variations in the partnership agreement, operations, and maintenance, depending upon the number of partners.

TWO PARTNERS

If you can afford it, a partnership of two partners is the best of both worlds. Depending upon the amount of flying each partner plans to do, it can be almost like being a sole owner without carrying the full financial burden. It is also likely to instill a sense of mutual loyalty. You will each feel bad if you let the other partner down. There is no third or fourth partner to whom you can complain or rationalize. The two-person partnership will work very well right away, or it will not work at all.

There is a lot of room for being informal, for keeping structure and bureaucracy to the bare minimum. If you have similar flying objectives, you can fly the heck out of the airplane as a team and get far more out of it than either partner would as sole owner. Or, if you prefer, you can arrange the partnership in such a fashion that you hardly ever see each other and fly the heck out of the airplane individually, practically as sole owners.

Two-person partnership agreement

The two-person partnership provides the greatest flexibility regarding the partnership agreement. The important objective is to set up an effective mechanism to resolve disputes and handle the dissolution of the partnership. Beyond that, it can be as minimal or as detailed as the partners prefer. "A schedule mutually agreeable" is just fine if you know that the time slots you each want are complementary.

Finances can also be handled in simple fashion. It is wise to include language that all shares of expenses are due immediately and that no partner will pay any-

The Swiss Datwyler might soon become a welcome new entry into the two-seat trainer market.

thing on behalf of the partnership prior to receiving the other partner's share of the payments. But how strictly you enforce these terms is up to you. A requirement to periodically settle accounts is also worth including.

An often ticklish aspect of the two-person partnership is the issue of engine and maintenance reserves. Based upon what they think they know of each other, two partners frequently trust each other to come up with the big bucks at maintenance and overhaul time, and surprise, surprise, someone can't deliver. Even the closest partners might want to set up a reserve account and fund it periodically, based upon the amount they fly. Nickel and dime checks probably do not need to be sent in every time you fly around the patch, but you should both be obligated to make a deposit once the reserve amount you owe reaches a certain level.

A good plan for two partners is to sit down with the partnership agreement chapter and go down the items one by one to decide the extent of detail required. A word of caution. If you don't know your partner too well, but necessity has brought you together and initial impressions are good enough to try a partnership, opt for greater detail.

In the end, the two-person partnership is truly a personal relationship, and no matter what your piece of paper says, ultimate success or failure depends on the nature of your relationship.

Operations considerations

Simplicity in operations is also the desirable and easily attainable goal of the two-person partnership. Keep your fuel bills separate and keep good records of

This well maintained Bonanza first flew in 1957 and is an ideal choice for a low-cost high-performance partnership.

who flew when (through a logbook kept in the airplane), and usually all will be well.

The easiest scheduling method is the priority system, where each partner has the airplane exclusively for alternate weekends or days, whatever works best. Beyond that, informal contact can always let the nonpriority partner know if the airplane is available. It is important for the nonpriority partner to be diplomatic. "I'll wait for you at the airport to get back, but take all the time you want at the beach," might make the priority partner feel unduly pressured.

Maintenance considerations

The big maintenance question is how much or how little to do yourself under the supervision of an airframe and powerplant mechanic working alone, independently of a big maintenance facility, and how much work do you want done in a fancy maintenance shop. You can learn a lot about the airplane working alongside an independent mechanic, and can keep the bills down but there are also drawbacks. The mechanic might not always be readily available (many of them have full-time jobs besides moonlighting on airplanes like yours), so repairs and annuals might take longer than you would like.

Alternatively, the fancy maintenance shop will service your airplane thoroughly (though not always speedily, depending on backlog) for big bucks and no effort on your part except a few phone calls.

Maintenance expenses are one of the biggest aircraft expense items, so even the most informal two-person partnership should have a clear understanding of committing to maintenance work only after mutual agreement.

Friction on maintenance issues can arise if one partner is an incorrigible tinkerer and the other one is terrified if anyone but an A&P lays hands on the airplane, even for preventative maintenance authorized under FAR 43 (appendix E) to be performed by the owner. Again, either approach is fine; the real issue is partner compatibility.

THREE OR FOUR PARTNERS

Three- or four-person partnerships are very popular because costs are greatly reduced yet the number of partners is sufficiently small to allow excellent aircraft availability. But when a partnership has more than two partners, considerably more formal structure and organization is usually required. Demand for the airplane is higher, the chance for misunderstandings greater, the administrative workload heavier.

Partnership agreement

The best advice for the three- or four-person partnership is to address everything in detail in the partnership agreement. Aircraft scheduling, expense billing and accounting, decision-making, fueling, dispute resolution, the departure of partners, and partnership dissolution all need to be spelled out with great care.

The relationship among the partners might be and often is very personal, but the partnership should be organized and run in an entirely businesslike fashion.

Operations considerations

While the three- or four-person partnership demands a certain degree of formal organization, it is still small enough to function effectively on a priority pilot basis if the partners' interest is to have access to the airplane for long stretches of time. A priority schedule can be laid out a month in advance and distributed among the partners. Some mechanism should be worked out to handle competition for the airplane among nonpriority pilots in case the priority pilot isn't using it. A first-come first-served arrangement through positive contact with the priority pilot, and a maximum nonpriority time limit usually does the trick.

If long-term use is not an objective, the partnership should have some simple scheduling arrangement, even if it is an informal phone check by a certain time of day with a partner designated to coordinate the schedule. The requirement to check in by a certain time frees the scheduling partner from sitting by the phone all day.

Fuel bills are still best kept separate, the partners being required to return the airplane refueled.

A responsibility that needs to be formally assigned to a partner is the partnership accounting. All partners should be kept informed of their account activity periodically (at least quarterly is recommended). All partners should pay their share of any expense promptly, and a mechanism for specific expense approval should be in place.

Engine and maintenance reserve accounts are highly recommended. Periodic payments of accumulated reserves due is probably an effective means of collection, as long as the maximum limit on amounts outstanding is kept small.

It is an excellent idea to hold quarterly get-togethers with the express purpose of catching up on partnership matters, including the review of accounts.

Maintenance considerations

Maintenance considerations for the three- or four-person partnership are really no different from the two-person partnership. The greater number of partners might have more opportunity to do their own work on the airplane. The partnership might want to consider arranging periodic airplane washing and waxing outings.

LARGER PARTNERSHIPS

Partnerships much beyond five or six members in size are beginning to assume the characteristics of a flying club. Most insurance companies consider a partnership of more than five members a club. From a legal standpoint, it is also advisable for the larger partnerships to incorporate, though the airplane can be the club's single asset and the members can retain equal percentage shares in it as in the traditional partnership.

Organizationally, the larger partnership needs to assume some of the more structured characteristics of the flying club. If it is incorporated, the partnership will have to have a minimal number of directors and hold periodic meetings documented by minutes as proof of legitimate corporate existence, though the group will still be small enough to make decisions through universal participation. More importantly, the workload of running the partnership will require the formal assignment of more duties to specific partners. A formal scheduling system needs to be set up and run, accounting becomes a more labor intensive responsibility, and the group might need to formalize checkout and currency requirements. The partnership agreement has to cover all aspects of the organization in great detail, and might need to be supplanted by operating rules.

Larger partnerships are feasible and are especially popular as a means of providing an opportunity to fly more sophisticated equipment, such as a Bonanza or a light twin. But undoubtedly, such partnerships require the adoption of at least some characteristics of the flying club. If you are contemplating the formation of a larger partnership, you might more precisely be contemplating a flying club, and part III is the place to start planning.

13

Creative partnerships

ENTERPRISING UTILIZATION of an aircraft partnership opens ownership doors that otherwise would be closed and locked to the individual pilot. Beyond the tasks of assessing all the aspects of a partnership, getting the most aircraft for your money, and considering production aircraft, it would be worthwhile to look at creating partnerships to learn to fly, to build and fly a homebuilt, or to fly a warbird. These examples are meant to stimulate personal creative alternatives and solutions to suit your fancy. Take the numbers not at face value, but as an approximation of what is possible. Collect the data applicable to your environment and make an in-depth analysis to unlock and open the doors.

A PARTNERSHIP TO LEARN TO FLY

Well, why not? If there are several of you who have put off learning to fly because of earthly constraints, but are serious about correcting this grave error, you should certainly take a good look at owning a trainer in partnership as an alternative to learning on rental airplanes. The basic idea is this: you and your partners buy an older model, but mechanically sound trainer for as little money as possible, learn to fly in it, and as soon as you all have your licenses, you sell it for about as much as you bought it. Will it cost less than the rental alternative? Only the numbers will tell.

A prerequisite for making such a partnership work is the commitment of all partners to be serious about learning to fly. You must also be realistic about your assumptions regarding the time it will take you to get your respective licenses and you must also make a proper airplane purchase; price should not be above the current market price or else you will have a hard time recouping your investment when you sell it. To further protect your investment, you must choose a model that has a history of a high resale value.

Another essential requirement is the reliable mechanical condition of the airplane. A hangar queen is never fun to own, but can be especially detrimental to your progress when you are learning to fly and lesson continuity is of the essence. The airplane should have plenty of hours left on the engine to cover

Round up a few partners and buy this Cessna 150 to learn to fly.

your needs and still be saleable at the end of your lessons. Buying one with a fresh annual, or having an annual performed at the outset is highly recommended. You don't want the airplane in the shop just when you are about to solo.

Don't be concerned with cosmetics. Many perfectly sound trainers have worn paint jobs. Pretty paint will only add to your costs and can wear off while you own the airplane, decreasing the value of your investment. Pretty paint on a trainer can also be a dastardly attempt to gloss over darker secrets awaiting the bright-eyed first-time buyer, which brings us to another important point. How to go about buying the airplane.

It is traumatic enough to be a first-time airplane buyer when you already have a license and some experience with airplanes, but it can be a real trap if you have no experience at all. To minimize the chance for surprises, there is only one alternative. Seek the assistance of someone experienced in buying airplanes whom you can fully trust.

A good plan is to make a package deal with an instructor to give you your lessons. Shop around among the many instructors who contract directly with airplane owners, and try for a discount (including a good deal on ground school) by committing the partnership to the instructor for all training needs. If you make such an arrangement, the instructor may also be able to help in selecting the airplane.

Let's take a look at some numbers. Cessna 150s are the stereotype trainer and retain their value well. They have also been around for decades, so the selection is wide. Let's say that three of you want to buy one to learn to fly. First, you will have to make a realistic assumption of how long it will take each of you to earn your licenses. Then, you will have to see how much it would cost under the rental option, and compare this figure to the costs of the partnership alternative.

The regulations allow you to get a private license in as little as 35 hours, but this figure is generally believed to be unrealistic if you can't fly practically every day. Scheduling constraints and weather delays will increase the number of hours most students will need. An average time often mentioned is 75 hours. The availability of your own airplane should give you the flexibility to keep at it consistently, so let's use 75 hours as the time each member of your partnership would require. At $80 per hour for dual at a rental establishment, the private pilot's license would cost each of you $6,000. This is the figure to beat.

Let's use the financial analysis model to see how much 75 hours per partner would cost in a three-way Cessna 150 partnership (Table 13-1, page 112). The purchase price of the 150 is $15,000, requiring $5,000 per partner. From beginning to end (including finding, buying, and selling the airplane) it would comfortably take you at the most a year, and probably less to earn your licenses, so it is assumed that you hold the airplane for one year.

Look at the last three lines of the example. The savings are considerable, assuming that you can sell the airplane in one year with another 300 hours on it for the same price you paid. If you bought well, this may be quite possible. But even if you take a $2,000 haircut on the total resale price, your net savings over the rental alternative are reduced only by $666 per person, which still puts you ahead by $895 ($1,562 − $666 = $895).

In this example, the partnership didn't borrow to buy the airplane. If you finance 50 percent ($7,500) of the airplane, each partner would have to come up with an initial investment of only $2,500. Annual payments on a loan of $7,500 for 10 years at 10 percent, would be $396 per partner (total annual loan payment of $1,188 divided by three). Without a resale haircut, the savings would be $1,166 per partner ($1,562 − $396). With a $666 loss per partner on the resale of the airplane, each partner would still be $500 ahead on a net basis ($1,166 − $666).

The savings could be larger if the partners completed their licenses and the sale of the aircraft in a shorter period of time. Tiedown fees would be less, and up to a point, there would also be an insurance refund if the whole year's worth of insurance was not used.

A very wide range of prices and equipment alternatives is out there, so do your homework and be careful. But with a little creativity and perseverance you might find the alternative of buying a trainer in partnership preferable to renting one on your own.

A PARTNERSHIP TO CONSTRUCT A HOMEBUILT

It is a fascinating thought to fly in something built by your own hand; in the minds of most pilots that is exactly what it remains, a thought. Building an airplane alone is an immense job requiring a lot of technical skill and at least access to a suitable workspace and a good set of tools. Even among those who try, the completion rate is not that high. Then there is the problem of money. Certain homebuilt kits, excluding the engine, can cost as much as a good, used, production four-seater.

Table 13-1.

	Total Cost	3 Pilots, per pilot
ANNUAL FIXED EXPENSES		
Tiedown/Hangar	960.00	320.00
Insurance	750.00	250.00
State Fees	120.00	40.00
Annual	450.00	150.00
Maintenance	900.00	300.00
Cost of Capital non-cash	1,050.00	350.00
Total Fixed Expenses / yr	4,230.00	1,410.00
HOURLY OPERATING EXPENSES		
Fuel	13.00	13.00
Oil	0.31	0.31
Engine Reserve	5.00	5.00
General Maint Res	2.00	2.00
Total Op Exp / hr	20.31	20.31
TOTAL HOURLY EXPENSES		
75 Hours		39.16
TOTAL ANNUAL EXPENSES		
75 Hours, Own		2,937.25
Plus instructor @ $20.00*75		1,500.00
Total License Cost		**4,437.25**
Total License Cost, Rental		**6,000.00**
Savings		**1,562.75**

If you can't go it alone, but are determined to construct an airplane, consider a partnership to build one. In many respects, such a venture is no different from a run-of-the-mill airplane partnership. Compatibility with your partners is just as important, perhaps even more so, considering that you are not only sharing a piece of equipment, but actually have to work together and rely on each other to complete a variety of fairly demanding tasks. Once the airplane is complete, the financial and most operational aspects of a homebuilt partnership become just like any other. What has to be sorted out at the outset is how it will function during the construction process and when complete, which partner or partners would be responsible for maintenance that is applicable under the experimental airworthiness certificate. Perhaps prospective partners should find a nearby Experimental Aircraft Association chapter; each person would join and start researching the matter independently, eventually pooling information for the partnership to make a proper airplane selection and fully understand every aspect of amateur-built aircraft.

The big risk is that you are making a considerable financial and nonfinancial commitment to something that doesn't even exist. You have to have very good reason to believe that the project will be completed. You should be able to see a credible path that will get you there, and you should also be prepared to handle setbacks; if it is a composite aircraft, one partner might develop an allergy to the construction materials. When you build an airplane on your own, you have only yourself to blame for not living up to your goals. In a partnership, there are always the partners, and the finger pointing can easily escalate out of control when the wheels miss the wheel wells by a fraction of an inch.

A good way to help you and your partners focus on the task, the responsibilities, and the pitfalls, is to work out a partnership agreement for the construction phase of the venture just as you would for a regular aircraft partnership. In broad scope, the aircraft construction partnership agreement should cover at least the major considerations.

Detailed specifications of the aircraft to be built. Spell out the design and model, the plans to be used, the kit or prefab components to be used, the engine (specs, used or new, how many hours), and the accessories and instrumentation to be installed.

Costs. Have as detailed a breakdown of the costs as possible. In the case of kitbuilt airplanes, this task is fairly easy. For scratchbuilt aircraft, the costing of the raw materials might be more difficult if you are not sure how much stock you will end up using and how much wastage you will have. A problem with costs is estimating future costs of components you will not need until much later in the building process. Considering that some projects can take many years to complete, there is a lot of room for error.

Construction schedule. Map out, as any businessperson would, the completion schedule of your project. Set target dates for phases to be completed. This requires a good understanding of the labor and time requirements of your project.

Funding. Establish each partner's financial commitments and when such commitments are due. Usually, the big expenses are made stage by stage as each major phase of construction is begun. The partnership should also have an expense tracking system in place and limit the amount that each partner can expend on behalf of the partnership without the others' approval.

Cost overruns. Higher than anticipated costs can be a big bone of contention, and the partners should have an understanding of how they will be handled.

Commitment of partner time. Questions about who spent how much time on the project can sometimes cause friction. It is worthwhile to agree beforehand to some amount of time commitment per partner. Some partnerships make this simple by making each partner wholly responsible for completing certain parts of the project whatever time it takes.

Sweat equity. One common reason for forming airplane construction partnerships is because one partner has the money and the other partner knows how to build airplanes. If any partner is going to contribute labor in exchange for a share of the airplane, the terms and measure of that labor must be carefully defined and well understood by all partners.

Conflict, dissolution, arbitration. The ticklish question of how to deal with disagreements and how to dissolve the partnership if a partner wants out for whatever reason, must be addressed. A half completed miniplane doesn't do well at yard sales, which is why you have to have such a good idea, before you cut metal or start riveting, of your ability to see the project through.

These are just some of the issues you should be thinking about. Undoubtedly, there are many more, peculiar to your circumstances. Be sure to run any agreement by a lawyer before signing on the dotted line.

The idea of forming a partnership to build an airplane is a good one. The rewards can be immense in a sense of personal satisfaction and in aircraft performance. And at three o'clock in the morning when you are looking for that rivet gun you just know your partner was the last one to use, think of what that first landing at Oshkosh will feel like.

A WARBIRD PARTNERSHIP

How does the sound of 32,000 horsepower strike you? To some it's just a lot of noise, but if you are a warbird fan it might be music to your ears. Especially if emitted by growling, snarling radials as was the case during a recent flyby of more than 50 T-6 Texans at Oshkosh not so long ago. To many pilots watching from down below, the old war-horses seemed as inaccessible as an F-16, but that might be a mistaken impression. It doesn't take nearly as much as you might think to be up there flying one of them from the owner's seat. Although warbirds will never be inexpensive, a partnership will dramatically cut the costs of flying these exciting birds and put them in reach of someone accustomed to being a sole owner of a Saratoga or a Bonanza.

Warbird prices can run into the millions for rare, well-restored World War II bombers such as the B-17; a P-51 Mustang can go for as much as $500,000. But the lighter iron can be surprisingly reasonable by warbird standards. Some vintage jets, such as the Fouga Magister and Willy Messerschmitt's Saeta range in price from $100,000 to $150,000 in good condition, and a T-6 Texan can be had for fewer than $100,000. So why not instantly trade in the Bonanza for a Texan?

The big bugbear is operating cost and there is also the matter of getting good training. Even the less expensive warbirds consume enormous amounts of avgas, maintenance is hideously expensive, and parts might be hard to come by. But if you get a good price, and are willing to spread the costs around through a partnership, a warbird might not be out of reach.

Consider the T-6 Texan. The numbers presented in Table 13-2 are indicative (actual costs might vary widely depending upon circumstances and changing prices), but give a good ballpark idea of what a prospective T-6 pilot might face.

The T-6 in the example is in good average condition and goes for $95,000. Let's be daring and compare the T-6 partnership to the expenses of owning a Piper Arrow III alone. Key figures are the total hourly expenses for the number of total hours flown (50, 100, 150), and the total annual expenses. Let's look at 100

Table 13-2.

NUMBER OF PILOTS		T-6					Arrow
	1	2	3	4	5	6	1
ANNUAL FIXED EXPENSES							
Tiedown/Hangar	2,700.00	1,350.00	900.00	675.00	540.00	450.00	960.00
Insurance	4,000.00	2,000.00	1,333.33	1,000.00	800.00	666.67	1,500.00
State Fees	120.00	60.00	40.00	30.00	24.00	20.00	120.00
Annual	2,000.00	1,000.00	666.67	500.00	400.00	333.33	750.00
Maintenance	2,000.00	1,000.00	666.67	500.00	400.00	333.33	1,500.00
Cost of Capital non-cash	6,650.00	3,325.00	2,216.67	1,662.50	1,330.00	1,108.33	3,150.00
Total Fixed Expenses / yr	17,470.00	8,735.00	5,823.33	4,367.50	3,494.00	2,911.67	7,980.00
HOURLY OPERATING EXPENSES							
Fuel	80.00	80.00	80.00	80.00	80.00	80.00	21.00
Oil	2.00	2.00	2.00	2.00	2.00	2.00	0.13
Engine Reserve	25.00	25.00	25.00	25.00	25.00	25.00	7.50
General Maint Res	10.00	10.00	10.00	10.00	10.00	10.00	3.00
Total Op Exp / hr	117.00	117.00	117.00	117.00	117.00	117.00	31.63
TOTAL HOURLY EXPENSES							
50 Hours	466.40	291.70	233.47	204.35	186.88	175.23	191.23
100 Hours	291.70	204.35	175.23	160.68	151.94	146.12	111.43
150 Hours	233.47	175.23	155.82	146.12	140.29	136.41	84.83
TOTAL ANNUAL EXPENSES							
50 Hours, Own	23320.00	14585.00	11673.33	10217.50	9344.00	8761.67	9561.25
Own cash only	16670.00	11260.00	9456.67	8555.00	8014.00	7653.33	6411.25
100 Hours, Own	29170.00	20435.00	17523.33	16067.50	15194.00	14611.67	11142.50
Own cash only	22520.00	17110.00	15306.67	14405.00	13864.00	13503.33	7992.50
150 Hours, Own	35020.00	26285.00	23373.33	21917.50	21044.00	20461.67	12723.75
Own cash only	28370.00	22960.00	21156.67	20255.00	19714.00	19353.33	9573.75

ASSUMPTIONS:	T-6	Arrow		T-6	Arrow
Aircraft Value:	95000.00	45000.00	Maintenance/yr:	2000.00	1500.00
Hangar/Month:	225.00	80.00	Gen Maint Res/hr:	10.00	3.00
Insurance/yr:	4000.00	1500.00	Engine Reserve/hr:	25.00	7.50
Annual:	2000.00	750.00	Time Before OH hrs :	1200	2000
Fuel Cons gal/hr :	40.0	10.5	Engine MOH Cost:	30000.00	15000.00
Fuel Cost $/gal :	2.00	2.00	Cost of Capital Rate:	7.00%	7.00%
Oil Cons qt/hr :	2.0	0.13	State Fees/yr:	120.00	120.00
Oil Cost $/qt :	1.00	1.00			

hours because you would rarely want to own an Arrow alone if you are going to fly it less than that, and for safety reasons you shouldn't be flying a Texan if you can't fly it 100 hours a year. The Texan is $291 per hour if owned alone; the Arrow is $111. That is a big difference. Now look at four partners in the Texan. The rate drops to $161. That is only $50 per hour more than the Arrow, or, on a total annual basis at 100 hours, $5,000 more.

You might think that an extra $5,000 is a lot to come up with, but consider this: You have $45,000 in the Arrow. A one-quarter share in the Texan is only $23,750. That is a whopping $21,250 less than what you already have in the Arrow. Another way to look at it is that the excess investment in the Arrow is the

This T-6 Texan flies in a three-person warbird partnership.

source of the extra $5,000 per year for four years. Sure, by the end of the fourth year it would be gone, but you would have 400 hours of T-6 time and countless adventures in your logbook. And at the end, you will still have your one-quarter equity share in the Texan. Because they don't make Texans any more (or, for that matter, Piper Arrows) it will most likely have held its value. You can always sell it and because you have a fresh perspective about partnerships, buy a half share of another Arrow and fly it 100 hours a year, just as you were doing before your wild and woolly Texan days. If there is a will, there is always a way.

Training

Before you do sell that Arrow and jump into a Texan, take one point to heart. It is absolutely imperative that you get the appropriate professional training to fly a warbird before you blast off in one alone. That goes not only for soloing it, but also for all other types of operations such as maneuvering, dogfighting, and aerobatics. These machines are a joy to fly, but they were built for war, to be flown by highly trained military pilots. Your standards should not be anything less.

Part III
Flying clubs

14

Ask the
right questions

RECALL THE TECHNIQUE OF ASKING KEY QUESTIONS to focus upon choosing a partnership or a flying club. If, in principle, you lean toward forming or joining a flying club, you now need to go into much greater detail to make yourself aware of all the issues and options you face: decisions to be made about equipment, aircraft use, flying time, fellow flying club members, maintenance, scheduling policies, and the many tradeoffs posed by a dozen other questions. All this is against the backdrop of the financial resources you are able and willing to dedicate to the cause. The key to making rapid progress and navigating around the pitfalls is to know up front what questions to ask.

These questions are grouped by the topics you should be thinking about; selected questions are equally valid in several categories. Read them first, and as you move on through the stages of forming or joining a flying club, read them again and again. They are presented at this stage not to provide specific answers, but to get you to ask all the right questions and to inspire additional questions relevant to your particular circumstances.

If you are considering an existing flying club, the questions are equally valid.

A number of the questions have been asked before, appearing again because of the need to constantly reexamine and reevaluate the options in ever increasing detail and from different perspectives as you close in on the solution best for you.

FLYING OBJECTIVES

What kind of flying would I like to do? You asked this question when you were deciding whether to go the flying club or partnership route. You now have to ask it again, in greater detail, to be able to decide on aircraft for your flying club, and to help you find like-minded prospective club members. Do you want more flight training? Do you want to tour for days? Do you want short, inexpen-

The Tampico is Aerospatiale's entry into the flying club market.

sive, local hops on the weekend? Or would you like to do aerobatics, or fly an affordable antique like an Aeronca?

What aircraft type best suits my purpose? Once you pin down the type of flying you want to do, you will have to find the airplane or airplanes that best suit your purpose. You will have to do careful research on aircraft specifications and performance. If you are willing to do diligent research, you might find solutions to your flying needs costing thousands of dollars less than the cost of the obvious choices. For example, a restored Comanche might give you, for half the price, everything you want and thought you had to get out of a Lance. Or how about a restored Cessna 150 with a new engine compared to a late model 152? You'll just have to do your homework.

Would I like to fly more than one type of airplane regularly? A benefit of the flying club with a fleet of different aircraft is equal access to different airplanes. Now is the time to sort out in detail your objectives in this regard and see what it will take. For example, you might want to have access to a Mooney during the week for business flights, but would be content with a VFR Cessna 172 to go to the beach on the weekends. Quite a few flying clubs are serving such needs.

How much flying do I plan to do annually? Assess realistically how much flying you and prospective fellow club members expect to do every year. Your answers will have implications for the number of airplanes and club members your club should have, as well as the price you will have to pay.

How flexible am I in choosing the times when I fly? This is another question that will help you decide how many club members to plan for and what equipment to select. If you all want to fly on the weekends, maybe two airplanes of more modest cost are the answer. If a good number of you can fly any time during the week, maybe you should get that late model Mooney instead. Only a close examination of the numbers will tell.

What ratio of pilots to airplane do I think is appropriate? The desire to keep costs down might tempt you to load up the membership roster, but too many members might mean not enough airplane to go around. Conventional wisdom has it that more than 15 members per airplane is asking for trouble.

Will the club have a strong social orientation or will members come to the airport, fly, and leave? This question is important because every member must be sure to feel comfortable with the club's style. Flying and fleeing in a social club or attempts to socialize with a bunch of no-nonsense misanthropes might be equally frowned upon.

FINANCES

Where will the capital come from to acquire aircraft? Members might be able to afford maintenance and operation of the aircraft, but first they must be able to afford the purchase. Will the founding members each pitch in with their share of the purchase price? Will the club borrow part of the money? Will borrowings be from a bank or club members? If leasing the aircraft is an option, on what terms?

Will members be required to buy a refundable share in the club in addition to annual fees and dues? This question is related to how the club will be capitalized. The club can, over time, repay the original shareholders who came up with the money for the aircraft, or it can choose to maintain saleable membership shares, which joining members would purchase from departing members. Again, the choice depends upon each club's individual circumstances and the membership's interests.

What will be the approximate annual expenses per member, based upon the desired aircraft type(s) and club member to aircraft ratio, and a reasonable average number of flight hours per member? Once you have a good initial idea of what you and your fellow club members want, it is time to find out if you can afford it. This becomes the time to do the in-depth financial analysis a good chunk of this book is all about.

Of these expenses, what is the amount of annual fees and dues, and can I and other prospective members afford them? As you will see, all flying clubs have a minimum requirement in dues and fees depending upon the fixed annual costs of the equipment, which must be met. All temptation to charge annual dues below this minimum in the hopes of making up the difference in heftier hourly charges must be resisted because the amount of hours flown is unpredictable. Do an honest analysis, and go back to the drawing board until the numbers and the contents of your wallet are at least in balance.

STRUCTURE AND ORGANIZATION

Are there enough committed potential club members with whom I can form the kind of club that I want? It is fine to come up with the number of club members below which you can't make the flying club work, but are they all lining up out there? If not, you and your friends had better start beating the bushes to attain the minimum number of committed members necessary before you commit the club to any financial obligations.

Will the club be legally incorporated, will there be bylaws? If you don't have plans to incorporate, you might be exposing club members personally to great liability. You must absolutely seek a lawyer's advice on the question of incorporation. Bylaws are required of any incorporated flying club. Insurance companies will also want a copy of the bylaws as a condition of insurance.

What will the club's structure be, and how frequently will directors be elected? It is best for flying clubs to have an organization structure, and an elected board of directors; if the club is incorporated, a board of directors is a legal requirement. The structure, number of directors, and officer positions will depend mostly upon the size of your club and the inclination of members to do volunteer work.

Will there be a need to hire a paid manager? In the beginning the temptation might be great to hire professional help, perhaps only part time. But even modest salaries are one of the biggest expense components of the flying club budget. On the other hand, the club might become so busy, especially on the weekends that some help might be justified. Be sure you can afford it.

INSURANCE

What liability and hull coverage should the club get? Insurance is one of the least understood aspects of aviation, yet the consequences of an ill informed decision can be disastrous. It is important to understand all the options and obtain sufficient coverage.

Will members be covered by insurance or only the club? Some clubs don't carry all members as named insured, others do. If members are not covered, the insurance company might try to claim from them after paying out on a claim against the club. Renter's insurance purchased by members individually might provide protection. The decision to cover members by making them named insured is yours. Consult your insurance provider, and make sure the members understand whether or not they are covered.

OPERATIONS AND SAFETY

What skills can the membership offer on a voluntary basis? Member skills and volunteer work are a key ingredient of the successful budget flying club. Go out of your way to attract skilled members if budget flying is your main objective. Assess the willingness of all members to do volunteer work. Bear in mind that any meaningful level of volunteer work requires a significant time commitment. Many people tend to be too optimistic about the time they think they can commit, and the amount of time the tasks they volunteer for will take.

How will scheduling be handled? The flying club's scheduling system has to work flawlessly to keep everyone happy. Among other things, you need to make decisions about how far in advance the airplanes can be scheduled, for how long they can be scheduled, daily minimums if any, what happens to no-shows, how the system will work, and who will run it.

Will there be peak demand for aircraft, such as on the weekend, or will demand be spread out? This is another question with implications for the ratio of members per airplane and costs per member.

Is airport management open to having the club on the field, and how will the relationship with the local FBO and airport management be handled? This can be a ticklish question and should be answered early on. If you face a hostile FBO and airport management, your flying club might be grounded before you even form it. But initial hostility can often be turned around with tact and appropriate politicking.

Will the aircraft be rented wet or dry, and if wet, where will fuel be obtained? The fueling question is always an important one, and can be confusing. Would the club have access to fuel at a discount? Can it recognize a little extra income on fuel sales to the membership? Is it easier just to require everyone to leave the airplanes topped off? It all depends on your club's particular circumstances, but you better have a sound plan.

Will premises be rented? The rental of club space is expensive. Like salaries, rental expense can be a budget buster, so it should be scrutinized carefully. Small clubs might want to avoid space rental altogether. The occasional use of members' homes, part-time rentals, and free community space might be alternatives.

Will club members be expected to participate in formal work parties? A formal requirement for work parties might be excessive unless the club is doing a restoration. Scheduled duty officer stints on the weekends might be a more likely requirement.

Will aircraft be available for several days in a row? The length of time for which aircraft are available is a defining characteristic of your flying club. Deal with this question up front, and be sure that all founding partners are comfortably in agreement.

What minimum flight experience level will be demanded from the members? Many clubs consider FAA minimum experience requirements too lenient, and so do many insurance companies. The club has to establish clear experience minimums based upon its own standards, as well as insurance requirements.

What flight currency and safety policies and procedures will the club have? FAA minimums or more? The club might wish to establish more stringent currency minimums than those required by the FAA. Good clubs also have comprehensive safety policies and procedures.

Will minimum monthly flight hours be required of members? Some clubs require payment for a minimum number of flight hours per a set period whether or not a member flies during that period, as a way to encourage flight currency.

What instructors will the club use? There are various options for making arrangements for club instructors, depending upon club needs and insurance considerations. Review them carefully and make your own choice. At a minimum, be sure to have some club approval mechanism in place for instructors used by the membership.

MAINTENANCE

Will the club do its own maintenance, or will maintenance be contracted out? If you want to do in-house maintenance, you have to take a good, hard look to see if it can be justified. Does the club have volunteer maintenance skills (to keep the costs down), does it have access to the proper facilities (enclosed space and tools), is the fleet large enough to justify in-house maintenance?

If maintenance is to be contracted out, on what basis is this to be accomplished and with what type of maintenance facility?

These questions cover a lot of important aspects of a club; your own circumstances might call for many more questions.

15

Analyze the numbers

FLYING CLUB FINANCIALS are not all that different from partnership financials. As in partnerships, the core expenses of the flying club are related to acquiring, flying, and maintaining the airplanes. The categories of airplane related expenses are similar: tiedown or hangar, insurance, taxes and fees, inspections, maintenance costs, loan payments, and the direct operating expenses, as presented in chapter 3; however, the flying club faces additional expenses not directly related to its airplanes: office rental, accountant's fees, and professional salaries.

A flying club also handles the management of its financials differently in certain respects. A club needs to formalize income sources as dues and hourly rental payments because more members make informal collection impractical. As a corporation, the flying club should report its financial condition to members in greater detail than is necessary for a partnership. In addition to a periodic statement of income and expenses, the flying club should also disclose from time to time its balance sheet, a statement of its assets (what it owns), liabilities (what it owes), and net worth (what is left of assets after subtracting liabilities). As a corporation, the flying club must also account for, file, and (if not a nonprofit club) pay taxes.

Founders of flying clubs have to come up with a business plan specifying what airplanes to acquire, how many members to have, and what to charge the members for the use of the airplanes. This task might seem overwhelming if you are very enthusiastic about flying, but are unenthusiastic about business; usually, any apprehension is misplaced. If you use a simple building block approach by making the costs the center of your analysis, then adding the handful of general expenses to the airplane expenses, and treating the flying club as the basically cash business that it should be—greatly reducing or eliminating the need for complicated receivables, payables, and inventory accounting—you will have little problem understanding flying club financials and doing your own analysis.

Analysis is one thing, establishing and maintaining a financial recordkeeping system is quite another. An inexpensive accounting software package to be run by your club's treasurer is highly recommended. If your flying club has more than one airplane and approximately 15 members and nobody in the club has any hands-on experience keeping business records, you are strongly advised to seek the assistance of a professional bookkeeper or accountant to help you set up your financial recordkeeping system, and balance the books periodically. A few hours at the outset and an hour or two every month or quarter will usually suffice. Your time saved and the potential confusion avoided will be well worth the modest expense.

EXPENSES AND INCOME

As in the case of partnerships, expenses and income are at the heart of the flying club's financials. To acquire the airplanes you will have all the funds or borrow them in part at the outset. What you have to clearly understand and accurately anticipate to make your flying club financially successful is what you will have to spend to keep the airplanes flying and where that money will come from.

In assessing the flying club's expenses using the building block approach, we will use the airplane partnership financial model to determine airplane expenses per club airplane. Use the aircraft expenses worksheet in the appendices or the automated aircraft financial analysis spreadsheet to analyze aircraft expenses. We then build on these results by adding in general flying club expenses to arrive at total expenses and determine where the income will come from to cover these expenses. First, the analysis is done on a break-even basis. A percentage is then added to the income components to ensure the generation of excess income over expenses to create an increasing equity cushion for the club. This is not inconsistent with nonprofit status (if that is the club's structure) as long as no surplus is ever distributed to the shareholders.

The format used to project and analyze expenses and income is also used to record and present the flying club's annual expenses and income. It is the flying club's annual *income statement*, which, along with the *balance sheet*, is the club's *annual statement of financial condition*. This statement should be made available to the membership every year soon after financial year end.

We will use the example of a flying club with a Cessna 172 for basic pleasure flying and a Piper Arrow III for complex flying. Look at the next two tables to scan the full break-even and income generating financial analyses before we get into the details (Tables 15-1 and 15-2).

Let's consider expenses first. As in the case of partnerships, there are two types of expenses any operator incurs when flying an airplane: fixed expenses and operating expenses. Recall the respective definitions: *fixed expenses* are expenses that you have to pay regardless of the hours flown by the airplane (storage, insurance, state fees), commonly measured *annually*; *operating expenses* are expenses incurred directly as a result of operating an airplane (fuel, oil, tires), commonly measured *hourly*.

The tables present the flying club's fixed expense structure. The first column contains the totals of aircraft fixed expenses as well as the flying club's general expenses. Subsequent columns contain the individual fixed expenses per aircraft.

Table 15-1.

FLYING CLUB BREAKEVEN FINANCIAL ANALYSIS ($)

EXPENSES	TOTAL	AIRCRAFT #1		AIRCRAFT #2	
		Type	PA28-201	Type	C-172
ANNUAL FIXED EXPENSES		Hrs/Yr	500	Hrs/Yr	500
AIRCRAFT RELATED					
Tiedown/Hangar	1,800		900		900
Insurance, Aircraft	3,500		2,000		1,500
Fees and Taxes	240		120		120
100 Hour and Annual Inspections	3,500		2,000		1,500
Maintenance	0		0		0
Loan Payments	0		0		0
Depreciation	4,000		2,500		1,500
GENERAL EXPENSES					
Insurance, Club	0				
Office rent	0				
Accountant's Fee	250				
Manager's Salary	0				
Mechanic's Salary	0				
Supplies/Administrative	250				
Other	0				
Total Fixed Expenses/yr	13,540		7,520		5,520
HOURLY OPERATING EXPENSES					
Fuel	34		20		14
Oil	2		1		1
Engine Reserve	13		8		5
General Maint Res	8		5		3
Total Op Exp/hr	57		34		23
Total Op Exp/yr	28,250		16,750		11,500
TOTAL ANNUAL EXPENSES	41,790		24,337		17,066

INCOME			
FIXED: Annual Fees and Dues	13,540		
OPERATING: Annual Aircraft Rental Income	28,250	16,750	11,500

TOTAL ANNUAL INCOME	41,790	30	**NUMBER OF MEMBERS (enter)**
SURPLUS/DEFICIT (to general reserve)	0	451	**ANNUAL FEES AND DUES PER MEMBER/YR**

ANNUAL COST PER MEMBER, PA28-201

50 Hours	2,378	per hour:	47.55
50 hours commercial rental at $90/hr	4,500		

ANNUAL COST PER MEMBER, C-172

50 Hours	1,774	per hour:	35.48
50 hours commercial rental at $70/hr	3,500		

Table 15-2.

FLYING CLUB FINANCIAL ANALYSIS ($)

Tightly controlled General Expenses

EXPENSES	TOTAL	AIRCRAFT #1	AIRCRAFT #2
		Type PA28-201	Type C-172
ANNUAL FIXED EXPENSES		Hrs/Yr 500	Hrs/Yr 500
AIRCRAFT RELATED			
Tiedown/Hangar	1,800	900	900
Insurance, Aircraft	3,500	2,000	1,500
Fees and Taxes	240	120	120
100 Hour and Annual Inspections	3,500	2,000	1,500
Maintenance	0	0	0
Loan Payments	0	0	0
Depreciation	4,000	2,500	1,500
GENERAL EXPENSES			
Insurance, Club	0		
Office rent	0		
Accountant's Fee	250		
Manager's Salary	0		
Mechanic's Salary	0		
Supplies/Administrative	250		
Other	0		
Total Fixed Expenses/yr	13,540	7,520	5,520
HOURLY OPERATING EXPENSES			
Fuel	34	20	14
Oil	2	1	1
Engine Reserve	13	8	5
General Maint Res	8	5	3
Total Op Exp/hr	57	34	23
Total Op Exp/yr	28,250	16,750	11,500
TOTAL ANNUAL EXPENSES	41,790	24,337	17,066
INCOME			
FIXED: Annual Fees and Dues	15,571		
OPERATING: Annual Aircraft Rental Income	32,488	19,263	13,225

TOTAL ANNUAL INCOME 48,059 | 30 NUMBER OF MEMBERS (enter)

SURPLUS/DEFICIT (to general reserve) 6,269 | 519 ANNUAL FEES AND DUES, MEMBER/YR

ANNUAL COST PER MEMBER, PA28-201

50 Hours	2,445	per hour:	48.91
50 hours commercial rental at $90/hr	4,500		

ANNUAL COST PER MEMBER, C-172

50 Hours	1,842	per hour:	36.83
50 hours commercial rental at $70/hr	3,500		

Aircraft annual fixed expenses

The aircraft related fixed expense items are in most respects similar to those of the partnership financial analysis; however, the amounts per expense category for the same aircraft type might vary in comparison to a partnership (Table 15-3).

Table 15-3.

ANNUAL FIXED EXPENSES	Total	Type	PA28-201	Type	C-172
		Hrs/Yr	500	Hrs/Yr	500
AIRCRAFT RELATED					
Tiedown/Hangar	1,800		900		900
Insurance, Aircraft	3,500		2,000		1,500
Fees and Taxes	240		120		120
100 Hour and Annual Inspections	3,500		2,000		1,500
Maintenance	0				
Loan Payments	0				
Depreciation	4,000		2,500		1,500
GENERAL EXPENSES					
Insurance, Club					
Office rent					
Accountant's Fee	250				
Manager's Salary					
Mechanic's Salary					
Supplies/Administrative	250				
Other					
Total Fixed Expenses/yr	13,540		7,520		5,520

Insurance per aircraft for the flying club will be higher because of the greater number of pilots and generally higher total flying hours. In practice, insurance is issued on one master policy, but the option of allocating insurance per airplane is provided and used in the examples to understand costs in greater detail.

Inspection costs will be significantly higher if the airplane flies a lot; 100-hour inspections are required because the club is renting the airplanes to club members. No fixed maintenance expense is shown under the theory that in a flying club the aircraft will fly enough to pay for all annual maintenance through hourly maintenance reserves (an operating expense item). The space is provided for you to use if you want to be conservative and budget a fixed maintenance sum in addition to the annual reserve.

Note that the opportunity cost of capital is not listed in the flying club financial model contrary to the partnership model. The investment of each member in the flying club is relatively small. Calculating the opportunity cost of capital per member would only be confusing when we are examining the entire flying club. Potential club members wishing to calculate this cost for their investment should see the partnership model.

A flying club with enough members might afford a complex retractable at rates well below the hourly costs of a small partnership.

An item presented here that is absent from the partnership model is depreciation. It is an important item for the flying club because it allows the club to build a reserve fund to be used for replacing worn out airplanes. To put it rather simplistically, *depreciation* is a measure of the decline in the value, due to wear and tear over a period of time, of a capital asset such as a truck, a bottling machine, or, in the flying club's case, its airplane. Businesses are allowed to take out of income and put into a reserve account the value by which the asset declined during the period being measured. When the asset is fully depreciated, a time that should ideally coincide with the asset being no longer usable, the reserve can be used to replace it. For businesses, government accounting standards set strict depreciation rules and schedules that determine how quickly an asset can be depreciated. Note that depreciation is not a cash expense because the money never leaves the entity depreciating its asset. It is merely set aside in a reserve account within the entity. In the case of the flying club, annual depreciation amounts per airplane are factored into the annual membership charges and are set aside in the depreciation reserve upon receipt. Depreciation regulations in effect for aircraft may be obtained from any local accountant.

General annual expenses

As you can see, general annual expenses are quite simple, yet can add up quickly if not tightly controlled. Any insurance over and above the airplanes is included here, as well as rents unrelated to the airplanes such as club offices, salaries of any personnel the club sees fit to employ, professional fees such as

The new trigear Maule is equally at home in the bush and at the jetport.

accountant's or bookkeeper's costs, supplies and administrative costs, and a catch-all other category.

Total annual fixed expenses

Total annual fixed expenses are the sum of the fixed expenses per airplane and the general expenses. Remember, these annual expenses must be paid by the flying club regardless of whether or not any of its airplanes fly at all. For the flying club with the Cessna 172 and the Piper Arrow, the annual fixed expenses are presented in Table 15-4.

Table 15-4.

	Total	PA28 201	C-172
Total Fixed Expenses/yr	13,540	7,520	5,520

Hourly operating expenses

As in the case of a partnership, the next building block in determining flying club costs is figuring out the hourly operating expenses per airplane (Table 15-5).

These club expense categories are identical to the partnership's operating expenses. The amount reserved for maintenance per airplane might be higher than for similar airplanes in a partnership if the club chooses to use only an hourly maintenance reserve to accumulate all annual maintenance expenses. The total hourly operating expenses per airplane are a good indication of the hourly break-even rates to charge club members for each airplane.

Table 15-5.

HOURLY OP EXPENSES	Total	PA28-201	C-172
Fuel	34	20	14
Oil	2	1	1
Engine Reserve	13	8	5
General Maint Res	8	5	3
Total Op Exp/hr	57	34	23
Total Op Exp/yr	28,250	16,750	11,500

In case the club operates leased aircraft, lease expenses need not enter into this expense category because they are awash with the hourly lease income portion of the total hourly rental costs, and are directly passed through to the aircraft owner from whom the aircraft is leased; however, the club's billing and accounting system must accurately track the amount and flow of hourly lease payments taken from total hourly rentals and passed on to the aircraft owners.

Total annual operating expenses

Total annual operating expenses are the hourly operating expenses multiplied by the number of hours flown by the airplanes for the year (during the planning process, an estimate).

Total annual expenses

The total annual expenses for the flying club are the sum of the annual fixed expenses and the annual operating expenses. This amount of money is the amount the flying club must raise for the year in a foolproof fashion to remain in business. The example flying club in Table 15-6 has total annual expenses of $41,790, which is not a small sum to come up with for the operation of two airplanes. Let's see how best to go about it.

Table 15-6.

	Total	PA28-201	C-172
TOTAL ANNUAL EXPENSES	41,790	24,337	17,066

Income

Two sources of income meet expenses: annual fees or dues and aircraft rental income. Just like expenses, these sources of income can be defined as fixed income and operating income. Fixed income, the fees and dues, is received by the club whether or not the airplanes fly. Operating income, the airplane rental income, is received only when the airplanes fly. And herein lies two cardinal rules for running a financially successful flying club—failing to realize this is the main cause of flying club failures:

- Meet annual fixed expenses from fixed income (fees and dues)
- Meet operating expenses from operating income (airplane rental charges)

Fixed expenses must be paid regardless of the number of hours flown; therefore, if the fixed expenses are collected from the members in annual dues and monthly fees, the flying club will remain solvent regardless of the number of hours flown. Many flying clubs make the mistake of assuming that their airplanes will fly a certain number of hours, calculate the airplane rental charges to include a portion of the fixed expenses, and charge low annual dues and fees. When the airplanes fail to fly the required hours, the club is unable to pay its fixed expenses. There is then a mad scramble for membership assessments and bridging loans. In the end, when these efforts are unsuccessful, as they often are, the flying club goes out of business. Take this point seriously. Mismatched sources of income and expenses is one of the most common reasons for flying club failures.

Let's take a look at the flying club in our example (Table 15-7). It has total annual expenses of $41,790. Of this amount, annual fixed expenses are $13,540, and annual operating expenses are $28,250. How are these expenses met?

Table 15-7.

INCOME	Total	PA 28-201	C-172
Annual Dues and Fees	13,540		
Annual Aircraft Rental Income	28,250	16,750	11,500
TOTAL ANNUAL INCOME	41,790		
NUMBER OF MEMBERS	30		
ANNUAL FEES & DUES/MEMBER	451		

Dues and fees meet the fixed expenses and airplane rental income meets the operating expenses. Total annual income is exactly equal to total annual expenses. Furthermore, if the airplanes flew fewer hours, total annual expenses and income would both be less and would remain equal to each other because members pay for operating expenses as they go: less flying means lower operating expenses, which means lower operating income, dollar for dollar.

Assuming 30 members, based on a ratio of 15 members per airplane, the dues and fees work out to $451 per member, or $38 per month per member. To have sufficient cash up front, it is best to collect as much of the annual dues and fees as possible. Many flying clubs collect half up front in an annual fee, and the rest in monthly dues. In this case, each member would have to pay $225 in an annual membership fee, and $19 in monthly dues. In a moment, we will get to the bottom line for the individual members, the comparison of renting from a flying club or a commercial operator, but before that, we must cover one more concept to complete our understanding of the flying club financial structure, the built-in cash reserve cushion.

Build a general cash reserve

In the financial analysis of the flying club as presented so far, total annual expenses equal total annual income. This structure tells us the minimum income necessary to meet expenses; however, to be prepared for any unanticipated additional cash needs, the flying club should accumulate a general reserve, over and above the engine, maintenance, and depreciation reserves. The other reserves are already earmarked for specific expenditures the club knows in advance it will have to pay. The general reserve is truly a cushion. Failure to build a general reserve is another common mistake of flying clubs. When an unexpected expense arises, they have no choice but to eat into the engine, maintenance, or depreciation reserves and weaken the club's financial condition.

Another role for the accumulation of a general reserve is to become a financial source for growth. Carefully managed, ever increasing general reserves eventually enable the flying club to upgrade equipment or acquire new equipment out of its own resources.

A simple way to build a general reserve into the flying club's financials is to determine break-even as we have, and increase dues, fees, and airplane rentals by an appropriate percentage (Table 15-2). It is the same financial example used in this chapter with a 15 percent cushion built into income. As you can see, with this cushion, the club now has a $6,269 reserve for the year. Because it will accumulate this reserve every year, soon it should have a sizable amount in the bank available at its discretion. At the same time, dues increased from the break-even scenario by only $68, and the increase in the cost of flying either club aircraft 50 hours per year is marginal.

FLYING CLUB VERSUS COMMERCIAL RENTAL

And now for the bottom line. How does the flying club compare to renting airplanes commercially? Very favorably, if the club is properly managed financially. The airplanes' operating and fixed costs do not differ greatly between the flying club and the commercial operator. The big difference is in general fixed expenses. Even to allow for a modest living, the commercial operator's fixed general expenses will be well above that of the well run flying club. Full-time salaries, rent, and a reasonable profit margin quickly drive up these expenses for the commercial operator, whereas the well run flying club can keep them to a minimum. The difference translates into considerably lower club aircraft rental rates.

From your perspective as a renter, you have to compare the cost of hourly rental at the flying club plus your annual fees and dues to the hourly rental of an equivalent airplane at your friendly FBO. The hourly flying club rental will always be lower. The question then is, how many hours of flight time will result in savings equivalent to your annual fees and dues. This is your personal break-even point. Beyond this number of flight hours, you will be ahead in the the flying club. Consider hourly rentals of $35 at the flying club, plus annual fees and dues of $550, compared to a commercial rental rate of $55. The difference between the two rental rates is $20. This is your hourly operating savings at the flying club; however, at the flying club you also have to pay a fixed fee of $550 per year. The question is, how many hours do you have to fly at an hourly savings of $20 to pay for the $550 annual fees and dues? (Table 15-8)

Table 15-8.

FBO rental per hour:	$55.00
Flying club rental per hour:	$35.00
Hourly operating savings:	$20.00
Annual flying club dues:	$550.00
Hours to be flown in club to save the equivalent of dues (550/20):	27.5 hrs

The answer, 27.5 hours per year, is 2.5 hours per month. If you fly less than that, in this example you are better off renting; if you fly more, you are better off in the flying club.

FLYING CLUB VERSUS PARTNERSHIP

The comparison is equally favorable with the partnership. The simple reason is that in addition to not having the enormous capital expenditure per member as you do per partner to acquire the airplane, you are also spreading the fixed expenses around a greater number of people. Consider the example of an airplane that rents for $35 at the flying club, has fixed expenses of $5,500, and operating expense of $30. The club membership for this airplane is 15 and the annual dues are, again, $550 per member per year, comfortably supporting the fixed expenses. The same airplane has similar operating expenses in a four-way partnership, and marginally lower fixed expenses of, say, $5,000 because of lower insurance payments. The fixed expenses translate into $1,250 per partner.

As illustrated in Table 15-9, for an equivalent number of hours flown, the flying club's all in rate will always be lower, (although the difference will diminish with an increase in hours flown) given the big difference in annual fixed expenses per person.

From a financial point of view, if you fly between 50 to 100 hours per year, the flying club is the best alternative. But in the fragile world of finance, the advantage can diminish quickly if expenses are not tightly controlled.

Table 15-9.

	Club	**Partnership**
Hourly charge:	$35.00	$30.00
Annual fixed expenses per person:	$550.00	$1,250.00
Hourly all in cost, 25 hrs:	$57.00	$80.00
50 hrs:	$46.00	$55.00
100 hrs:	$40.50	$42.50

THE BALANCE SHEET

The flying club's balance sheet is a picture at a moment in time of its financial condition. It is really nothing more than a list of its assets and its liabilities, and the difference between the two, its net worth. On a very basic level, it tells the membership and the banks how indebted the flying club is, how much value is available to the club over and above its indebtedness, and how accessible this value is (*liquidity*). In this regard, the balance sheet is useful, but it is a static picture. The flow and magnitude of expenses and income as discussed in the previous section is far more important.

The B&C Flying Club's balance sheet (Table 15-10) shows that on 12/31/91 the club had $56,000 more in assets than in liabilities. Of this amount, $21,300 was current, which means accessible immediately or in the near future ($16,300 was available immediately, $5,500 was expected in the form of dues on the basis of bills sent out to the membership). On the liability side, the club is about to have to pay $9,400 in bills and loan payments. If the club satisfied these payments from immediately available sources ($16,300), it would have only $6,900 available immediately to spend as it chooses, even though its net worth is $56,300. The fact is that most of the club's net worth is tied up in its airplanes. To free up any substantial amount of net worth, it would have to sell an airplane.

This example is a simple summary. In reality, the accounts can be shown in greater detail, specifically identifying such items as engine and maintenance reserve accounts. Any accounting software will prompt you with templates for the day to day accounting entries from which it will automatically generate the balance sheet as well as the income statement.

A problem with balance sheets is that there is a lot they do not tell. A balance sheet is a snapshot at a point in time. Tomorrow the club might face a liability that is nowhere to be seen today. For a dynamic image of the flying club's financial condition, you must see its statement of expenses and income for the current and past years, and the projections for future years.

Table 15-10.

THE B&C FLYING CLUB

Statement of Condition, 12/31/91 ($)

ASSETS		LIABILITIES	
Current Assets		**Current Liabilities**	
Cash	6,300	Bills Payable	3,500
T Bills	10,000	Current Loan Payment.	5,900
Dues Receivable	5,500		
Total Current Assets	21,300	Total Current Liab.	9,400
Fixed Assets		**Long Term Debt**	
C-172	28,000	C-172 Loan	11,800
PA 28-201	45,000	PA 28-201 Loan	18,800
Less Depreciation	(8,000)	**Total Liabilities**	40,000
Net fixed assets	65,000		
		NET WORTH	56,300
Total Assets	96,300	**Total Liab. and Net Worth**	96,300

CONTROLLING FLYING CLUB EXPENSES

The temptation is great to spend generously when establishing and running a flying club. Pinching pennies can be downright depressing and might compromise safety. Pleasure flying should be fun and safe, so why not do it right and spend what it takes? This attitude is fundamentally sound as long as you spend only what it takes and not a penny more. Financial problems arise when the flying club spends beyond its means, when it borrows too much, or rents a lavish clubhouse and buys a limited edition Barnburner lithograph to decorate it, or hires a full-time manager and mechanic for too few airplanes.

It doesn't take much to send costs spiralling skyward. Compare Tables 15-2 and 15-11. In the first case the club has not borrowed to buy its airplanes and has kept general expenses trimmed to the bone. In the following case, the club has borrowed 50 percent of the cost of each airplane and has spent generously, but not excessively, on general expenses. It has also increased the hourly operating reserves it charges. The end results are fairly startling. The cost of flying each airplane has almost doubled, and is barely below commercial rental rates.

Controlling fixed expenses

The two areas where the flying club can control its fixed expenses most effectively are borrowing and general expenses. The effect of borrowing is easily illustrated. Take a look at the payments on 10 year loans at 10 percent for the two airplanes (Table 15-11). They are a whopping one-third of total aircraft fixed expenses. During the first five years of the loan, most of your payments will be for interest under the usual repayment rules of banks who would like to get paid for the use of their money first. Given that the club might not keep the airplane for the life of the loan, little equity might have been built in it by the time it is sold. And the amounts borrowed are only 50 percent of the airplanes' value, a conservative amount by bankers' standards. This is not to say that you shouldn't borrow. Borrowing is meant to close the gap between your resources and the object of your desires, but only if you can afford the cost of borrowing.

The flying club that borrows heavily can get into financial trouble if it experiences a decline in membership. It is the members' dues that repay the loan. If, for whatever reason, membership declines, the dues per individual member have to rise to service the loan. This might cause remaining members to decide that the increased dues are more than they care to spend and soon income might be too low to make the loan payments. This is why all good bankers demand the airplane as collateral as a condition for making a loan.

General fixed expenses are the other source of significant potential cost savings. The small, disciplined flying club should be able to keep these expenses to a minimum; a larger flying club can also do better than the membership might first think. The rental of premises and salaries are the big savings opportunities.

The rental of premises is expensive, and all but the largest flying clubs have little need for permanent full-time space. Great savings can be had by cutting a part-time rental deal for underused premises. Rent a room at the airport only for the weekends. Don't rent a room if a counter will do. Investigate the possibility of a mobile clubhouse in the form of a member's rarely used motor home. For off-airport meetings, use the homes of various members and look into using community space at the local schools, town hall, or VFW post. Such community space is often available free. If you do rent full-time space, try to sublet it during unused periods.

Volunteer work is the key to salary control. A flying club has to get very large before even part-time salaried positions are justified. Scheduling and administrative functions are easily performed by most members. Tasks requiring specialized skills, such as maintenance and accounting, are harder to fill on a volunteer basis, but a determined effort to attract members with such skills in exchange for some form of concessionary flying will usually do the trick for considerable savings over salaried positions.

There is also room for savings on some of the other fixed expenses. You shouldn't skimp on insurance and there is little you can do about state fees and

Table 15-11.

FLYING CLUB FINANCIAL ANALYSIS ($)

Generous Expenses and Reserves

EXPENSES	TOTAL	AIRCRAFT #1	AIRCRAFT #2
		Type PA28-201	Type C-172
ANNUAL FIXED EXPENSES		Hrs/Yr 500	Hrs/Yr 500
AIRCRAFT RELATED			
Tiedown/Hangar	1,800	900	900
Insurance, Aircraft	3,500	2,000	1,500
Fees and Taxes	240	120	120
100 Hour and Annual Inspections	3,500	2,000	1,500
Maintenance	0	0	0
Loan Payments	5,788	3,568	2,220
Depreciation	4,000	2,500	1,500
GENERAL EXPENSES			
Insurance, Club	1,000		
Office rent	2,400		
Accountant's Fee	250		
Manager's Salary	5,200		
Mechanic's Salary	4,160		
Supplies/Administrative	250		
Other	1,000		
Total Fixed Expenses/yr	33,088	11,088	7,740
HOURLY OPERATING EXPENSES			
Fuel	34	20	14
Oil	2	1	1
Engine Reserve	26	16	10
General Maint Res	16	10	6
Total Op Exp/hr	78	47	31
Total Op Exp/yr	39,000	23,500	15,500
TOTAL ANNUAL EXPENSES	72,088	34,682	23,302

INCOME			
FIXED: Annual Fees and Dues	38,051		
OPERATING: Annual Aircraft Rental Income	44,850	27,025	17,825

TOTAL ANNUAL INCOME	82,901	30	NUMBER OF MEMBERS (enter)
SURPLUS/DEFICIT (to general reserve)	10,813	1,268	ANNUAL FEES AND DUES, MEMBER/YR

ANNUAL COST PER MEMBER, PA28-201

50 Hours	3,971	per hour:	79.42
50 hours commercial rental at $90/hr	4,500		

ANNUAL COST PER MEMBER, C-172

50 Hours	3,051	per hour:	61.02
50 hours commercial rental at $70/hr	3,500		

Table 15-12.

FLYING CLUB FINANCIAL ANALYSIS, FIVE AIRPLANE CLUB ($)

EXPENSES	TOTAL	AIRCRAFT #1	AIRCRAFT #2	AIRCRAFT #3	AIRCRAFT #4	AIRCRAFT #5
Type		C-150	C-150	C-150	C-172	PA28-201
Hrs/Yr		500	500	500	350	300
ANNUAL FIXED EXPENSES						
AIRCRAFT RELATED						
Tiedown/Hangar	4,500	900	900	900	900	900
Insurance, Aircraft	7,400	1,300	1,300	1,300	1,500	2,000
Fees and Taxes	600	120	120	120	120	120
100 Hour and Annual Inspections	7,050	1,350	1,350	1,350	1,500	1,500
Maintenance	0	0	0	0	0	0
Loan Payments	5,788	0	0	0	2,220	3,568
Depreciation	7,000	1,000	1,000	1,000	1,500	2,500
GENERAL EXPENSES						
Insurance, Club	1,000					
Office rent	1,200					
Accountant's Fee	500					
Manager's Salary	5,200					
Mechanic's Salary	4,160					
Supplies/Administrative	500					
Other	1,000					
Total Fixed Expenses/yr	45,898	4,670	4,670	4,670	7,740	10,588
HOURLY OPERATING EXPENSES						
Fuel	70	12	12	12	14	20
Oil	5	1	1	1	1	1
Engine Reserve	25	4	4	4	5	8
General Maint Res	14	2	2	2	3	5
Total Op Exp/hr	114	19	19	19	23	34
Total Op Exp/yr	46,750	9,500	9,500	9,500	8,050	10,200
TOTAL ANNUAL EXPENSES	92,648	14,208	14,208	14,208	15,836	20,856
INCOME						
FIXED: Annual Fees and Dues	52,783					
OPERATING: Annual Aircraft Rental Income	53,763	10,925	10,925	10,925	9,258	11,730
TOTAL ANNUAL INCOME	106,545					
SURPLUS/DEFICIT (to general reserve)	13,897					

NUMBER OF MEMBERS (enter): 75

ANNUAL FEES AND DUES PER MEMBER PER YEAR: 704

taxes, but you might save on tiedown at a smaller airport, and voluntary or concessionary maintenance work can decrease inspection and annual cost (though such arrangements should never be at the expense of safety).

Operating expenses

There is less room to save on operating expenses, but there are possibilities. Try buying flying club fuel and oil in bulk for a discount. Take a good look at the engine and maintenance reserves to make sure you are not overreserving (though the usual tendency is to underreserve, a temptation to be avoided). Prudent budget maintenance arrangements will also reduce the need for maintenance reserves.

Increasing income

When the club has done all it can to cut expenses and they are still considered too high per member, an option is to sign up more members. This increases fee and dues income to cover the same amount of fixed expenses, reducing the share per member of these expenses and keeping individual fees and dues in check. Be careful not to unreasonably compromise aircraft availability by signing up too many additional members.

DIFFERENTIAL DUES

A legitimate claim of members who exclusively fly only a less expensive aircraft in a flying club that operates several aircraft types is that they are subsidizing the fixed expenses of those members who fly the more expensive types. Consider the sample financial analysis of a flying club with five airplanes presented in Table 15-12. The club has three Cessna 150s, a Skyhawk, and an Arrow. As you can see, dues per person work out to $704; however, fixed expenses are $4,670 for the 150s; $7,740 for the Skyhawk; and $10,588 for the Arrow. To ensure a fair allocation of expenses, this club should charge proportionally less in annual dues for pilots signed off to fly only the less expensive airplanes.

16

Legal structure, organization, and operating rules

A FLYING CLUB'S FUNDAMENTAL OBJECTIVE is similar to that of the partnership: A number of like-minded pilots wish to make flying affordable through a joint-venture. In concept, the flying club faces the same legal and organizational issues as the partnership. The form of legal existence has to be addressed, and the club's policies and procedures have to be put in writing; however, the greater number of members in the flying club makes the less formal structure of the partnership unworkable.

While incorporation and the attendant transfer of liability from the members to the corporation might be optional for the partnership, it is practically mandatory for the flying club. The risk of being held liable for the actions of another member in an unincorporated flying club is greater than it is in a partnership because of the greater number of members, many of whom probably hardly know each other.

While the partnership can comfortably involve all partners in all decisions, the flying club has to delegate many decisions to function efficiently; therefore, it has to develop a structure of officers authorized to make those decisions.

And while the partnership can get by with a fairly basic agreement that leaves a lot of room for interpretation (as long as the mechanism to resolve differences is effective), the flying club needs to spell out its policies and procedures in much more detail for the benefit of its larger membership.

Legal incorporation and a structure of officer positions provides the flying club with the framework that enables it to function effectively. Bylaws define the flying club's purpose, its organizational structure, its policies regarding all aspects of its activities, and the responsibilities of its officers. Operating procedures are the flying club's operating manual. They spell out for the membership the day-to-day operating rules: scheduling procedures, payment procedures, experience requirements, currency requirements, and the like.

As you plot to establish a flying club, do not be intimidated by all this legal and organizational paperwork. This chapter shall help you find that it is all logical and very easy to understand. This material is intended only to provide guidance; it is imperative that you seek the assistance of a lawyer to handle the specific needs of your fledgling flying club; what you most need is a good dose of common sense. And, as in the case of setting up a partnership with the help of a lawyer, you will get the best results for the lowest legal fee if you are well informed, specific and detailed in your objectives, and willing to make decisions based upon your lawyer's advice instead of looking to your lawyer to make the decisions for you.

INCORPORATION AND ORGANIZATION

The main reason for incorporation is to limit the liability of the individual members of the flying club. When the club is incorporated (registered with the appropriate authorities as a corporation), it becomes a separate and distinct legal entity. It enters into commitments on behalf of its members, and it owns the assets of the club, such as the airplanes. The members own a share in the club, rather than shares of the airplanes directly. As a legally incorporated entity, the club, rather than its constituent members, is legally liable for any commitments made by it and for any consequences of the activities performed under its auspices.

If a member of an incorporated flying club causes damage or injury while operating a club aircraft, the victim's legal recourse is limited to the club, and under certain circumstances, the member causing the problem. The other club members are shielded from liability by the incorporation. Were the club not incorporated, all club members could, under a variety of scenarios, be found liable personally for the actions of any one member. The victim could come after all personal assets of every club member, easily causing personal financial ruin. In the same vein, if the incorporated flying club defaults on the payment of any money it owes, the creditors cannot demand payment from the individual members, as they could in the case of an unincorporated club. So, incorporating your flying club is not only desirable, but essential.

How to incorporate

The specific procedures vary from state to state, but incorporation is an easy administrative procedure everywhere. The founding document of a corporation is its articles of incorporation. This document usually defines the flying club's purpose and its right to enter into commitments to meet that purpose, such as acquire assets, enter into contracts, and borrow money. The document also identifies the club's place of business, its incorporators, its directors at the time of incorporation, its share structure and property rights, its nonprofit nature (if applicable), and the manner of its dissolution. As you can see from the sample articles of incorporation in the appendices, it is a straightforward and simple document. The actual format and content requirements vary from state to state, so you must work through a lawyer. You should also consult a lawyer to find out what the requirements are in your particular jurisdiction to acquire nonprofit status; a nonprofit corporation can save a bundle on taxes, but usually the club has to meet numerous legal means and organizational purpose requirements.

The actual act of incorporation usually consists of notarizing the articles of incorporation to verify the signatures, and filing it with the state registrar of corporations along with some other simple supporting documents depending upon the state, and paying a registration fee. In certain states, registering as a nonprofit corporation might be different from filing a regular registration.

When incorporated, the entity has to fulfill certain minimal requirements regarding board of directors' meetings evidenced by official minutes to prove that the organization is truly a corporation rather than a legal shell established for some murky business convenience.

Organization

The corporation (the flying club) is the sum of its shareholders (the members) who make a financial commitment when they become shareholders with the expectation that the club will be operated in their best interest and they will be able to influence how it is run. Ideally, every club member could vote on every decision, but this is impractical, given the size of most clubs and the limited amount of time most members have that they would prefer to spend flying rather than voting. So, similar to the shareholders of corporations and constituents of democratic governments, flying club members elect representatives from among themselves for a period of time to run the club on their behalf. These elected members form the club's governing body, the board of directors. Election of the board of directors is usually held annually or biannually with provisions for extraordinary elections under certain circumstances. The board oversees the management of the club and makes all major decisions for the club. It is empowered to appoint officers who are responsible for the day-to-day performance of the function to which they have been appointed. Given the needs of the average flying club, officer positions typically should be filled:

- president
- vice president
- secretary
- treasurer
- maintenance officer
- operations officer
- safety officer
- chief pilot
- membership officer

Not all clubs will find a need for all these functions, and being a director does not preclude someone from serving as an officer as well. Many smaller clubs that don't have the bodies to go around, don't bother with distinguishing between directors and officers. Members are nominated as directors and as officers at the same time. In larger clubs, where the membership might not be well informed about the technical skills of individual members, it makes more sense to elect the directors, and let them appoint the officers after a careful evaluation of the experience and the dedication of the applicants.

Elections

In small clubs of up to 15 members, the elections can be conducted less formally than required by the bylaws, provided the membership is in agreement. The members might discuss who would like to do what, find out if there are competing candidates for a particular position, and then vote on the entire slate for the sake of good order. If there are more candidates than one for a particular position, a vote may be taken for that position. Names in a hat will usually do the trick.

In larger clubs, elections are a more elaborate affair. The club should establish rules for nominating candidates for the directorships. A decent interval should pass from the close of nominations to the elections to give the candidates ample time to make their views and objectives known among the club members. Candidates could mail out letters to the membership or make statements in the club newsletter. Election day could be a big, festive get-together at which the members vote by secret ballot and the votes are counted and the winners announced as the evening's highlight. Provisions should be made for absentee balloting for members who cannot attend.

Paid employees

A payroll is an expense a flying club should avoid as long as possible. For smaller clubs, the expense of even a part-time salary might be prohibitive, and for the larger ones it will be one of the biggest single annual expenses; however, there comes a time when a flying club gets too large to be run by members alone on a voluntary basis and the hiring of a salaried flying club manager is justified. The failure to recognize the need for a paid manager can be just as damaging as lavishly hiring one when there is no need.

When the decision is made to hire a manager part-time or full-time, the manager has to report to someone. There should be one boss from the manager's point of view because answering too many chiefs always turns into a big mess of competing agendas. The best solution is to have the manager report to the president, through whom the membership can address any major grievances, should they arise.

Additional salaried employees should report to the club manager.

BYLAWS

The bylaws of a flying club define and govern everything it does. It is as important a document as a partnership agreement is for an aircraft partnership. When you establish a flying club, setting up the bylaws will be one of your most important tasks and will have to cover practically every aspect of your club's structure and activities; therefore, a careful review of this section even before you are ready to draft your own club's bylaws is an excellent way to become familiar with everything you need to think about when setting up a flying club. A sample bylaws document may be found in the appendices.

As in the case of partnership agreements, it is highly recommended that you seek professional legal advice in setting up your club's bylaws. But prior to seeking the assistance of a lawyer, prepare a detailed draft summary of what you want each section to accomplish. Your lawyer will be grateful for the guidance and you will save on the legal expense.

Purpose

The statement of purpose can be as broad or specific as you want it to be, but it should capture the spirit of your flying club. You can distinguish between general flying, touring, aerobatic flying, the preservation of antiques, instructional flying, the objective of providing flying as inexpensively as possible, or whatever else your club endeavors to accomplish.

Meetings

Meetings are an important feature of flying clubs because they provide a forum for communication between members and the resolution of outstanding issues. By formally committing to regular meetings, this forum is assured.

Type, time, purpose, and place. Two types of meetings are general membership meetings and meetings of the board of directors, which might be addressed under subheadings or in separate sections of the bylaws. Regularly scheduled meetings should be at predetermined intervals, and provisions should be made for calling extraordinary meetings. The provisions for calling extraordinary meetings should be worded to ensure sufficient advanced notice to give all potential attendees enough time to make arrangements to attend. The bylaws should state the time, purpose, and place of the regular meetings: second Thursday of each month at a member's or director's house at 7 p.m.

Annual meeting. One of the general meetings should be specified as an annual meeting. At this meeting, the board of directors should report to the membership on the club's general condition. Topics to be covered should include financial condition and financial results for the year, substantial achievements, issues requiring resolution, plans for the coming year, and the like. This meeting is considered by some clubs to be the ideal venue for the election of the next year's board of directors. Year-end need not coincide with calendar year-end.

Chairperson. The bylaws should specify who will run the meeting and provide a mechanism for alternative arrangements (for example, the members present could elect a chairperson for the meeting if the person who should be running it is absent).

Decisions, quorums, votes. Meetings should be held to make decisions (a novel concept often forgotten); therefore, a mechanism should be put in place to enable meeting participants to make decisions. Decisions vary in levels of importance and all members must have an opportunity to participate; thus, the first order of business is to define elsewhere in this document the level of participation required for various categories of decisions and the advanced notice required to be given to participants. Once it is clear what kind of gathering is empowered to make what decision, a *quorum* has to be established. A quorum is the minimum number of members present necessary to make a decision. Certain situations might require the presence of two thirds of the total membership, other situations might require the presence of half of the board of directors. The definition of a quorum is entirely up to your club. Just be sure that all club members clearly understand the definition and are agreeable.

Many flying clubs simply require that for there to be a quorum—the ability to make decisions—at least 50 percent of the members must be present at general membership meetings, and 50 percent of directors must be present at directors' meetings.

For the sake of good order, it should be formally stated that each member has one vote in any situation requiring votes.

The bylaws should specify the majority necessary for passing a resolution and for electing officials. Simple majority of those present (provided there is a quorum) is a popular choice. In the case of smaller clubs, a two-third majority vote for resolutions might be more appropriate to ensure greater harmony—it is easier to agree to disagree in a larger organization. For a directors' quorum to make routine decisions, a presence of less than 50 percent of the directors might be acceptable.

Meeting procedures. It is best to conduct meetings according to some established code of procedures, such as parliamentary procedures or *Roberts' Rules of Order*, so stated in the bylaws. The advantage of this provision is that if you encounter a procedural stumbling block not covered in the bylaws, you can rely on these rules.

Directors

This section of the bylaws specifies the number of directors the club has, the manner in which they are elected, the length of their term of office, and the scope of their powers and responsibilities. The basic idea is that they can make all the decisions necessary to enable the club to function, including the buying and selling of assets, committing the club to borrowing money, enforcing FAA and club rules and regulations, and hiring paid employees. If the club prefers, the bylaws may specify that the directors seek the membership's majority approval for truly major decisions, such as the selection and purchase of new

Ragwing antiques are available at a number of flying clubs.

equipment. This might be especially desirable in a small flying club for the sake of harmony.

An important role of the directors in the bigger flying clubs is to select the club's officers, usually by majority directors' votes. Depending on club preference as specified in the bylaws, the directors may select officers from among themselves, or may also consider candidates from the membership at large. The timeframe within which the board is obligated to select officers should also be specified.

The directors are required by this section of the bylaws to maintain accurate records of their meetings, votes, and decisions. This information is to be available to the membership for review at any time. Many clubs mail the board of directors' meeting minutes to the membership.

It should be stated that directors serve without any compensation; however, if they personally incur expenditures on behalf of the club with prior approval, they may be reimbursed.

Officers

This section identifies the officers the club is to have, the manner of their selection, and the scope of their duties and responsibilities. It also addresses the issue of officer compensation. Most officers in most clubs serve for no compensation at all. In selected larger clubs, officers fulfilling labor intensive functions, such as treasurer, might get a number of free flying hours per month in exchange for their services.

Some of these functions might be combined, especially in smaller clubs with fewer members. Popular combinations are vice president and treasurer, treasurer and secretary, or vice president and secretary.

Officers should be required to attend the periodic directors' meetings and report on the status of the club functions under their responsibility.

President. The president is the flying club's chief executive officer, in effect, the flying club's boss. He or she is the link between the board of directors and the club, being charged with implementing the board's directives. If the board selects a new airplane to be bought for a specified amount, it is the president's responsibility to make sure that it is done. The president is always a board member and generally presides over all meetings of the club.

In addition to implementing the board's directives, the president is also responsible for reporting to the board any concerns of the membership, any problems with club operations, and from time to time the general condition of the club. The president can call extraordinary meetings unilaterally as needed.

An important responsibility of the president is cosigning all checks issued by the club.

Vice president. The vice president is the president's stand-in. When the president is absent, the vice president inherits all his or her powers. Because the president is unlikely to be absent often from what is a part-time responsibility to begin with, the vice president's job is suited to be combined with another function such as treasurer.

Secretary. The secretary is the flying club's recordkeeper. The secretary keeps the minutes of meetings, membership lists and records, an original set of bylaws, and the flying club seal if there is one. As part of his or her corporate duties, the secretary also cosigns with the president all contracts and other legal instruments following board approval.

Depending upon club size, the secretary's function might be combined with that of the operations officer, the membership officer, or the vice president.

In the absence of the treasurer, the secretary is the stand-in, according to typical bylaws.

Treasurer. The treasurer is the club's financial manager. He or she collects the dues, fees, and payments, pays the club's bills, keeps the books and receipts, and makes sure it all balances at the end of the day.

The treasurer is responsible for providing periodic financial reports on the club to the board of directors and the membership. Common reporting periods are monthly to the board and quarterly to the membership. The minimum information to be provided should be the club's balance sheet and income statement. Statistical reporting on flight activity, such as total hours flown, hours per airplane, hours per member, and the profitability of club aircraft given certain levels of utilization, could also be required of the treasurer.

An important function of the treasurer is to maintain delinquency records and report all member delinquencies to the president within a specified period of time.

The treasurer issues all checks that must be cosigned by the president. Most clubs put a dollar limit on the size of expenditures that may be paid without board approval.

The treasurer must be chosen with great care, and should preferably be someone who has had solid experience in keeping financial records. Corporate treasurers and bank operations officers are usually good candidates. Beware of bank lending officers; they are good at analyzing credits and giving money away, but are rarely required by their job to personally keep detailed, up-to-the-minute financial records and can really make a mess of things before they or anyone else recognizes it.

If there is no in-house treasurer talent, have a bookkeeper set up a system, show someone what records to keep, and come in once a month to balance the books. The bookkeeper's modest fee will be worth its weight in avgas.

Considerable sums of money might flow through the treasurer's hands; therefore, to guard against any possibility of financial monkey business, it is fairly common to have the treasurer bonded. Bonding agencies provide the service for a reasonable fee; contact the club's bank or the local chamber of commerce for referrals.

Maintenance officer. The maintenance officer is responsible for ensuring that all aircraft are properly maintained, and that maintenance takes place in a timely fashion. The maintenance officer schedules all maintenance and subcontracts the work to the appropriate mechanics, or supervises the work of in-house mechanics, if there are any. He or she is also responsible for tracking squawk reports and expeditiously arranging the performance of unscheduled maintenance.

The maintenance officer should watch for unsound operating practices by the membership that might lead to increased maintenance problems (poor leaning techniques, misuse of brakes, improper cold start procedures, and the like) and should take countermeasures by making known and enforcing proper operating procedures.

If the club has an airplane captain program where a member is assigned to each airplane for a period of time to keep it clean, fueled, oiled, and ready to go, the maintenance officer should be the supervisor of this program.

Operations officer. The operations officer is responsible for scheduling and day to day relationships with the local FBO and other airport tenants. This function is especially important in a big flying club, where even a weekend duty officer position might be justified. The operations officer would farm out the duty officer position on a rotational basis, but would be responsible for supervising the duty officer program, and passing the weekend schedule to the duty officer.

Safety officer. Some clubs have a separate safety officer, charged with watching over the flying club's operations and bringing to the attention of members, officers, and directors alike issues of safety. Usually the safety officer's role is best served by implementing preventative safety measures, and fostering a general atmosphere of safety consciousness throughout the club. Examples of preventative safety measures are sending in November to all members a comprehensive article on winter flying, arranging a presentation on go-arounds, and arranging member participation in the FAA's aviation safety programs.

Chief pilot. The chief pilot is responsible for developing and managing a flight proficiency program that ensures that all members have the appropriate levels of experience and currency for the flying they do. The chief pilot is in charge of all the club instructors, if there are any, and should ideally also be an instructor. If there are no instructors in the club, it is the chief pilot's responsibility to ensure the availability of qualified and reliable outside instructors for club members to do whatever flying requiring a flight instructor is authorized in the bylaws.

Membership officer. A separate membership officer position is justified only in a large flying club where keeping track of the membership and recruiting new members is a time-consuming responsibility. The membership officer is responsible for keeping club membership records up-to-date and tracking membership levels and any other membership statistics the club might find useful. It is also the membership officer's responsibility to provide information packages to prospective members, and recruit new members if the club wants to increase the membership level.

This description of officer positions, duties, and responsibilities is rather extensive. Not all positions might be appropriate for your particular flying club, so be flexible in designing your club's structure and let common sense rule.

Vacancies

It is important to have a mechanism in place for dealing with vacancies that arise on the board of directors or among officers when someone is unable to serve out a full term. The usual solution is to have the board approve an interim successor to complete the unfinished term. Vacancies on the board of directors might reach a level that, in the view of the club's founders, justifies extraordinary elections. The bylaws should define that level and establish procedures for extraordinary elections. A good rule of thumb is to hold new elections at anytime when more than one-third of the board positions becomes vacant.

Safety board

Safety should be of paramount concern for a flying club as it is for professional aircraft operators. When an incident or accident happens, there can be a lot of maneuvering to obscure facts or shift blame for a variety of reasons. The safety board's role is to independently and objectively investigate incidents and accidents and report its finding and assessment of responsibility to the board of directors within a specified time after the event.

The bylaws should state how many members the safety board has and which officer positions constitute it. Typically the safety board could include the chief pilot and the safety officer or maintenance officer, as well as another officer or two with no role overseeing day-to-day aircraft operations. Selected clubs don't have a permanent safety board, but have the board of directors assemble an ad hoc board when an incident or accident occurs.

The bylaws should explicitly state that an individual involved in an accident cannot serve on the safety board investigating it.

Hearings

Hearings are the next logical step to the findings of a safety board. Hearings are before the board of directors, and are the opportunity for the other side to present its case: the chance for the person involved in the incident or accident to challenge the safety board's findings.

This section usually includes provisions for the board of directors to reach a conclusion and also defines what penalties and remedial action it can impose. Monetary payments are usually imposed only for violations not covered by insurance. Nonmonetary requirements might include refresher training and temporary restriction of certain flight privileges.

Responsibility

Some club bylaws state in a separate section what financial responsibility a member has who has caused damage to and with club equipment. The standard approach is to hold the member responsible based upon the findings of the safety board, for deductibles and whatever is not covered by insurance due to a violation of regulations. If you do not break out this section separately, be sure to incorporate it somewhere else in the bylaws.

Membership

This section specifies how many members the club is willing to accept (usually expressed in number of members per aircraft), what qualifications applicants must have to be eligible for membership, and how new applicants are approved.

Many flying clubs require a vote by the full membership on the acceptance of any new member. Information on the applicant is made available for a period of time and the application is voted on at a general meeting. In smaller clubs, unanimous approval is recommended. Larger clubs might find some form of majority approval or approval by the board of directors more convenient.

In some clubs, new members might be on a probationary status for a period of time before becoming permanent members.

This section also defines procedures and notice required for resigning from the club. If there are specific procedures for disposing of a member's share, such as the club's first right of refusal, to prevent the shares from being sold to anyone, here is the place to address the issue.

An unpleasant and thankfully infrequent task in flying clubs is the occasional need to expel a member, and this section should provide for such an eventuality. Usually a two-thirds majority vote of members is required, reasonable notice should be given (10 days is common), and the member being expelled should have the right to a hearing prior to being expelled. If the flying club is the kind where members own saleable shares, an automatic, no questions asked buyout of the member being expelled will make things a lot smoother.

Disposition of a member's share upon the member's death should also be addressed here.

Member payments

This section spells out what payments members are required to make for the privilege of flying with the club. It should address initiation fees, share payments if any, refundability at the termination of membership, annual dues, monthly dues, rates for aircraft, payment due dates, and delinquencies and their consequences.

It is a common practice to require joining members to pay the annual fees, as well as the first and last month's dues upon joining. This provides a financial cushion for the club in case members get into payment problems for whatever reason.

If the fleet is large and rates are likely to fluctuate, it might not be practical to list individual aircraft fees in the bylaws. In that case, the bylaws should refer to an attached fee schedule, approved by the board of directors and amended from time to time.

For most payment categories, the bylaws should specify immediate payment (a short cash cycle is the key to a flying club's financial health). Delinquencies should be dealt with swiftly, stiff penalties imposed, and if a delinquency is not cured in short order, flying privileges should be withdrawn.

Club finances

Some flying club bylaws address all expenditure limits by the club in this section instead of referring to them in the sections covering the members and club officials who make the expenditures.

Here is the place to define what expenditures can be committed to on behalf of the club by the treasurer and maintenance officer without seeking specific approval by the board of directors. It also addresses any reimbursement of members for expenses incurred at the club's request, and sets a limit (usually very low) for expenditures a member can authorize for field repairs necessary to get the airplane back to home base.

It is a good idea to state that no expenditures or financial obligations may be incurred on the club's behalf by any club member except as provided for by the bylaws.

Flight proficiency program and operating rules

Regarding flight proficiency, this section states the club's obligation to establish minimum requirements for qualifications, flight experience levels, minimum periodic flight time requirements, currency requirements, and checkride requirements.

The section's second function is to state the club's obligation to establish a set of operating rules by which the members are to conduct their flying.

It is not unusual for flying clubs to require much higher levels of proficiency and currency than called for by the FAA regulations. Flying club members might be required to take an annual checkride in the most advanced type of club aircraft they fly, and might have to fly a minimum number of hours per month or quarter. In the case of complex aircraft, they might be required to have substantial complex experience before acting as pilot in command, usually motivated by insurance requirements in addition to club safety considerations.

Surplus

If the flying club is well managed, it will have a running cash surplus after taking in all income and paying all expenditures. The surplus should increase as time goes by. This section of the bylaws specifies that this surplus is the club's, to be used as seen fit by the club per the bylaws (for example, to buy new equipment or upgrade equipment), and is not to be distributed to individual members except in case of the dissolution of the club.

Amendments

As in the case of all legal agreements, there have to be provisions for amending the bylaws. The entire membership should vote on any amendments, and to ensure a high degree of consensus, the requirement of a two-thirds majority is recommended.

OPERATING RULES

The operating rules are the manual that the members should use in conducting their day to day flight activities. Some clubs break out nonflight rules, such as billing and scheduling procedures, from flight rules. Others combine all operating rules into one document. In any event, operating rules should address the following topics.

Flightline

A good idea at the outset is to list all available aircraft, their major specifications, their equipment, and rental rates.

Compliance

The rules should explicitly require that all members must adhere to all FAA laws and regulations, as well as any club rules and procedures.

This section should also specify temporary flight suspension policies for violations.

Beech Aircraft Corporation

The club bylaws should specify the fields where club aircraft may land.

Use of aircraft

This section of the operating rules deals with all aspects of aircraft use, including but not limited to the following:

- It outlines the purposes for which aircraft may be used and cannot be used. You might find it useful to list explicit prohibitions on aerobatics, air show flying, commercial use of the aircraft, and the like.
- It specifies pilot qualifications and currency requirements for the use of particular aircraft, checkride requirements to fly specific aircraft, and periodic flight review requirements (usually annual). Some clubs require separate checkouts for night flying.
- It requires members to meet all aircraft operating manual requirements and limitations, conduct thorough preflight checks to verify airworthiness, and report all maintenance discrepancies to the maintenance officer. A squawk sheet system is highly recommended.
- It specifies rules and regulations regarding the use of instructors by club members.
- It defines access by student pilots to aircraft, and flight limitations on student pilots, if any.
- It defines weather minimums for flying club aircraft. Club weather minimums might be considerably more conservative than FAA minimums. Examples are higher and farther VFR and night VFR ceiling and visibility minimums.
- It specifies which airports may be used by club members in club aircraft. Many clubs have restrictions on the use of marginal fields in the area or fields with runways shorter than a certain length.
- It outlines refueling policies and procedures.
- It specifies postflight duties regarding the aircraft.

Scheduling

The scheduling section of the operating rules describes how to schedule aircraft and what the consequences are for not living up to the schedule either by the member or the club. This section usually addresses with whom to schedule the aircraft, how far in advance aircraft may be scheduled, and for what period of time aircraft may be scheduled.

It also specifies cancellation policies and alternatives available to a member if the scheduled aircraft is not present at the appointed time.

Finances, payments, billing

This section lists all annual fees, monthly dues, and aircraft rental rates in effect. It describes payment procedures, payment due dates, delinquency charges and the consequences of uncured delinquencies.

Being grounded away from home base

Some clubs break out this topic separately, others address it under use of aircraft. The idea is to design a policy that discourages flying in marginal weather, or with a marginal mechanical condition just to get home, but provide a disincentive to extend beyond a scheduled slot because the sky is so blue and the water is so warm in the Bahamas this time of year; thus, no extra charges should be levied for verifiable weather or mechanical delays, but a hefty surcharge should be forthcoming if a trip is extended for other reasons.

It is imperative to require immediate reporting to the club of any delays due to grounding away from home base.

Lease agreement

In addition to providing each member with the operating rules, most clubs require all new members before their first flight in a club aircraft to sign a lease agreement, explicitly committing themselves to adhere to the terms of renting and operating club aircraft, including but not limited to the following points:

- Operate the aircraft in a responsible fashion (including thorough preflight checks and not permitting others to fly the aircraft).
- Comply with federal, state, and local regulations.
- Land only at airports approved by the club.
- Report all accidents promptly.
- Pay bills promptly.
- Abide by the club's bylaws and all other club policies, procedures, rules, and regulations.

The wording of this lease agreement, specifically the term lease, should be examined by an attorney or CPA. In some jurisdictions, the wrong use of the term might have unforeseen tax and legal consequences. It should be explicitly clear that the aircraft are available for use only to club members and the club is not in the business of leasing aircraft to the public.

17

Financing the flying club

FINANCIAL ANALYSIS OF THE FLYING CLUB that you would like to establish is complete and the projections tell you that the plan would work. Now you have to find the money to acquire the airplane or airplanes for the club. You face the classic problem of the startup business. You need sources of capital. Because the club has no track record, banks are unwilling to provide financing except under special circumstances; thus, the choices are to raise the money entirely among the prospective members of the club in the form of share subscriptions, to finance a part of the airplanes by meeting the banks' special requirements, or to borrow from club members.

Another possibility for acquiring the airplanes is to enter into lease arrangements with private owners. While these leases have largely lost their attraction as money-making propositions for the airplanes' owners (because there are no longer tax advantages since the demise of the investment tax credit and changes in accounting for equipment leases), a flying club lease can still result in a substantial subsidy of the owners' cost of flying. This chapter reviews all four options.

PRIVATE SOURCES OF CAPITAL

When a flying club is started from scratch, the simplest option is for all the prospective members to pay in their share of the airplane's purchase price. In exchange, the members become shareholders in the club. This arrangement is not much different from the capital structure of an airplane partnership, except that the cost of the airplane is shared by a greater number of people. The shares are transferable, and are paid for over and above the annual fees and dues. When a club member leaves, he or she sells his or her shares. The club should have first right of refusal. If the club chooses to buy the departing member's shares, it can sell them to a new member or can reduce the number of shareholders by buying the shares via an assessment of the remaining shareholders. Under this structure, no person can join the club without purchasing a share. The bylaws should specify some sort of periodic share valuation based on changes in aircraft value and the other assets of the flying club (reserves, and the like).

A $30,000 Cessna 172 bought by 15 members requires an initial investment per member of $2,000. This is a lot of money, but far less than the $7,500 required per partner in a four-way partnership. Nevertheless, it is more than many pilots interested in joining a flying club would like to pay. As the flying club matures, individual share contributions can be reduced. From annual fees and dues, the club can buy back for its own account over time the shares held by the individual members. Say, of $600 in annual dues per nonshareholding member, $200 is used to buy back $200 worth of shares from the founding members, reducing the shares per member from $2,000 to $1,800 in the first year. The net effect is to fully buy back individually held shares per member or reduce the amounts individually held to levels more easily saleable to prospective new members upon the departure of an original shareholder. It is not unusual for a fairly mature flying club to require a $500-750 refundable fee from joining members over and above annual fees and dues. This amount is essentially the purchase of a share in the flying club, and was probably arrived at by some variation of the capitalization scheme just described.

Over time, the flying club may choose to fully repay the original shareholders, and avoid any need to require joining members to come up with a hefty refundable fee.

One way to ease the financial burden of coming up with big chunks of capital is to borrow part of the airplane's purchase price from a bank. If the 15-member club borrows $15,000 on the $30,000 Cessna 172, the initial capital contribution of each member is reduced to $1,000. The trouble is that banks don't have much faith in recreational flying clubs.

The Cessna singles are also a familiar sight on flying club flightlines.

BANK FINANCING

It is often said of bankers that they are willing to lend money only to people who don't really need it. A loan request from a nonprofit flying club about to be established seeking money to buy its first airplane is not what a run-of-the-mill banker wants to find inside the in-box on a Monday morning. The start-up flying club is like the start-up business, virtually unfinanceable on conventional terms by commercial banks until there is a solid track record; however, an alternative is provided by the handful of banks that specialize in aircraft financing.

From these banks, the fledgling flying club will at least get a fair hearing, and, under the right conditions, even a loan. The catch is that certain members of the flying club will have to go out on a limb and provide personal guarantees of the club's obligations. That is quite a responsibility to undertake for little personal return.

The aviation-minded bank's approach to financing a flying club is no different from financing an airplane partnership. The bank will usually not, on principle, provide the club a loan for general purposes, not tied to a specific aircraft. It will finance the purchase of an aircraft, taking it as collateral. The maximum percentage of the purchase price the bank is willing to finance is determined as it is for a partnership (usually a percentage of the retail or wholesale bluebook price). In addition to taking the airplane as collateral, the bank needs to see a clear source of repayment.

In the case of partnership borrowings, the source of repayment is each partner's personal income, sufficiently large to allow for loan payments after meeting all other obligations. In the case of a loan to the flying club, the only source of repayment is the club's income from fees, dues, and aircraft rentals. This is not a source that even an aviation-minded bank considers reliable, and rightly so. From a business standpoint, even commercial aviation businesses are viewed as high risk, let alone a noncommercial flying club established purely for the pleasure of its members; hence, the need for reliable outside sources of repayment and the requirement for personal guarantees from financially strong club members, even in the case of flying clubs that have been around for a few years.

(Incidentally, the local FBO or other small businesses don't have it any easier. In practically all instances, for general purpose borrowing, the principals must provide not only their personal guarantees to the bank, but also some other form of collateral, such as their house.)

So where does this leave the flying club? What inducement is there for any member to put personal assets on the line to guarantee the performance of the club? The big incentive is to make possible a way of flying unavailable otherwise, and if the arrangement is properly structured, the members providing the guarantee can minimize their financial exposure.

Another inducement lies in the nature of the guarantee. Given the collateral value of the airplane, in case of loan repayment problems, the bank stands to recover most if not all of its loan by selling the airplane. In a liquidation, the guarantors will be required only to make up any shortfalls between the outstanding loan amount and the sale price of the airplane. If the loan amount is conservative (say 50 percent of the wholesale value), the guarantors' risk exposure is moderate.

If the flying club experiences financial problems and is unable to make payments on the loan, from the guarantor's point of view it might be preferable in some cases to pay off the bank, take over the loan to the club and get a better price on the orderly sale of the airplane compared to a foreclosure liquidation price.

A risk run by the guarantors is finding themselves on the hook for the whole amount of the loan in case the airplane is destroyed and the insurance claim is denied. All guarantors of flying club obligations should absolutely seek the advice of a lawyer before committing to any guarantees.

Once the decision is made to seek financing and there are willing guarantors, the application process, the evaluation of the borrower and the guarantors, and the terms and conditions for the loan are similar to a loan made to an airplane partnership, as described in great detail in chapter 8. Study this chapter carefully and use the same loan worksheet to gather information from lenders. Prepare an application package that is professional in appearance. In addition to the information required for a partnership loan, be prepared to provide the flying club's income statements, balance sheets, and tax returns, for the last three years if available. The bank will most likely also want a copy of the club's articles of incorporation, bylaws, and membership roster.

An alternative to bank borrowing by the club is for the individual members to take out general purpose personal loans to finance their share of the flying club; however, in this case, each member has the responsibility of evaluating whether or not he or she considers the club an acceptable risk. Remember, if the club folds, the bank will still collect on your personal loan.

BORROWING FROM MEMBERS

As do some partnerships, the flying club might want to consider borrowing from its members. There is a financial advantage to the club and the member. There is usually a difference of several percentage points between the interest rates banks charge for loans and are willing to pay for deposits. A loan from a member to the club, priced between the bank's lending rate and its deposit rate, will result in a lower borrowing cost to the club and a higher return to the member in comparison to the bank option.

If the club borrows from a member, it should be at arms length, similar in structure to a bank loan, properly documented by a loan agreement similar to one required by the bank, and collateralized by the airplane under the appropriate security agreement and filed liens. An attorney's assistance in setting up a loan between a member and the flying club is essential.

While financially convenient, a loan from a member might cause friction in the flying club if the member expects (wrongly) any special status, privileges, or influence for having made the loan. Both parties should enter into such an arrangement with their eyes wide open.

THE LEASE OPTION

The least expensive way to get a flying club going is to avoid the need for capital or financing altogether. This can be accomplished by leasing an airplane from a private owner. Once upon a time such arrangements were very popular because of the investment tax credits which, along with a little lease income, actually allowed an owner to make some money. The investment tax credits have long been eliminated, and in the vast majority of cases the reduced lease income that remains is not and never has been sufficient to allow the owner to break even on the costs of owning the airplane; however, under the proper structure and circumstances, leasing an airplane to a flying club can amount to a significant subsidy of the owner's costs.

Lease terms are whatever the owner and club make them. The general idea is that the owner receives an hourly income from the entity leasing the airplane. A lease agreement can leave the owner responsible for all expenses related to the aircraft (insurance, maintenance, tiedown, fuel, oil), and pay a substantial percentage of the hourly rental income to the owner. This was the favored arrangement in the tax-driven heydays of leases, and frankly, more often than not, excluding the tax advantages, it was a ripoff. The owner had to pay the fixed expenses whether the airplane flew or not (he was relying on variable income to pay fixed expenses, always a risky business), selected FBOs tended to go to town on the maintenance, and many of them grossly overestimated the amount of time the airplanes were expected to fly.

A more desirable alternative from the owner's point of view is to lease the airplane under terms that require the club to pay the tiedown, insurance, inspection and annual fees, all labor on maintenance, and fuel and oil. In addition, the owner is paid an hourly fee for engine reserve and wear and tear. In turn, the owner pays for any parts. This arrangement is fair, because the flying club gets use of the airplane, yet has an incentive to control expenses tightly because it is paying them directly. The owner gets to use the airplane and pay for it just like any other member.

Owners with underutilized airplanes are the best potential source of airplanes available for lease. Many of them love the idea of owning an airplane, but have difficulty justifying it. A lease to a club that defrays a lot of their expenses, yet enables them to fly the modest number of hours they desire, might be just the reason they need to keep the airplane.

Flying clubs and owners have great flexibility in structuring a lease agreement. It is important that both parties act in good faith and genuinely believe that they are getting a fair deal.

Any lease arrangement between a club and the owner should be in writing and subjected to legal review before being signed.

18

Insuring the flying club

IN MANY RESPECTS, insuring the flying club is similar to insuring the partnership. The flying club requires hull insurance to protect it against damage to the aircraft; liability insurance is required to protect it against liabilities incurred as a result of damage or injury caused to others by club-related activities. Other insurance options, such as medical coverage for the aircraft occupants is also available, as it is to partnerships.

This chapter explores the differences between flying club and partnership insurance and comments on insurance issues specific to flying clubs. Chapter 9, regarding partnership insurance, is a primer on aircraft insurance.

RATES

The biggest difference between partnership and flying club insurance is in the insurance rates. Insurance companies perceive a higher risk beyond a certain number of pilots flying the same aircraft. At that point the insured entity is considered a flying club, regardless of its legal form of existence, and insurance rates increase dramatically. At the time of this writing, most insurance companies consider any cooperative flying venture with more than five or six pilots a flying club. Club insurance rates compared to noncommercial partnership rates for pilots with similar experience flying similar equipment are, on average, almost double. Flying club rates are nearly identical to the commercial rates for comparable pilots and equipment because in the insurance company's eyes, the risks are similar.

Rates are calculated according to actuarial formulae, taking into consideration the number of pilots, pilot experience and record, proposed use, amount of hours to be flown during the insured period, and the type and value of the aircraft.

Deductibles apply as they do to aircraft partnership insurance.

COVERAGE

If a flying club has only one airplane, little is different from the partnership in the way it is insured, except for the heftier insurance premium. If the club has more than one aircraft, all the airplanes are usually put on one master policy. This arrangement is quite similar to the concept of having more than one car on your car insurance policy. There is one common liability limit that applies to all aircraft, and hull amounts are set separately for each aircraft depending upon value.

Forms and levels of coverage

The structure of liability and hull coverage for the flying club is relatively similar to partnership insurance. Liability limits may be combined with no restrictions per claimant, meaning that if there is only one claimant on a $1 million limit, the entire limit is available to satisfy the one claim. Alternatively, limits might be set per person per occurrence. Beware of inexpensive coverage with low limits per person per occurrence that might leave the club inadequately covered.

Although the incorporated flying club's liability beyond the liability insurance limits is limited to its assets, no club wants to run a high risk of being put out of business in case of trouble, just to save a few dollars on premiums. A generous level of liability insurance is highly recommended. Be aware that there are also upper limits beyond which insurers are unwilling to provide coverage. At the time of this writing, these limits for flying clubs were in the $2 million range. Members might not be able to purchase additional coverage individually, depending upon the status of the insurance markets. Check with your agent or insurance company.

Hull insurance options are similar to those available to partnerships. To review, there are two considerations: the phase of operations for which the hull is insured, and the manner in which hull value is calculated. *All risk* covers the aircraft under all circumstances, in motion or not in motion, in flight and on the ground; *all risk not in flight* provides coverage only on the ground in motion and not in motion; *all risk not in motion* provides coverage only when the aircraft is stationary on the ground (usually selected when the aircraft is grounded for a prolonged period). Given the relatively large number of pilots flying in even a one-airplane club, anything but all risk coverage for the average flying club is shortsighted.

Aircraft valuation is on an agreed value basis, similar to partnership aircraft valuation. Basically, the insurer expects you to insure the aircraft for a value within ± 10 percent of retail bluebook value. (Additional details are in chapter 9.)

Flying club insurance and the membership

An important question for individual members in any flying club is whether or not the insurance company, after paying out the club, can come after the member who caused the accident or incident. Unless all members are named insureds on the policy, the insurance company can sue the offending member to recover amounts forked over to the club. If members are not named insureds, they can purchase renter's insurance for individual protection. Flying club insurance is rarely written without all members being named insureds, but markets can change quickly, so check with your insurance provider.

The Aerospatiale Trinidad, a slick, complex single, should be accessible to budget pilots through a well organized flying club.

Insuring aircraft used but not owned by the flying club

Many flying clubs lease the aircraft they fly, rather than own them outright. In this case, the aircraft may still be put on one master policy arranged by the club, with the owner clearly identified as the beneficiary. Some savings might result in comparison to the owners insuring the aircraft on their own account.

Information requirements

Insurance company information requirements for flying clubs are basically the same as it is for partnerships. The flying club must submit detailed pilot data sheets on all club pilots and detailed information on the equipment to be insured. In addition, the club must usually provide a copy of its bylaws, and a summary membership roster.

Flying club insurance and the bank

The fact that a bank financed airplane flies with a flying club should pose no insurance difficulties. Naming the bank as loss payee on the master policy for the particular aircraft it is financing is no problem; however, the flying club might have to meet the bank's insurance standards, which might be more stringent than the club would prefer on its own.

Insurance cost reduction

It would be foolhardy to try and save money by deliberately underinsuring, but a sensible tip reduces the cost: exceed insurance company requirements. The club should require a higher experience level from members who want to fly progressively more complex aircraft. To some extent, insurance companies set fairly rigorous experience requirements anyway, but exceeding them with club policy might result in substantial savings.

Pilots often wonder if a higher deductible results in savings. The difference is negligible in the 1990s insurance market.

Agency or company?

Insurance agents and companies provide equally good service, but there might be an advantage to going through an agent, especially if your club is large and has complex insurance requirements. The agent's ability to shop around can be especially useful, compared to the restriction of the companies to their own policies.

THE IMPORTANCE OF MONITORING PILOT QUALIFICATIONS

A flying club needs to keep careful track of its pilots' qualifications, flight currency status, and medical currency to avoid unpleasant insurance surprises. It is especially important to confirm at the outset, prior to the formal checkout, that a pilot meets the insurance requirements for the aircraft to be flown.

A member's failure to meet insurance requirements might invalidate a flying club's insurance policy in case of an accident or incident. Such risks depend upon the terms of individual policies. Review carefully with your agent or insurer the circumstances under which the club's policy might not apply and be sure to clearly communicate these terms to the membership.

An insurance presentation to the membership with your insurance agent's assistance at one of the club's regular meetings might be a worthwhile event. Most members are woefully ill-informed about their flying club's insurance arrangements.

POINTS TO REVIEW

Beyond the issues discussed above, you are again encouraged to study chapter 9, regarding partnership insurance, for a detailed discussion of insurance concepts, terms, and conditions. Use the worksheet presented there to gather information.

As you work on obtaining insurance for your flying club, bear in mind the following questions:

- Do the liability and hull limits under consideration provide sufficient protection?
- Are there per person, per occurrence liability limits? If so, are they too low, and do they erode the protection promised by the full liability limit?
- Can the club point the members in the right direction to individually purchase additional liability coverage?
- Are deductibles reasonable?
- Is hull coverage all risk? If not, why not?
- Are members named insureds? If not, can the club offer suggestions for obtaining renter's insurance?
- Are all exclusions clearly understood? Are there no easy escape clauses, especially slippery FAR violation exclusions?
- Are experience level requirements reasonable? Can insurance premium levels be reduced by raising experience requirements without imposing undue restrictions on the membership?
- Does the club have a system to effectively monitor membership compliance with insurance requirements regarding experience, flight currency, and medical currency?
- What is the geographic extent of coverage? Is the membership clearly aware of it?
- Has the club shopped around for the best deal possible?
- Would an insurance presentation to the membership be useful?

19

Operations and safety

OF ALL THE TOPICS TO BE CONSIDERED in setting up and running a flying club, operations and safety are the most familiar to prospective members. In our experience with commercial operators, most of us have had at least some exposure to operations issues in a multipilot, multiairplane environment, and have had safety drummed into us throughout our flight training; thus, the transition to functioning under the particular operations and safety requirements of the average flying club will be relatively easy.

Operations, as the term implies, encompasses flying of the airplanes and such related issues as tiedown and fueling arrangements, preferred operating procedures, and compliance with laws and regulations. Safety is directly linked to operations. Poorly conceived operating procedures, minimal experience and currency requirements, and lax adherence to laws and regulations will greatly diminish the safety of any operation.

OPERATIONS

In a setting where several pilots fly one or more airplanes, the objective of operations is to provide all club members the opportunity to do their fair share of safe flying with the least amount of fuss. This goal is achieved by addressing the key operations issues on several levels. It is an operations responsibility to establish a stable, cost-effective home for the flying club's airplanes: to find an airport where rates are reasonable, facilities meet the flying club's needs, and the club is welcome. It is an operations responsibility to set up and administer a system that results in effective scheduling and smooth flight operations. And it is an operations responsibility to set safety standards that meet or significantly exceed the standards imposed by legal and insurance requirements.

Operations officer

The operations officer is the person responsible for devising an operations structure appropriate for the club in view of its size and objectives, and making

A good checkout program is essential for safe flying club operations.

sure that it works. While the operations officer relies heavily on the contribution of the entire membership in achieving the flying club's operating objectives, he or she has to be a real leader. The operations officer should enjoy taking charge, aggressively identifying problems, devising solutions, and overseeing their implementation. At the same time, he or she also has to have a lot of tact, an ability to deal with a large number of diverse people brought together on an entirely voluntary basis, as well as airport officials who can be difficult, and FBOs that might view the presence of a flying club on the field as unfair competition.

The operations officer works closely with the maintenance officer and treasurer to coordinate aircraft availability and the timely collection of rental receipts, payment of bills, and renewal of insurance.

Scheduling

An effective scheduling system is a must for any flying club. Unlike partnerships that can function quite informally through a designated priority pilot system, flying clubs have to ensure equal access to a lot more pilots per airplane. The first thing the club has to consider is what the rules will be for access to the aircraft:

- What is the minimum length of time for which an airplane can be scheduled? Typical time slots for training airplanes are two-hour blocks: a half an hour for the preflight, an hour for the flight, and another half an hour for postflight. Pilots of touring clubs, on the other hand, might want to be assured of having the airplane for at least half a day. Opportunities for longer rentals should also be provided.

- What is the maximum length of time for which an airplane can be rented? If demand for longer term rentals is high, it might be equally important to specify a maximum rental time slot, beyond which special arrangements need to be made. One way to ration long-term rentals is to set a limit on the number of times a member can rent long-term each month, unless the airplane is available anyway. Another, more common form of control, is to specify a minimum number of flight hours for which a member will be charged per day on long-term rentals. Another option is to allow a long-term rental booking to be made provisionally, to become final perhaps 24 hours before the flight, if no other reservations have come in for the airplane by then. Another alternative is to restrict long-term rentals to off-peak usage perhaps during the week.

- How far in advance can a booking be made? Advanced booking is a great convenience up to a point, but if too many members book too far in advance, it can be a source of annoyance. Members should have reasonable lead time to plan their flying, but if the system is abused, a limit might be necessary.

- How many consecutive bookings can one member make? Again, if there is an airplane hog in your midst, a limit on the number of reservations at any one time per member might be useful. Carefully monitor reservations around holiday weekends; repetitive usage by one member should be discouraged.

- What are the consequences of canceling a reservation? All club members have to change plans from time to time and should be able to cancel aircraft reservations with some advanced notice without penalty. On the other hand, a cancellation time limit beyond which a penalty must be paid might be desirable to discourage last minute cancellations that might leave the airplane idle when it could have been rented by other club members.

- How are no-shows handled? No shows should be strongly discouraged. A no-show is unfair to other club members who might have wanted to fly in the same time slot had the airplane been available on the schedule. A common policy on no-shows is the requirement to pay the club for the hours booked, up to a maximum number of hours, perhaps the daily minimum.

- How are late returns handled? Late return charges should depend upon the reason for the late return. Absolutely no penalty should be levied for mechanical or weather delays. No member should ever be under any pressure to push to get home under such circumstances. Late returns due to a pilot deciding to extend a trip for reasons other than mechanical problems or weather delays should carry a hefty surcharge, unless no other club members want the airplane during the extension period (this is easier to arrange in smaller clubs). Any late return should be immediately communicated to the club.

- How are instructors scheduled? Instructors may be scheduled in a variety of ways. Many clubs prefer that the instructor and student deal directly with each other to establish a mutually convenient time, and put it on the schedule. Another alternative, especially suitable for larger clubs, is to have the instructors listed in the scheduling book, just like the airplanes, and have the pilots book instructors when booking the airplanes.

A word of caution: It is important not to overstructure scheduling. Most fledgling clubs will be surprised to find a considerably higher level of aircraft availability than first anticipated. Keep the rules simple and adjust them as needed based upon experience.

In addition to scheduling policies, the flying club needs to develop a reliable scheduling system. In clubs with no airport presence and no permanent manager, scheduling responsibilities can be rotated, perhaps two months at a time, among volunteer members that are accessible on the telephone. Another alternative is an answering service. Larger clubs with a permanent manager or presence at the airport might handle scheduling just like a commercial operator. The club should have a scheduling book, as outlined in chapter 28, regarding flying club records.

Flight operations

In small self-service clubs where the scheduled member simply shows up at the airport, unties the airplane and goes flying, there is little scope for flight operations. Larger clubs with enough rental activity to require a presence at the airport at least on weekends, need someone to man the operations counter and make sure that the airplanes are ready for action in the morning and are properly put away at day's end. Such responsibilities can be assigned to volunteer duty officers, or paid part-time help.

Among the responsibilities of the duty officers might be the requirement to ensure that aircraft are ready to go in the morning with gas and oil topped off, the windshield clean, the tires inflated, the cockpit clean and orderly, and the flight logs up-to-date. If the flying club is exceptionally large and busy, requiring the duty officer to man the desk full-time, these duties may be relegated to volunteer airplane captains appointed from among the members on a rotating basis.

It is an important operations responsibility to ensure that the members are current and qualified according to club requirements for the aircraft they fly. While it is cumbersome to check this information every time, the operations officer and duty officers should have the records available and should review them periodically.

Administration

Operations responsibilities in the flying club require some administration. It is the treasurer who pays the flying club bills and deposits the payments made to the club, but the operations officer who is responsible for making sure that the system works. Operations has to keep the airplanes and the counter stocked with the appropriate forms, operations has to get the collected payments and supporting data to the treasurer, operations has to keep an eye on expiring insurance policies, and operations has to pull the airplanes off the line for maintenance, scheduled and unscheduled. It is also an operations responsibility to collect the raw operational data for analyzing the flying club's flight activities.

Chief pilot

It is desirable that a flying club's members meet the same standards of competence for the type of flying done in the club. The standard of instruction offered by the club should also be uniform and high. It is the chief pilot's responsibility to ensure that these standards are sufficient and are met. In smaller clubs, the chief pilot might have other responsibilities, but in the larger clubs it is worthwhile to leave the chief pilot free to concentrate entirely on piloting standards.

The most effective means for the chief pilot to maintain club flying standards is to administer many of the checkrides personally, which can be done only if he or she is a certified flight instructor.

If the club offers instruction, the chief pilot should check out each instructor, manage them, and set and periodically review standards of instruction with them.

But what if your club does not provide instruction and does not have a certified flight instructor among the members? Then it is best to make an arrangement with an outside flight instructor to act as chief pilot, paid independently by each member for checkrides administered. Members can certainly use other instructors to receive instruction (as permitted by the insurance policy), but to maintain uniform standards, the instructor designated as chief pilot should be used to give periodic recurrent checkrides and to check out members in club equipment.

Flying club instructors

Flying clubs handle their association with flight instructors in a variety of ways. Some have members who also happen to instruct, others may keep instructors on staff, and still others maintain a list of approved outside instructors with whom club members make arrangements on their own.

There are no hard and fast rules about which option is best, but it is fair to say that having instructors contract their services as independent contractors directly with members has some advantages. By eliminating the "haircut" that the club would take from the instructors' fees, it saves money for the club members but puts more money into the instructors' pocket, making both parties better off. It also saves on the paperwork the club would have to do if it were to contract the instructors, so the club is better off.

Should the club choose to employ the instructors, it is advisable to hire them on a contract basis rather than as direct employees. Direct employment would require too much government paperwork to make the effort cost-effective.

Field relations

Good field relations are an important aspect of the flying club's longevity. Field relations encompass the flying club's relationship with everyone on the field from airport management on down to the local lineboys. Airfields have specific rules about the activities and businesses authorized at the field, so it is imperative for the flying club to understand them up front and get approval for its proposed activities. It might be that an airport has regulations prohibiting the existence of a flying club. It is embarrassing to find out about them when the airport manager strolls over to see what your first open house is all about. Don't laugh. At a big airport, it is perfectly plausible that a collection of pilots pool two airplanes and declare themselves a flying club without saying "boo" to anyone, only to find that they are not welcome. It has happened before.

FBOs don't always welcome a flying club at the local field, especially if it offers flight instruction. A lot of hostility can be overcome by cultivating good relations, backed up with using certain services of the FBO, such as fuel sales and perhaps maintenance.

Once established at a field, the flying club must work hard to maintain good relations with management and other tenants. Have frequent contact. Be as constructive as possible when any issues arise. Look for ways to cooperate rather than reasons to say no. Be sensitive to any potential friction while sticking up for the club's rights. Signing up airport personnel as members can go a long way to accomplish this goal.

SAFETY

Preventive measures are the most effective tool for ensuring a high level of safety in the flying club's operations. Good training, experience, and currency are the prerequisites of safe flying. A high degree of safety awareness fostered by the club through safety seminars helps.

FAA-required minimum experience levels are just that: minimums. Prudent flying clubs will often demand more. The same goes for operational minimums, such as VFR visibility and ceiling minimums and IFR approach minimums. Overseen by the operations officer, the chief pilot, or the safety officer, the flying club should carefully evaluate these factors in view of the members' experience and the kind of flying the club does, and set its own standards as it deems appropriate.

Experience and checkout requirements

Many clubs set higher levels of experience than required by the FAA to check out in club equipment, especially complex airplanes; insurance companies also might require higher experience levels. For a complex single-engine retractable-gear airplane, 200 hours of total time and 10 hours of instruction and 25 hours in type are not uncommon. Some clubs require an instrument rating for the more powerful singles, such as a Bonanza or a P-210. For twins, as much as 500 hours of total time and 100 hours of multiengine time might be required. Fairly demanding minimums may also be set for tailwheel checkouts.

Clubs may also have separate checkout requirements for different types of flying, such as night flying, mountain flying, overwater flying, aerobatics, or procedures specific to a particular airport, such as flying in a TCA environment. Clubs based at airports with very long runways might require a short-field checkout before allowing members to shoehorn club airplanes into the neighborhood's smaller strips. Some particularly hairy airports might be placed entirely off limits for club aircraft.

Flight review and currency requirements

Complementing, perhaps exceeding, FAA regulations, it is common for flying clubs to require at least an annual flight review. When you fly a variety of airplanes and do not fly very often (as might be the case for quite a few club members), an annual clearing of the cobwebs makes a lot of sense. An option is to waive club review requirements for club members that fly a specified minimum number of hours during the year; however, at a minimum, FARs must be followed to the letter.

As a way of maintaining the highest levels of safety, it is hard to beat currency. A big concern in flying clubs is the lengthy interval that can pass between flights for many club members. More stringent currency requirements than mandated by the FAA are a common technique employed by flying clubs to keep the membership's flying skills sharp. The three takeoff and landing requirement in the preceding 90 days to carry passengers might be shortened to 60 days and extended to include solo flight; minimum flight hours during the period might also be required. Members who fail to stay current under the club's rules need a checkride to get back in the air. If the club has student pilots, student pilot solo currency requirements should be carefully considered.

Some flying clubs charge a monthly flight time minimum regardless of whether or not a member flies, as a means of encouraging members to keep current. A mechanism for encouraging flight is to rebate a percentage of the dues if a minimum number of hours are flown by the member in a predetermined period of time.

IFR minimum time requirements to maintain currency are also often expanded beyond FAA requirements.

Flight plan requirements

A common technique to heighten safety awareness is to require the filing of a flight plan for any flight more than 50 miles away from home base. This is a good idea, because besides the safety advantage, it also gives the club a record of where its airplanes have wandered.

Flying club weather minimums

Many flying clubs set higher ceiling and farther visibility minimums than specified by regulations, especially for night VFR and IFR flights. Five-mile visibility and a 2,000-foot ceiling for night flying is commonly required. IFR ceiling minimums of 750 or 800 feet are also a popular choice. It is entirely up to your club to set higher minimums. Given that many prudent pilots already observe higher minimums in their own flying, it might be a popular idea with the entire membership and is highly recommended.

Violations

The flying club should have a mechanism to deal with violations of its operating standards and rules, as well as FAA, state, and local regulations. Temporary withdrawal of flight privileges and/or monetary penalties are the common methods of handling violations. Prior to judgment, the alleged violator should have an impartial hearing to argue his or her side of the story. Violations provisions are usually spelled out in the club bylaws or operating rules that are fully explained elsewhere in this book.

Safety seminars

An excellent way to heighten safety awareness is to have members regularly attend the FAA's safety seminars, and arrange in-house seminars tailored specifically to the club's circumstances. Some clubs require attendance at a minimum number of safety seminars per year.

Role of the safety officer

If the club does not have an in-house chief pilot, it might be a worthwhile idea to appoint a safety officer that oversees the issues raised above and would develop specific safety standards for the club. The safety officer could also be the club's contact person with the outside chief pilot.

20

Maintenance

MAINTENANCE OF THE FLYING CLUB'S FLEET is a big responsibility. The quality of maintenance has implications not only for safety, but also for the efficient use of the club's aircraft and the flying expenses paid by the members. It is advisable for a flying club of any size to have a stated maintenance policy and a maintenance program run by the club's maintenance officer. The maintenance officer's responsibilities depend upon the size of the flying club's fleet and whether maintenance is contracted out or performed in-house.

MAINTENANCE POLICY

A maintenance policy is a statement of the flying club's maintenance objectives. Distributed to the membership, it clarifies for everyone the club's approach to maintenance. The objective of providing quality maintenance is a given, but how this is accomplished can vary greatly depending upon the flying club's purpose and resources.

A training and pleasure flying club formed specifically to provide inexpensive flying for members on tight budgets might want to state explicitly in its maintenance policy that quality maintenance is to be provided at the lowest possible cost. It might also want to specify that members under the supervision of a mechanic are to perform as much maintenance as possible. It might lay down guidelines for expected amounts of volunteer work per person per month or quarter. Such a policy will make it clear to members that if an airplane is down, the maintenance officer's top priority will be to get the most economical fix available, but it might take a little longer than if the sick bird was wheeled into a million-dollar maintenance facility.

A flying club of high-priced IFR touring aircraft flown primarily on business by pilots with relatively deep pockets might have a different approach to maintenance. Its policy might state that in the normal course of the club's business, maintenance problems are to be fixed under a maintenance contract by a full-service professional maintenance facility of the club's choice as expeditiously as possible. This policy will put members on notice that the airplane will be quickly

FAR Part 43 allows the partners and the flying club's members to perform some preventative maintenance.

fixed and they will never have to get their hands dirty, but the maintenance bills will be hefty.

Or consider the maintenance objectives of a large West Coast flying club with more than 50 aircraft and an in-house maintenance staff of 12 that includes a full-time avionics technician:

- Quality maintenance, clean reliable aircraft
- Professional maintenance at nonprofit prices
- Full-time dedication to club aircraft; no maintenance performed for outside clients
- Maintenance available seven days a week
- Unique preventative maintenance program designed to increase aircraft up-time, reduce costs, and preserve asset value

The policy is brief, to the point, and gives everyone a good idea of what makes this flying club tick.

OUTSIDE MAINTENANCE

Maintenance performed for the flying club by an outside facility or mechanic is usually the most effective arrangement in all but the largest flying clubs. Few clubs have the skills and fleet size that would justify an in-house maintenance program.

It is best to have a long-term arrangement with a facility or a mechanic for routine maintenance and the unscheduled glitches that pop up from time to time. A well developed relationship with the maintenance people is essential for trouble-free, reliable service. Maintenance personnel value the steady flow of bread-and-butter business and will be careful not to risk losing it. The club in turn can expect service of a known quality at predictable prices within a reasonable timeframe.

Maintenance shops

A convenient but pricey arrangement is to contract out all the club's maintenance to a reputable full-service maintenance shop. When maintenance is due, the airplane disappears into the shop. You are informed of a list of items that need fixing, you are quoted a price, and you approve the work. Soon the airplane reappears on the line, ready to fly in exchange for a check. Nothing could be simpler, and if the membership is able to foot the bill, this option is highly recommended.

Of course, from time to time you might discover that all sorts of extra work was done and the bill is twice the size you expected; or you might find a screwdriver left inside a wing or landing light wires that were not reattached. Or the airplane might not reappear for weeks when it was due back on the line in three days. This is why a solid long-term relationship with your maintenance shop is so important.

Shop around carefully when you select a maintenance facility. Talk to as many of their customers as you can. Check out their reputation for quality work, turnaround time, and prices. Ask customers if they had any experience with excessive amounts of maintenance pushed by the shop. Ask for the shop's price list. See if you can get a discount for giving the shop all your routine maintenance business.

Don't restrict your search to maintenance facilities only at your home field. Check out all area airports, especially the smaller ones, where overhead expenses are lower and might be reflected in the shop's rates.

Less expensive alternatives

There are several ways to reduce the maintenance costs charged by full-service maintenance facilities. One alternative is to have the work done at a shop

Maintenance costs are higher for twins than singles.

that allows club members to participate under the supervision of an A&P. A big part of maintenance work is the performance of simple time-consuming tasks: opening inspection panels, taking out and reinstalling seats, decowling and buttoning up the engine compartment, and the like. The actual inspection and servicing can take less time than getting at the component to be serviced. The volunteer help of the membership with simple labor intensive tasks such as removing and reinstalling inspection panels can save a bundle. Certain shops will permit such participation because it allows the skilled mechanics to spend more time on complex maintenance items instead of being tied up with no-brainer apprentice tasks. Other shops are prohibited by their insurance policies from letting anyone but their own mechanics work on the airplanes. You are most likely to get a receptive hearing at a small shop run and staffed by one or two mechanics.

Another possibility for reducing the cost of maintenance is to contract with a mechanic who freelances during off hours. Many mechanics would like to run their own shop instead of working for a maintenance facility, but cannot afford to. For the more ambitious mechanics, the first step is to freelance on the side. Others choose to freelance to earn a little extra income over their company salaries. Still others might have a job in a corporate flight department but would like to keep their hands in maintaining light airplanes on their own time. Some have an arrangement with their employer that permits them to work on the side (say, the weekends) and even use some of the employer's equipment and facilities. The point is, there is a whole army of good mechanics out there looking for freelance opportunities at hourly rates well below the commercial shop rates. Seek them out. Tools are not a problem because all self-respecting mechanics own their own. Concessionary flight privileges are often an attractive inducement for a freelance mechanic.

A pitfall of giving the club's business to a mechanic freelancing on the side is workload. The mechanic might not always have the time and his or her full-time job will almost always take precedent; however, a club with only one or two airplanes can usually work out a satisfactory arrangement with a little planning, especially for routine maintenance.

Working with a freelance mechanic lends itself to volunteer member participation, and this combination is one of the better budget deals you can arrange. To avoid frustration, the club should make sure that the members assisting the mechanic know their way around airplanes and can use a screwdriver efficiently. Inexperienced volunteers should at first be paired with an experienced member.

The flying club can also save money by performing its own preventative maintenance as permitted by FAR Part 43 (appendix E), which can be interpreted to include changing the oil (refer to a current edition of FAR Part 43 for up-to-date guidance).

Maintenance officer responsibilities

When maintenance work is contracted to the outside, one of the most important responsibilities of the maintenance officer is to be the club's representative to the maintenance entity. He or she should play a key role in selecting the maintenance facility or mechanic to be given the club's business and negotiating the terms of the relationship. Once the maintenance arrangements are in place, the maintenance officer schedules the work to be done, approves work and cost estimates presented by the mechanics, and accepts work completed.

It should be explicitly clear to the membership that all contact with the maintenance provider is to be by the maintenance officer. The maintenance provider will soon get annoyed if bombarded by uncoordinated requests from all sides.

Authorizing expenditures for maintenance work is also an important responsibility of the maintenance officer. Above a certain amount, the concurrence of another club officer (usually the president or treasurer, as defined in the bylaws) is required to contract work. After the work is completed and accepted by the maintenance officer, he or she should inform the treasurer that the bill should be paid.

To fulfill these tasks effectively, the maintenance officer has to be the keeper of the club's maintenance records. He should have all the airframe and engine logs and should make sure that they are kept up-to-date. He should have a recurrent maintenance schedule for each airplane, and should anticipate and schedule routine maintenance with sufficient lead time to avoid frustrating delays and maintenance backlogs.

The maintenance officer should be contacted immediately in case of a mechanical malfunction that grounds the aircraft and should be prepared to handle it. He should also receive all squawk sheets, and should handle, as expeditiously as possible without disrupting the club's activities, squawks that do not ground the aircraft.

The maintenance officer is responsible for scheduling and supervising volunteer maintenance work by members, including preventative maintenance done under FAR Part 43, and the day-to-day care, washing, and waxing of the airplanes.

The maintenance officer should also carefully monitor trends in club maintenance expenses. In cooperation with the club's treasurer, he should compare actual expenses to budgeted expenses and should monitor engine and maintenance reserves. Any deterioration in reserves should be promptly reported to the board of directors to provide sufficient time to take effective countermeasures, such as increasing the per hour engine and maintenance reserve charges.

Other duties of the maintenance officer include maintaining an up-to-date list of airworthiness directives and service bulletins, ensuring compliance, monitoring the club's operating practices, and organizing maintenance presentations. An extraordinarily conscientious maintenance officer might periodically request service difficulty reports that pertain to specific makes and models of club aircraft. The reports are on file with the FAA; contact a local maintenance facility for information about obtaining the reports.

Airplane captains

An occasional problem faced by flying clubs is keeping the airplanes orderly, clean, and presentable. Leaving the airplane in a civilized condition is usually the user's responsibility, but the results are not always satisfying. A flying club might find it useful to assign members on a rotating basis as airplane captains, charged with the responsibility of going over their assigned airplane once a week with a fine-tooth comb, cleaning the windshield, resolving any cosmetic discrepancies, and checking the documents and squawk sheets on board. This arrangement is especially useful if the airplanes are used frequently on short flights as would be typical in a club that provides a lot of training.

IN-HOUSE MAINTENANCE

A flying club is most likely to do maintenance in-house if a practicing A&P is a club member with access to a suitable maintenance space and is willing to donate time, or if the club is large enough to afford a salaried in-house professional maintenance staff.

Some clubs might be large enough to justify a paid in-house A&P, but not full time. These clubs might make an arrangement with an A&P to work for the club, say, three or four days out of the week, and allow him to take on private clients on the remaining days (making the A&P the ideal freelance candidate as described in the previous section). Such an arrangement works well only if the A&P has his priorities straight, is a good judge of workload, and does not take on more private clients than he can handle.

The club fortunate enough to have professional in-house maintenance should be in good hands. The A&P can run the maintenance program pretty autonomously, as he would any commercial business; however, some A&Ps are not as well organized as others, so the club should be prepared to provide administrative help if necessary.

Maintenance officer responsibilities

When maintenance is done in-house, the club no longer needs a maintenance officer in addition to the in-house A&P. In fact, the A&P (or the senior A&P) can be formally appointed maintenance officer or maintenance manager by the board of directors, combining the position's responsibilities as outlined above, with the day-to-day maintenance work. Oversight would continue to come from the board.

Room for innovation

An innovative and enthusiastic in-house A&P/maintenance officer can be of great benefit to the flying club in devising a maintenance program that will result in great savings. An outstanding example is a phased maintenance program developed by the professional maintenance manager of the West Coast flying club whose maintenance policy is stated in this chapter.

The maintenance manager, ever keen to reduce high costs, looked into the FAA's 100-hour inspection requirements and uncovered some interesting facts. His club is nonprofit and does not directly provide instructors for its students. Rather, it maintains a list of instructors that are independent contractors hired directly by the students. This situation is just the same as a private aircraft owner hiring a paid instructor to provide flying lessons. The aircraft owner does not need to perform 100-hour inspections. So, because it is not supplying the instructor and provides the airplane on a nonprofit basis, why should the flying club be required to do 100-hour inspections?

The manager asked the FAA, and received a ruling that, indeed, the club did not have to perform 100-hour inspections. Instead, the maintenance manager devised a phased program (similar to the airlines' and the Air Force's progressive maintenance programs) consisting of a full annual-type inspection every 300 hours and five inspections of various detail in between. The savings have been impressive.

As is the case with so many other aspects of forming and running a flying club, the choice of flying club maintenance arrangements is wide. No rock should be left unturned in search of the best safe solution. A creative attitude can deliver a lot of bang for the buck.

21

Flying club records

A FLYING CLUB CANNOT FUNCTION PROPERLY without an effective record-keeping system: dues and aircraft rental income must be collected, flying club bills must be paid, aircraft use must be tracked to ensure the timely scheduling of inspections and maintenance, and membership records must be maintained. Recordkeeping beyond the flying club's day-to-day activities is also important; periodic statistical reviews of hours flown, costs per hour, and costs per member tell the club how well it is doing and where it might want to find ways to improve. Aircraft records must also be maintained to satisfy FAA requirements; the flying club's legal documents and records must be properly maintained.

The extent to which a flying club is likely to want to keep records will depend mostly on club size. In many respects, the recordkeeping needs and chores of any flying club are a more elaborate offshoot of the records kept by the prudent partnership. A small club with approximately 15 members and one airplane will be quite satisfied to keep its records similar to the way they are kept by a partnership, as recommended in chapter 11 regarding partnership records. A club with hundreds of members that between them fly thousands of hours a year will want a lot more. But even its sophisticated recordkeeping system, not unlike the accounting and management reporting systems of a corporation, will have at its roots the elements of the basic partnership records.

A good rule of thumb is to always try to meet the club's needs with the minimum amount of recordkeeping necessary to do the job. Consider the guidelines below, and devise a system that gives your club the most return with the least amount of fuss.

MEMBERSHIP

Members are the flying club's foundation and more members mean that it is proportionally more important to keep track of a variety of data on them to enable the club to function effectively.

Demographic data

At a minimum, every flying club should have an official list of its members' names, addresses, and telephone numbers, freely available to the membership. Certainly in the interest of privacy, any member that does not want an address or telephone number made available might be represented in the list with a work telephone and/or work address; a limited number of club officials might have access to the member's home telephone number and address for last minute rescheduling or an emergency. Additional information presented might be any special skills and any affiliation with businesses, companies, and professional organizations and associations that might be of help to the flying club. Some clubs also like to present each member's original date of membership.

Flight experience, checkout, currency, and medical records

It is ultimately each pilot's responsibility to meet all the licensing, currency, and medical requirements appropriate for each flight, but these are records that flying clubs, especially the bigger ones, might also wish to track. Clubs often have more stringent experience and currency requirements for certain types of flying than is required by the FAA, based upon personal preference and because of insurance requirements. Pilots usually have no trouble remembering FAA-mandated checkout and currency requirements, but find it more difficult to keep abreast of club standards. A good way to ensure that members meet club standards is by keeping a current log of licenses and ratings held, club checkout dates, and the club aircraft each member is authorized to fly, and the expiration dates of club annual checkouts, flight reviews, and medical certificates. If the club is large enough to have a dispatch counter, it might be a good idea to have these records at the counter on a printout, or in electronic form, to be checked when an airplane is signed out.

Member ID cards

Even for relatively small clubs, a member ID card might be a worthwhile investment, and for the larger clubs it is strongly recommended. The card is easily designed to contain the appropriate checkout and currency information. It can be reissued every year when annual dues are renewed. A current card is an indication of being current on annual dues. Such a membership card system can be used in lieu of records at a dispatch counter. The card should be presented when an airplane is signed out.

Red flags

Given the forgetfulness of some club members, it is best for a club to implement some form of red flag system, to identify members not in compliance with important club requirements. Unpaid dues, past due bills, expired annual checks, flight reviews, and medicals are the obvious items. The system should be designed to identify culprits to club personnel in charge of airplane rentals and suspend rental privileges until the problem is cured.

The membership database

By far the easiest way to track membership information, is through a membership database on a personal computer. Anyone with the most rudimentary computer skills can set up a basic database that easily meets the requirements of smaller flying clubs. For the more complex tasks, inexpensive commercial software is available to create menu-driven databases with greater flexibility. The ideal choice is to select accounting software that is capable of also providing detailed nonaccounting information both at the individual account (member) level, and also in summary report form.

AIRCRAFT OPERATIONS

The flying club's basic purpose, the operation of its aircraft by the members, could not be met without some recordkeeping regardless of the club's size. Every club must keep a schedule and signout documentation. Squawk sheets and aircraft performance logs are also in widespread use.

Scheduling

The extent of the scheduling book depends upon the club's size and the length of time for which members rent the aircraft. Clubs with a few aircraft, rented by the members for at least half a day at a time, might get by with a weekly or even a monthly calendar kept by the scheduler. If the membership rents for shorter periods of time, a calendar that divides each day into hours might be more suitable. If your club has a number of aircraft and the members take frequent, short flights, your best bet is to get an aircraft scheduling book used by the commercial flight schools in which you can reserve each airplane in two-hour blocks. You might also want to enter the club's instructors in the scheduling book, parallel to the airplanes.

Another useful function of the scheduling book besides telling everyone who is to fly next, is serving as a check on who flew when, if any confusion arises. To work effectively, a scheduling book should record cancellations and no-shows, as well as original bookings. In the case of flying clubs where the scheduler is not always physically present at the airport, the schedule can be compared to payments received for flights to check for no-shows and charge whatever is appropriate according to club policy. When maintained at the airport, no-shows can be entered directly into the book, as well as the pilot's account.

If the flying club has more than one airplane, it is best to make up columns for each airplane in the scheduling book for an entire year in advance. When an airplane is supposed to be off the flightline for maintenance, that should be represented in the scheduling book as far in advance as possible. The person that oversees scheduling should monitor aircraft flight times to anticipate blocking out time for regular maintenance prior to scheduling by the membership.

Aircraft logs and signout sheets

Important information for any flying club is the record of hours flown by its aircraft. In the case of smaller clubs, this might be best accomplished by a flight log in the aircraft, similar to the ones recommended for partnerships in chapter 11. Flight time can be periodically transferred from the logs to the club's accounting records.

When a flying club's airplanes are checked out from a dispatcher or duty officer, signout cards similar to the ones used by commercial operators are a good way to keep track of aircraft flight time; record the airplane's N number, the beginning tach or hobbs time, the renter's name and account number, the ending time, and the total flight time for the rental. The card is turned in at the end of the flight, and the information is used for billing and statistical records.

The signout cards can be used even if the airplanes are not checked out from a dispatcher at the airport, but are taken on a self-service basis. Make sure to leave a large supply of cards and require a filled out card to be sent in with the payment for each flight.

Selected flying clubs—primarily clubs outside North America—keep a logbook for each airplane in the same detail that a pilot keeps a personal logbook. Every flight is entered, including date, destination details, pilot, and duration. While some fliers might find this level of recordkeeping excessive, the more detail oriented types might want to bear it in mind.

Aircraft performance records

Similar to certain private owners and partnerships, certain flying clubs might want to keep track of particular aircraft flight and engine performance parameters per flight along the lines of the records kept by professional operators. When airplanes are flown a lot by many different pilots, a trend is easy to establish and a useful reference source for pilots that might not know a particular airplane as intimately as if they owned it. These performance records are no different from those recommended for partnerships, which are described in chapter 11.

Aircraft squawk sheets

Squawk sheets are even more important for flying clubs than they are for partnerships. The greater number of pilots per airplane makes informal communications less reliable. The squawk sheet is the best method of ensuring that all pilots about to fly a particular airplane are made aware of any potential mechanical problems with it. Flying club squawk sheets do not differ in concept from those recommended for partnerships, which are described in chapter 11.

It is worth recording what the engine gauges say to track performance trends.

ACCOUNTING

Accounting is a dreaded word, conjuring up images of undecipherable figures and humorless bores with sharp pencils forever on the case of anyone daring enough to spend money for fun. Like all stereotypes, this one is also misguided. Accounting for the simple financial activities of the flying club is easy, as long as you observe a handful of recordkeeping principles and maintain good financial records. If you don't have financial experience, you should seek at least the advice of an accountant or bookkeeper in setting up your accounting system and periodically checking the books. Many accountants, bookkeepers, bankers, and finance managers love to fly and you might well find one in-house, among the membership, just waiting to be named treasurer.

General ledger and treasurer's role

The most important financial recordkeeping task of the flying club is to keep a very detailed and accurate record of income and expenses, money taken in and paid out. Each income and expense should be recorded in a book, the club's general ledger, which is a glorified checkbook. The difference between the income and expense columns in the general ledger is the club's account balance, and it better be a positive balance. Other financial records must be compiled, but the general ledger is the heart of the matter. If it is accurate, any bookkeeper can easily sort out the flying club's financial position. If it is a mess, the club might never find out where all the money went.

In addition to the dollar amounts of income and expense items, the general ledger should identify each item in detail and code each item by category to facilitate the generation of summary information. Most flying clubs have typical income and expense categories:

Income
Annual membership dues
Monthly membership fees
Aircraft rental
Miscellaneous (merchandise, ground school fees)

Expenses
Tiedown/hangar
Insurance
Fees and taxes
Maintenance
Loan payments
Rent
Salaries
Telephone, answering service
Supplies/administrative
Miscellaneous

Parallel to the general ledger, accounts should be kept for each club member. In these accounts, all member payments (income for the club), including payments due but not yet received, are recorded. When the payments are received they are entered in the general ledger. The members' accounts enable the club to track overdue payments and provide periodic individual statements.

The treasurer's most important roles are to devise a system that reliably captures all income and expenses, and to maintain the general ledger. From this information the treasurer also compiles other financial records from time to time (such as annual balance sheets and income statements), and fills out the club's annual tax returns.

The key to the treasurer's effectiveness is the central control of financial flows. On the income side, all payments should flow to the treasurer to be deposited in the club's account and entered into the general ledger. On the expense side, the treasurer should make out all flying club checks. If the club is large enough to justify a treasurer's assistant, the treasurer should still be the one to sign all checks.

Options for collecting money due to the club and making payments are outlined below. The flow of income is broken down into two broad categories, income from aircraft use and income from other sources. Expenses (payments) are treated as one topic.

Billing and collection procedures, aircraft use

The most desirable option in collecting money due is to get it as quickly as possible. In the case of aircraft rental, this means requiring the membership to fork over a check at the end of each flight. If the club operates on a self-service basis (no club dispatcher or duty officer at the field), the checks, along with supporting documentation such as a flight card and an invoice filled out by the pilots can be dropped in a strong box or mailed to the treasurer. The strongbox option is recommended to avoid mail delays and the tendency of some people not to mail their bills on time. If the checks are mailed in, a record of the flight (the flight card and a copy of the invoice made out by the pilot) should be left in the airplane or a drop box for the treasurer to collect and know what payments to expect.

Some clubs might prefer to bill members for aircraft use as an option to collecting payment up front. This alternative is fine, especially for a club with many active members who would prefer to write one large check per month instead of several small ones. The drawback is the increased potential for late payments. Short payment terms, perhaps 15 days, and a strictly enforced rule of suspending flying privileges in case of bills past due, will control this problem. A small discount for immediate payment is an excellent incentive to speed up payments and is usually very effective.

Billing and collection procedures, other charges

The other big charges faced by flying club members are annual dues and monthly fees. For these charges, members should be billed through the mail. Prompt payment should be expected, the same tight payment terms applied to aircraft rentals should be the standard, and past dues should swiftly result in the suspension of flying privileges.

Flying club payments

Prompt receipt of income from the members is extremely important. The club has payments to make and is also expected to make them promptly. All payments should be made by the treasurer by check. For control purposes, expenses above a certain amount (usually a rather small amount) should require the signature of another club official vested with check signing authority by the bylaws, in addition to the treasurer. Opportunities to take advantage of discounts for prompt payment should not be missed. Records of payment are the club checkbook, the entries in the general ledger, and the supporting invoices. The invoices are proof of the legitimacy of the expenses being paid.

Member statements

Members like to know their account activity with the flying club, and it is the club's financial responsibility to keep them informed. Depending upon membership size, preference, and available labor, statements may be sent monthly or quarterly. The statements should list all charges and payments for the period, and any balance due.

Financial statements

Besides their individual financial status with the flying club, members like to be kept informed of and have a right to know the club's overall financial condition. This information should be made available in the form of financial statements periodically compiled from the club's financial records (the general ledger), the member accounts, the record of assets owned, and liabilities (such as loans) incurred. The presentation format of the financials consists of an income statement and a balance sheet as discussed in chapter 17 regarding flying club financials. The usual practice is to provide members with an annual financial statement at the end of the fiscal year.

Annual outside review

It is a normal procedure for any business to periodically get an independent outside review of the accuracy of its financial records, and is highly recommended for the flying club. While one objective of such a review is to check for any monkey business, the general intent is not to automatically cast suspicion on the treasurer's integrity. Rather, it is to take a professional look from a distance at how well the club's system of financial recordkeeping is working, and see if it needs any enhancement. Most treasurers are proud of their work and welcome an outside review as independent confirmation of the good job they are doing.

Accounting software

If it isn't obvious by now, then it needs to be explicitly said. Do your club a big favor and get an inexpensive desktop accounting software package. Once properly set up, these menu-driven systems require only the entry of raw data in the appropriate boxes, and will immeasurably simplify the flying club's accounting chores. Most systems will not only link accounts and provide up-to-the-minute information on any account or financial statement at the push of a button, but will also prepare periodic account statements and invoices, print checks, and even generate statistical summaries of financial trends.

FLYING CLUB STATISTICS

One recordkeeping role goes beyond the day-to-day operations of the flying club. It is developing summary information about flying club activities over time, usually on a monthly, quarterly, or annual basis depending upon need. Commonly measured items are hours flown and costs per hour, presented in a variety of ways. Such information will tell a club if its airplanes are being used as efficiently as was hoped, if costs are where they should be, and if members are flying enough to make the club option their continued logical choice.

The information can also be used to plan for the future. It helps the club understand where there are unrealistic assumptions about its flying costs, and enables it to fine-tune the numbers used to set rental rates, dues, and budgets going forward.

There are no hard and fast rules about what statistical summary information to track. As long as the data comparisons are valid, the content is up to your needs. Whatever numbers you choose to track, it is worthwhile to distribute them to the membership from time to time, accompanied by some analytical commentary:

- Total hours flown by the club per year and month
- Hours per aircraft per year and month
- Operating expenses per hour per aircraft
- Fixed expenses per hour per aircraft
- Total expenses per hour per aircraft
- Maintenance expenses per aircraft
- Maintenance expenses per hour per aircraft
- Income per hour per aircraft
- Income and expense trends
- Financial reserve positions, adequacy, and trends

FLYING CLUB LEGAL DOCUMENTS

Flying clubs should be careful to keep the original copies of important legal documents in a secure place: articles of incorporation, bylaws, loan agreements, and the like. A safe is a good choice. Aircraft documents that should receive equal care are the engine and airframe logs and the insurance policies. It is best to appoint a club member (usually the secretary, or in the case of the airframe and engine logs, the maintenance officer) to be in charge of these records.

22

The flying club newsletter

EFFECTIVE COMMUNICATIONS is one of the most important characteristics of the successful flying club. Keeping in touch with the flying club's affairs is not always easy for pilots who have limited time to spend on their flying, and can become especially cumbersome in large flying clubs with a big membership list. But an excellent solution to keep the flow of communications going is the flying club newsletter. For larger clubs, it is indispensable in getting out the word and a modest newsletter is a worthwhile effort for flying clubs with as few as 10 or 15 members.

The flying club newsletter's primary function is to inform the membership about flying club issues that directly affect their activities in the club. It reviews the proceedings at recent general meetings and directors' meetings, and summarizes the important decisions. It brings news of recent flying club participation in aviation events and informs the membership of equipment upgrades and new equipment put on the flying club's line.

It alerts members to changes in operating procedures and highlights any maintenance issues. It presents the members with a schedule of upcoming events, such as flyouts, picnics, ground school sessions, safety seminars, guest speakers, and field trips to aviation facilities or flying museums. It prominently announces upcoming general meetings with ample lead time and presents the agenda. At the end of each fiscal year, it prints the flying club's annual financial statement. In other words, it brings all the flying club news that's fit to print.

A newsletter does have two other important features: education and entertainment. In its educational role, the newsletter can have a major positive effect on the way the flying club's aircraft are flown. A steady diet of articles dealing with operating technique and safety will surely rub off on the members and the way they fly. Cautionary articles before the onset of seasons that place particular demand on specific flying skills, such as winter flying and thunderstorm avoidance, will also be welcome by the membership. Regular maintenance, safety, and chief pilot columns are a good way to handle educational material.

The newsletter's entertainment material is often one of its most popular features with the membership. First-person descriptions of member experiences on club flights are especially well liked. Flyout suggestions, airport restaurant experiences, and aviation history related in some way to the club are also good bets.

EDITING AND PUBLISHING THE NEWSLETTER

Editing and publishing the newsletter is a big job, bigger than most people realize who accept the responsibility without previous experience. It can be great fun for the editor, but care must be taken to keep the process of writing and production to manageable levels. The newsletter is like a little business. Raw material must be gathered, it must be turned into a finished product, which must then be reproduced and shipped out, all on a deadline. During the year, indeed, the editor's entire tenure, the process must be punctually repeated again and again according to regular deadlines.

Most editors who accept the job do so because they enjoy writing and editing. Yet, a big part of the job is on the production side, reproducing the master copy and getting it into the mail. It is in production that most newsletters tend to run into delays. This was especially true before the ascent of the personal computer.

In our high tech age, a personal computer is indispensable in publishing the flying club newsletter. Any average personal computer with a standard word processing program will reduce the production time of the newsletter's master

The flying club newsletter is the place to report on the members' exotic flight experiences.

copy dramatically in comparison to the tiring old days of typing, cutting, pasting, and lugging it all to the print shop. When you print the newsletter, make sure to use one of the many readily available laser printers. Though dot matrix printers can also get the job done, the laser printer yields production results equivalent to the slickest professional newsletters. If you really want to get fancy (and you can with little effort and expense), work with one of the popular desktop publishing programs.

A flying club should examine certain important aspects of editing and publishing the newsletter.

Frequency

Most enthusiastic fledgling clubs would like to have the newsletter appear monthly, but this might be a trifle ambitious because of the high workload for the inexperienced, part-time volunteer editor. More often than not, the newsletter ends up being delayed. It is much better to start slowly, aiming for an edition every two months, and going to a monthly schedule if and when experience and demand warrants.

Length and content

It will also pay off to start with a newsletter of modest length. Your initial objective should be to provide essential flying club news. Learn to do an outstanding job with the basics and proceed to the secondary stuff slowly.

For starters, be sure to always have a lead article, which should be the centerpiece of each issue, and a calendar of upcoming events. Develop the secondary articles and columns as you go along.

At first you might find that one page, front to back, is sufficient. Few newsletters are more than four pages. The less paper you can get away with the lower your mailing costs will be.

Gathering material

Part of being the editor is being a reporter. Plan newsletter issues in advance. Anticipate events and plan coverage. A pattern will emerge. Certain types of information will be dated and will be of primary importance, while other topics will give you the luxury of time.

An important source of material is the membership. As discussed below, assign columns to various members, and ask others for occasional articles. Before you know it, the less date-sensitive material will be writing itself, and you can concentrate on the "hot" news and production.

Layout and composition

It is up to you how fancy you want to get with the layout. Study other newsletters and try to develop a style. The visual appeal of the newsletter is also important. A nicely laid out newsletter can be good for club morale.

A good desktop publishing computer program will have numerous type fonts and letter sizes available. To hold down paper needs and mailing costs, use small, dense type, but make sure that the size you choose is reasonably readable.

Develop a mast, incorporating the club logo and lay out a template first page. Scan this page, including the mast, into the computer and use it as a template. Number the volumes and issues of the newsletter.

If your computer does not have graphics capability that allows you to store the front page template including the mast, have the layout run off in quantity at an instant print shop, as you would with personal stationery, and use these sheets to feed the computer for each issue's first page. If you have access to a high quality photocopier, you might be able to run off the front page stationery yourself.

Keep styles and color simple. Black-and-white is the way to go to keep expenses under control. Some flying clubs run off their newsletters on colored paper to add a personal touch.

Reproduction

The personal computer and the laser printer make it easy to produce a finished master copy suitable for reproduction. If your newsletter has only simple artwork along with the text it is easily reproduced on a quality photocopier, either by yourself or an instant print shop. The advantage of having the print shop reproduce the master copy if there are a lot of copies to be sent out is that the shop can also fold the copies for a small fee, and deliver them ready for the address labels and mailing.

Pictures

Getting pictures into the newsletter is ambitious and can be somewhat costly if you have to have half tones prepared (the camera-ready copy the printer needs to print). If you choose to include pictures and don't have a scanner and a graphics program on your computer that enables you to print the picture directly through the computer onto the master copy of the newsletter you will have to use the services of a printer. Leave space in your layout for the pictures, and deliver the original photos to the printer who will scan them and "drop" them into position.

With a scanner, and a graphics program on your computer, it is as easy to print pictures directly onto your master copy as it is to print the rest of the newsletter.

If you don't have a scanner, it is best not to fool with pictures initially, given the time and cost considerations.

Mailing

Cost and labor are the issues you have to deal with when you mail the newsletter. For a small membership mailing is a simple, relatively low cost affair. But if the membership is large, the mailing of the newsletter can be a major, labor intensive undertaking. For this reason, the automatic folding of the newsletter at a printer might be worth the extra expense.

Design the newsletter to be folded just like a letter. Never use an envelope. Make sure that one outside surface is blank, with the possible exception of a return address, when the newsletter is folded, and use it for the mailing address label. Staple the newsletter shut with one staple at the top (bulk mailing regulations might not permit stapling, in which case a peel-off sticky tab will accomplish the same purpose).

Preprinted address labels are a must and should be available from the person handling membership.

On large-volume mailings, you can realize considerable savings on mailing if you get a bulk mailing permit and mail out the newsletter third class. You need a minimum number of pieces mailed regularly to qualify for bulk mailing. Ask at any post office for bulk mailing information, and the application forms.

Timesaver tips

Organization is the key to success. Have the newsletter template set up on your computer.

Have separate desk files by topic and build up an inventory of articles to be ready to go leaving you free to concentrate on the more pressing, dated items.

Develop a list of articles to be written and add to it constantly. You can practically plan the contents that are not date-sensitive for each issue a year in advance as do the many magazines.

Badger the membership for written contributions.

Be careful with copying articles from other sources. You might be breaking copyright laws.

Cover a lot of ground in regular columns.

COLUMNS

Columns are an excellent device for covering specific themes regularly. Depending upon how elaborate your newsletter is, you may have as many or as few regular columns as you see fit. If the scope of your newsletter is too limited for a wide range of regular columns, be sure to cover suitable themes in occasional columns.

The beauty of the columns is that they can be delegated to other club members.

Club news. This column is a good place to present brief, run-of-the-mill news items that do not warrant feature coverage.

Chief pilot's pointers. This is the chief pilot's chance to speak out on any topic that is timely or important regarding the membership's flying habits. Topics could be instructional, operational, or theoretical. Brief pieces on better crosswind landings, go arounds, plans to sign up more instructors, and critical engine considerations on the club twin are some examples of ideal topics.

Safety tips. This is the domain of the safety officer, if there is one, and is the place to address timely safety topics and issues pertinent to the club's operations. This is the place for brief pointers on the pitfalls of night VFR, educational comments on incidents and accidents, tips on guarding against fuel contamination, and similar topics.

Maintenance corner. This is an important column to be written by the maintenance officer. It should offer pointers on operating procedures that would reduce maintenance costs, and should address bad operating habits, especially if widely practiced by the membership. Proper leaning techniques, proper use of the brakes, club policies on the use of autogas, and potential damage due to improper ground handling are all ideal topics for this column.

Members in the news. This column is usually popular with the membership. Everyone likes to be recognized for any exceptional achievement inside or outside the club. This is also the place to welcome new members.

Calendar of events. This is one of the most useful columns. It should include not only upcoming club events, but also any outside aviation events of note within your area.

A word from the president. This column provides the president with the opportunity to reach the membership directly with whatever is on his or her mind. It should not be abused. It should be an occasional column to be presented only when the president really has something to say.

Book review. Hundreds of aviation books are out there, new and old. Spread the word about them. Remember, for someone new to aviation, every aviation book is new. Brief, one- or two-paragraph reviews are always popular and several can be written in advance.

Part IV
Buying an airplane

23

Researching and finding the aircraft

WHEN YOU HAVE A GOOD IDEA of the kind of flying you want to do and how much money you have available, you need to decide on the aircraft make and model that would best meet your performance requirements within budget, and you have to find a specific aircraft to buy. Comprehensive information and good planning are essential to move quickly and smoothly from your initial thoughts of make and model to flying away with a freshly signed bill of sale and the just completed aircraft registration naming you and your partners as the co-owners.

You need to know how to find detailed specifications and performance information on the greatest number of makes and models that are within range of your objectives. You need to find reliable pricing information. You need to line up financing and insurance as far in advance as possible to avoid delays once you have located a specific aircraft. You have to identify aircraft for sale worth looking at, and after all that work you should really buy one. This chapter shows you how to conduct the initial research of aircraft specifications and performance, how to develop pricing information, and how to find aircraft for sale worth investigating.

RESEARCHING AIRCRAFT SPECIFICATIONS

Chances are that a wide variety of aircraft types will fit your mission requirements. Whether training, touring, or even aerobatics, there is a vast private air force for sale out there ready to meet your needs. How to be aware of all the options and how to choose? As you conduct a systematic, carefully researched comparison of all the options, you will suddenly reach a point where the ultimate choice will become obvious.

Pilots are a conservative and loyal lot. They tend to stick with what they know. If they learned to fly in Cessnas, they will most likely buy a Cessna. If they have been renting Cherokees from the local FBO, that is what they will want to buy. Yet there might be other alternatives worth considering. In the late 1980s, for example, many pilots purchased used Piper Arrow IIIs and IVs, unaware that for a time a used Grumman/Gulfstream Tiger was an excellent and considerably less expensive alternative. The price was lower because the Tiger had been out of production for some time raising spare part questions, it was not well known, especially by pilots who came on the scene after its production had ceased, and it had an undeserved reputation of being a hot ship. Yet if your performance and specifications research had identified the Tiger as an alternative worth investigating, you would have been pleasantly surprised when you looked into prices, to find the option of Arrow performance for up to $10,000 less. And how flying fortunes change. As of this writing, the Tiger is back in production and the future of Piper production is unclear.

Being aware of all the aircraft types available to meet your needs based upon comparative performance is only one aspect to research. For each type you consider, you should also find out how well it has done in service, what airworthiness directives and service bulletins have been issued on it, and what quirks, if any, is the airplane known for.

Technical specifications to consider

The technical specifications you will find most relevant will depend upon your intended use of the aircraft, but there are a number of standard specs you should look for when you develop the information to make comparisons. Specs such as dimensions, which are nice to know but are of little help in comparing types, are not presented.

- Aircraft make, model, year
- Seats and configuration
- Powerplant make, model
- Horsepower
- Type fuel used (80, 100LL, auto-STCd)
- Propeller make and model
- Weights and loadings
- Gross weight
- Empty weight
- Useful load
- Payload, full fuel and oil
- Fuel capacity (gallons and pounds)
- Baggage capacity
- Performance
- Maximum speed, sea level
- Cruise speed 75 percent power
- 65 percent power
- 55 percent power
- Range 75 percent power
- 65 percent power

- 55 percent power
- Rate of climb, sea level
- Service ceiling
- Best angle of climb speed
- Best rate of climb speed
- Stall speed, clean
- Stall speed, gear and flaps down
- Approach speed
- Takeoff distance over 50-foot obstacle
- Landing distance over 50-foot obstacle

Sources of information

Technical information on aircraft is available from a variety of sources. Some are legendary tomes, such as *Jane's All the World's Aircraft* (updated annually), or, for older aircraft, Juptners' many volumes. They are prohibitively expensive for infrequent use, but any good library should be able to chase them down for you. (Jane's occasionally puts out condensed paperback extracts but these are not sufficiently detailed to be of use by purchasers of aircraft.) To meet the needs of most of us, there are other, more readily available sources.

Books. Several good books are on the market that are exclusively compilations of information on general aviation aircraft. These books group aircraft by class (single-engine, multiengine) and type within class (two-seat trainer, four-seat fixed gear, and the like). They provide brief histories as well as all the important technical specifications.

Aviation Consumer. This publication is perhaps the most comprehensive source for not only technical information on an airplane type, but especially on how well it has done in service. Technical reliability, maintenance problems, its safety record, major ADs and service bulletins, and handling are all addressed in comprehensive pilot reports. The publication accepts no advertising, which puts conspiratorial minds at ease. Most production aircraft have been covered at some time or other, and many are covered again and again periodically. TAB-McGraw Hill has issued in book form a large collection of the *Consumer's* reports.

Aviation magazines. Aviation magazines are in the business of writing pilot reports on practically every type of general aviation aircraft from antique Piper Cubs to hefty brand new twins. The latest offerings of the airplane manufacturers and used aircraft are given equal time. The more popular used types are reviewed every three to four years. A good strategy is to get copies of all the articles over time on a particular type. Periodically, magazines also publish articles comparing the competing models of several manufacturers. Some magazines provide copies of pilot reports for a fee. Many publish indexes from time to time, where pilot reports are easily located. If you have difficulty finding back issues, your librarian might be able to help. Although most aviation magazines are too specialized to be in many libraries, perhaps the librarian can research which library closest to you has back issues.

Aircraft manuals. It is relatively easy to borrow the manuals of the aircraft in which you are seriously interested. Many manuals are also available for purchase, but it makes more economic sense to borrow them.

Airworthiness directives

During your initial research, you can familiarize yourself with the most important ADs from the books and magazine articles. But such secondary sources of information are inadequate when you settled on a particular type of aircraft you expect to buy. Books and magazines are dated. ADs might have been issued after their publication. They might cover only the major ADs.

To be fully informed of all ADs issued on an aircraft type, you need to order an official list of ADs. This list is obtainable from your local flight standards district office, the FAA in Oklahoma City, or through AOPA, which provides a special AD list service for a modest fee. For an additional fee, AOPA will also provide service difficulty reports filed with the FAA by mechanics.

It is crucial that you get an official, up-to-date AD list for the type of aircraft you decide to buy. The comparison of the AD list to the aircraft logs is the only effective means of independently verifying compliance with all ADs of the aircraft you will buy.

FINDING AND PRICING THE AIRCRAFT

Developing a short list of aircraft types based upon technical specs, performance data, and pilot reports is only half the task. You also have to develop reliable price information to establish the going rate, and you have to start looking for specific aircraft for sale.

Aircraft advertised for sale

Several publications are dedicated wholly to advertising aircraft and related products for sale. The most well known and comprehensive among them is *Trade-A-Plane*. Its newspaper-size yellow pages carry literally thousands of aircraft advertisements in each issue. *Trade-A-Plane* is reasonably priced, it appears three times a month, and is available by subscription for periods as brief as three months, which is an ideal time period for most private buyers. The ads generally contain sufficient information to group the offered airplanes according to your ballpark specifications, and will enable you to develop a very good idea of the range of prices.

Other good sources of airplane ads are regional aviation papers such as the *Pacific Flyer* and *Atlantic Flyer*, which carry a big classified section. For home-builts, the classified sections in *Kitplanes* and EAA's *Sport Aviation* magazine are helpful. *Soaring* magazine lists gliders for sale.

There are a number of glossy ad magazines, such as *A/C Flyer*, with pages and pages of pretty color pictures of aircraft for sale. These publications list aircraft offered by dealers and cover mostly corporate aircraft, but they also carry

Be sure to find the right airplane from among the hundreds of choices presented in the aviation ads every week.

some single-engine light aircraft, especially the more expensive ones, such as Mooneys and Bonanzas. Inevitably, prices are at the high end due to hefty dealer markups.

Computer listings are a relatively recent source of aircraft advertisements. Most list aircraft for sale by owners (no dealers). The lists themselves are advertised in the classified sections of most popular aviation magazines.

Aircraft Bluebook Price Digest

The best source of current price information is the *Aircraft Bluebook Price Digest*; however, it is available only to aviation businesses: dealers, aircraft financiers, and insurance companies. It is also very expensive. The *Aircraft Bluebook* appears four times a year. It tracks in great detail the wholesale and retail prices of virtually every aircraft make and model produced, adjusted for engine time, equipment, and general condition. It is not easy to read. There is a complex adjustment process to the basic prices, and the prices are in code because the price book is intended to benefit the business users (especially aircraft dealers) that pay the hefty subscription price, at the expense of the less well informed consumer who will not realize he is being overcharged by a dealer.

In spite of all the secretiveness, there are informal ways for private individuals to obtain *Bluebook* information. Some subscribers might see a business reason to reveal retail prices to you. Contacts with personnel working at firms that subscribe might lead to a willingness to provide counsel on aircraft prices implicitly understood to be based upon *Bluebook* values. Information can also be obtained from your friendly banker. Ask what maximum percentage of the going price the bank is willing to finance, and is the price wholesale or retail. Then submit a list of aircraft types with desired avionics and engine and airframe times, and ask the banker for the maximum dollar amount he or she would be willing to finance on each type. You can then easily figure out the approximate *Bluebook* price.

Other sources of information

Other sources you should cover in your search are the traditional ones, such as word of mouth, the region's FBOs, and bulletin boards at airports. Bulletin boards can be an especially helpful source of information on pilots seeking partners. A twist on the bulletin board approach is putting up an airplane wanted buyer's ad.

FINANCING AND INSURANCE HOMEWORK

It is advisable to line up financing and insurance as early as you can, to minimize delays when you find the aircraft that will be the one. When you decide to buy a particular aircraft, you will most likely be required to put down a deposit that will hold the aircraft for a specified period of time while you complete the necessary arrangements. If, at this stage, you run into delays through no fault of the seller, you might risk losing your deposit.

The best time to start working on financing and insurance is when you have made a decision on the type of aircraft you want to buy, and have defined such criteria as total time, engine time since major overhaul, and avionics requirements.

Financing preapproval

Most banks are willing to prequalify you for a certain amount of financing, based upon predetermined criteria for the aircraft. You fill out all the loan applications and provide all the other information the bank needs, and you define in great detail the specs of the aircraft you are looking for. The banker can then preapprove a loan for you, which will be immediately available upon the location of an aircraft that fits the predetermined criteria, and completion of a satisfactory title search.

Banks can usually approve an aircraft loan in 48 hours, so why the need for preapproval? You need it to find out that you qualify for a loan. Some pilots make the mistake of not getting preapproval because of the fast turnaround in bank approvals, only to find out that they don't qualify for a loan on the terms they would need. That starts a mad scramble for alternative financing that might not work out in time, threatening loss of the deposit given to the seller.

Lining up insurance

Insurance can be lined up much in the same manner as bank financing. The drawback of not lining up insurance ahead of time is not that you would not get coverage, but that coverage might be on less favorable terms than you expected. Determine the levels and types of coverage you want, define the specifications of the aircraft you are looking for, ask how much coverage will cost, and have your insurance provider standing by on your terms and conditions.

BEGINNING THE SEARCH

When you have completed your research of aircraft specifications, performance, and prices, and made a decision on what to look for, it is time to see what's available. Again, a systematic approach will yield the best results. Draw up a list of likely airplanes from all the sources available to you, and start making some phone calls.

The Cherokee 180 is an outstanding low-cost four-seat partnership or club airplane.

24

Checking them out

GEOGRAPHICAL LOCATION OF AIRPLANES for sale is an important question when deciding which ones to check out. To have the widest choice available, it is best to be as flexible as possible in how far you are willing to travel to inspect the airplanes. A good rule of thumb is to have the airplane brought to you if it is within reasonable flying distance from your home airport. You have the advantage of home turf for the test flight and your mechanic will be on the spot for the prepurchase inspection; however, if the airplane is far away, or demand for it is great, you and your mechanic might have to go to it. Define what expense you consider reasonable for such travel, consider it part of the costs of buying an airplane, and set your geographical limits accordingly. Sometimes it is possible to make arrangements with the seller to fly to your home field for preagreed expenses if you decide not to buy the airplane following the prepurchase inspection. An inexpensive but somewhat limiting solution is to restrict yourself to checking out airplanes only within day-trip range.

INITIAL CONTACT WITH THE SELLER

A lot can be learned from the first telephone call. If you are well organized and ask the right questions, you can quickly screen your initial list and decide which aircraft merit further follow up. You might want to fill out a screening worksheet for each aircraft and keep a record of the responses to your questions. The questions below are available as a worksheet in the appendices, suitable for reproduction.

- How many owners has the airplane had?
- Where has it been based geographically during its life?
- Has it ever been used for training or rental flying?
- Total time, airframe.
- Total time, engine.
- Total time, engine since major overhaul.
- How many times has the engine been overhauled?

- Who performed the overhaul? The choices are the factory (the best but most expensive alternative), an FAA certified repair station (many specialize in engine overhauls and are perhaps the best buy for the money), or an FBO or independent mechanic (who do some of the best and some of the worst work around; the problem is knowing who does the best and who does the worst).
- Was the overhaul to factory new tolerances or service limits? Factory new tolerances mean that the main components meet the standards of new components. Service limits mean that wear and tear is within the limits within which the components may be kept in service, but the components might be considerably below factory new tolerances.
- Were the accessories also overhauled? If not, how many hours are on the accessories? (Starter, alternator, magnetos, vacuum pump, and the like)
- Are all ADs complied with and entered into the aircraft logs?
- Has there been a top overhaul since the major overhaul?
- Is there any damage history?
- How old is the paint and interior?
- Rate the exterior and interior on a scale of 1 to 10
- Has the airplane been hangared?
- When was the last annual?
- Who did the last annual?
- Is the oil sent out for analysis at oil change and are the results available?
- How many hours has the airplane flown since the last annual?
- How many hours has the airplane flown in the last 12 months?
- When was the most recent transponder and static/altimeter check?
- What major maintenance items have been logged in the last 12 months?
- What make and model avionics does the airplane have? (navcom, HSI, ADF, loran, RNAV, GPS, and the like)
- Are there any maintenance issues with the avionics?
- Does the airplane have an intercom (does it work)?
- Are the airframe and engine logs complete?
- Have the airframe or engine been modified in any fashion and is any modification represented in the logbooks? Why was the modification performed?
- Are pictures available? (exterior, interior, and instrument panel)
- What is the asking price?
- Does the airplane have EGT and CHT gauges?

Which airplanes you decide to follow up on depends upon the standards of acceptability you have set for yourself: limits on total time, time since engine overhaul, acceptance of engine overhauls done to factory new tolerances by at least an FAA authorized repair station, no use of the airplane as a trainer or rental aircraft, limits on geographical location during the life of the airplane (you might not want to consider an airplane that has spent the last 10 years unhangared in a saltwater coastline environment), and getting together with the seller for the prepurchase inspection.

THE PREPURCHASE INSPECTION

A thorough prepurchase inspection is absolutely imperative prior to buying an aircraft. If you do not have substantial aircraft maintenance experience, it is also imperative that an A&P mechanic of your choice perform the inspection. The small inspection fee is well worth the peace of mind it will bring, considering the size of your investment. The seller will often reassure you that an annual has just recently been done, or that the seller's mechanic will be happy to give an opinion. Most sellers are honest and are just trying to be helpful, but you can never be sure unless you use your own mechanic.

A prepurchase inspection should usually consist of three phases:

- Examination of the aircraft papers
- Mechanical inspection of the airplane
- Flight test

A basic guideline for each phase is helpful to get things started; rely upon your mechanic for best results: "Let the buyer beware."

An aircraft appraiser might assuage any doubts about the asking price. Many mechanics are qualified aircraft appraisers, so it might be quite possible to combine a prepurchase inspection with an independent appraisal.

Examining the aircraft papers

It is a good idea to start with the aircraft papers. If there is a problem with them, you might save everyone a lot of time by discovering it up front. The review of the papers is also important simply to decide if you feel comfortable with going on the test flight; if the aircraft is far away, have the seller send you photocopies of the aircraft papers prior to trekking out to see the airplane. You should concentrate on the airframe and engine logs, but you should also examine all the papers required to be on board by the FAA:

- Certificate of airworthiness
- Registration
- Radio station license
- Airframe and engine logs
- Weight and balance
- Flight manual
     Check for:
- Proper annual entries
- Evidence of 100 hour inspections indicating commercial use
- Compression (most recent and history)
- Amount of hours flown per year
- Evidence of unscheduled repair work
- Airworthiness directive compliance

- Engine major overhaul entry (when and where done, to what tolerances)
- Record of geographic movements
- Damage history and evidence of hidden damage, such as propeller replaced for no apparent reason
- Propeller and accessories overhaul record

The mechanical inspection

The mechanical inspection should be along the lines of a 100-hour inspection, following the manufacturer's 100-hour inspection worksheet. An especially important part of the inspection is the compression check. If the engine has been overhauled, be sure to verify overhaul information provided by the seller on initial contact (when was the overhaul done, by whom, to what tolerances, and the like).

The following guidelines are provided to familiarize you with the items your mechanic should be checking during the prepurchase inspection. Inspection criteria should include examinations for:

Airframe

- Wrinkled skin, loose rivets, dings, cracks, and corrosion
- Mismatched paint, which could be a sign of repairs
- All controls for free and correct movement
- All control hinges (ailerons, elevator, rudder, flaps) for looseness, play, and hairline cracks
- Vertical and horizontal stabilizer attach points for looseness, play, and hairline cracks
- Wing attach points for hairline cracks and corrosion (any looseness cannot be tolerated)
- Control cables for looseness and chafing; look inside fuselage and wings through inspection panels with a flashlight
- Fuel caps, quick drains, and fuel tank areas for signs of fuel leaks (brownish stains)
- Fuselage underside for cleanliness and signs of leaks from engine area
- Wing struts for any signs of damage, corrosion, or hairline cracks
- Fabric test, plus peeling fabric or synthetics on covered airframes and components
- Engine cowling for looseness, play, and cracks, especially at attach points

Landing gear

- Landing gear struts for leaks
- Tires for wear and bald spots
- Brake pads for wear, brake disks for corrosion, pitting, and warping, and brake hydraulic lines for signs of seeping or leaking fluid

Cockpit

- Cabin doors and windows for signs of water leaks
- Windows for crazing
- Seat belts for wear and tear; they can get caught and damaged in the seat rails
- Move all controls and trim to verify full control movement and check for binding
- Move all other knobs and switches to check for proper operation
- ELT for proper operation
- Entire aircraft for proper display of placards and limitations
- Look underneath the panel for the free and correct movement of controls, plus orderliness of components and wiring, and signs of leaks

Engine and propeller

- Compression check
- Baffles for damage or deformation; baffle irregularities can cause cooling problems
- Any sign of leaks, especially around the various gaskets; look for oil and fuel stains
- Lower spark plugs for proper condition (take them out and examine them)
- Wiring harness for signs of brittleness and fraying
- Induction/exhaust system for leaks, cracks, corrosion, and looseness
- Engine controls running to the cockpit for free and easy movement
- Battery for fluid level and signs of overheating
- Accessory attachments (alternator, mags, vacuum pump, starter, electric fuel pump, and the like); check alternator belt for fraying and tightness
- Propeller for nicks and spinner for cracks

The test flight

If the paperwork and mechanical inspection check out, you are ready for the test flight. Be insistent upon one, and offer to pay for the fuel, if necessary. Some sellers are wary of phony purchasers out to get some free flying.

The objective of the test flight is twofold. It is your means of verifying that the airplane works as advertised, and it is also your chance to see if you feel comfortable with the way the airplane handles, if it is really the type of airplane you want.

Handle the test flight systematically and professionally. For pilots inexperienced with test flights, a good way to go about them is to treat them as a VFR flight test. Such a test requires the pilot to operate the aircraft through the whole spectrum of its normal operating range and is as much a mechanical test of the airplane as it is of the pilot's abilities. There won't be an examiner prompting you to do this and that, so take with you a checklist of all the items you want to accomplish. With that in mind, consider these guidelines.

Beech Aircraft Corporation

Fly it before you buy it is a wise idea.

Preflight. Do a detailed preflight per the operating manual. Follow the manual's detailed checklist to be sure of covering everything.

Engine start. Note how easily the engine cranks and turns over.

Taxi. Perform radio checks on both coms. Test brakes. Notice engine response, steering, and suspension. (For safety's sake, someone else should taxi the airplane while you check cockpit equipment.)

Pretakeoff checks. Perform careful pretakeoff checks and runup, verifying aircraft behavior to operating manual standards.

Takeoff. Note if power settings reach required levels. Climb to a convenient maneuvering altitude.

Basic VFR maneuvers and handling checks. Perform steep turns, slow flight, and stalls. Cycle flaps and gear. Note if aircraft is in trim.

Cruise checks. Set up various cruise configurations. Note performance compared to operating manual standards. Check engine gauges.

Avionics checks. Check all avionics in flight. Do in-flight radio checks. Track VOR, localizer, and glideslope on all appropriate navigation receivers. Compare needle indication of each VOR set to the same radial. Check ADF and marker beacons as appropriate. Establish radar contact with ground control, compare transponder altitude readout reported by ground control to altimeter indication.

Miscellaneous checks. Check cabin lights, vents, and heating system.

Touch and goes. Perform two or three touch and goes to feel fully comfortable with the handling of the aircraft.

Postflight check. Remove the cowling or nacelle covers and check for evidence of any engine leaks. Turn on all nav lights, landing lights, strobes, and flashing beacon, and check for operation.

The prepurchase inspection **213**

DECISION TIME

If the test flight goes as well as the paperwork review and the mechanical inspection, and the price is where you expected it, it is decision time. Review carefully the results of the prepurchase inspection. Determine any grounds for a price adjustment; propose to the seller any price adjustments you feel are appropriate and inform the seller about any squawks that must be dealt with before the airplane would be acceptable to you. The preferable strategy is to reduce the price by the cost of fixing the squawks and have the repairs done yourself. This ensures peace of mind that the work is done to your satisfaction as opposed to a quick fix by a seller keen to move the aircraft. If you can reach agreement, ideally in writing restricted to a memorandum of understanding that holds the aircraft for you for a few days until you make a decision, it might be time to consider giving the seller a deposit and move on toward closing the deal.

The Beechcraft Skipper is an excellent choice for the VFR budget partnership.

25

Closing the deal

YOU HAVE FOUND THE AIRPLANE YOU WANT, and you and the seller are in agreement on the price, so what next? No need to panic. As with a car and a house, certain simple but essential steps are to be taken to complete the transaction and take possession. You need to do a title search to find out if the seller really owns the airplane free and clear of any liens; you need to complete your financing arrangements; you need to obtain insurance; and you have to set up the FAA paperwork to transfer title. During this time, the seller has to complete whatever additional repairs or inspections that were agreed to.

DEPOSIT, PURCHASE, AND SALE AGREEMENT

Buyer and the seller need to see commitment from the other party regarding the pending deal. This is accomplished by your giving a deposit to the seller and both of you signing a purchase and sale agreement. The deposit is evidence of your commitment. It holds the airplane for you for a set period agreed to by you and the seller. If you do not buy the airplane during the time the deposit is in effect, through no fault of the seller, you lose the deposit. The amount of time for which a deposit will hold an airplane is typically approximately 30 days.

The deposit need not be a big amount in relation to the airplane's price, but it should be big enough from the seller's point of view to keep you motivated to complete the transaction. Approximately two percent of the airplane's price is usually sufficient; thus, on a $50,000 airplane, a deposit of $1,000 would be appropriate.

Terms under which you and the seller agreed to the sale are documented in the purchase and sale agreement. It is the seller's commitment not to sell the airplane while the deposit is in effect. It spells out the purchase price, the terms of the deposit, and any other conditions you might mutually agree to. If you show up with the money before your deposit period expires, the seller has to sell you the airplane. If the seller reneges, you might have recourse in the courts. The purchase and sale agreement also gives you protection if you lay down conditions that must be met by the seller (such as fixing mechanical problems or having an annual done) before the deposit period expires. If the seller does not meet these conditions, you can back out and have your deposit returned; however, beware that when the agreement is signed, you cannot impose additional conditions not covered in the agreement and back out without losing your deposit.

Purchase and sale agreements should be tailored to meet your personal circumstances and should at least be reviewed by your lawyer. The agreement should be signed by buyer and seller and should be dated. Minimal elements of the agreement bring the transaction into focus:

- Aircraft make, model, serial number, and N number
- Detailed equipment description
- Sale price
- Amount of deposit
- Amount of time for which the deposit holds the aircraft
- Satisfactory title search
- Aircraft to be delivered in full working condition as it was at the time of the prepurchase agreement, subject to any special agreement and noted discrepancies addressed in the agreement
- Special conditions (fresh annual at the expense of the seller, repair by seller of mechanical problems identified during the prepurchase agreement, avionics repairs, a new paint job, and the like)

The escrow option

Aircraft purchasers have the option of making sure that the seller does not disappear into the sunset with their cashed deposit, never to be seen again, or optimistically spending the deposit money and not being able to return it when there are grounds for its return. This option is the escrow account, a practice popular in real estate and other business transactions. It is an account maintained by an impartial third party, usually your lawyer. The money is no longer under your control, but is not released to the seller until the deposit period expires and you fail to buy the airplane, entitling the seller to the deposit.

PAPERWORK

The big job after the deposit and associated paperwork is getting all the final sale paperwork lined up to complete the transaction. A most important piece of paperwork is the title search.

Title search

Title is proof of ownership of an asset. In the case of airplanes, title is filed with the FAA in Oklahoma City. The owner of the asset can pledge it as collateral against debt, giving the lender a right to the asset (a security interest). If the debt is not properly handled, the lender can take possession of the asset and sell it to extinguish the debt. The sale of the asset does not invalidate the lien; thus, the new owner can rudely have the asset snatched from him by the lien-holding creditors of the former owner without being able to do anything about it. The lender's agreement with the former owner probably forbids the sale of the aircraft without extinguishing the loan, so the buyer can also find himself a victim of a fraudulent sale; thus, it is essential that the buyer perform a title search to verify that title is clear, or has only a lien on it known to the buyer; the underlying debt is to be paid off from the proceeds of the sale in exchange for release of the lien.

Title can be further complicated by the ability of creditors to put a lien on a debtor's asset even if it is not pledged to the creditor. An example is a mechanic's lien for unpaid maintenance. If the case goes to court, and the lien holder wins, he can force the sale of the asset regardless of who the new owner is. A buyer would be insane not to run a title search before buying an airplane.

The easiest way to do a title search is to use AOPA's title search service for a reasonable fee. If you are getting bank financing for the airplane, the bank will do the title search.

What if the title search shows a lien unknown to you? It might be a deal breaker, but more often it could be an old lien that was not released upon payment of the underlying debt. The lien holder has to specifically request that the lien be removed and many lien holders never bother to do this. They then have to be contacted and asked to have the lien removed. If you encounter any liens, anticipated or unanticipated, make their removal a condition of purchase.

The ultimate payoff . . . in the air.

Title insurance option

A routine title search might not reveal some particularly ancient lien problem that could cause problems if it surfaces. Such occurrences among aircraft are extremely rare, but to put your mind completely at ease about any title problems, you can purchase title insurance. Ask your insurance provider for advice.

Completing finance and insurance arrangements

Upon placing a deposit on an aircraft, you should complete the financial arrangements if you are obtaining bank financing, and you should also arrange for insurance.

If you have preapproval, the financing arrangements will be closed quickly. You have to provide the bank with the details of the aircraft and they will run a title search and prepare the loan documents. When everything is ready, you have to sign the loan documents and will be given a bank check made out to you and the seller, which both parties have to sign before it can be cashed.

Insurance arrangements can also be quickly completed. You have to provide the insurance company the particulars of the aircraft and pay for the policy. In return, the insurance company will issue you a binder, a brief, temporary proof of immediate coverage pending the arrival of your policy later in the mail. If you are getting bank financing, the insurance binder must be delivered directly to the bank by the insurance company as a condition of disbursing the loan.

Bill of sale

This form transfers title to you from the seller. It is legal proof of your purchase of the aircraft. It is usually provided by the seller, but it doesn't hurt for you to have a blank form with you just in case. The form can be obtained from any flight standards district office or from the FAA's Mike Monroney Aeronautical Center in Oklahoma City (AC Form 8050-2). Instructions are on the form explaining how to fill it out and where to send it.

Registration

When the aircraft is sold, it has to be reregistered in the name of the new owners. This is done on the aircraft registration application (AC Form 8050-1). You must have this form with you to take possession of the aircraft, because the pink copy of this application will be your temporary registration on board the aircraft until the processed permanent registration is sent to you. This form also has instructions on how to fill it out and where to send it.

As of this writing there is a proposal to change the temporary pink copy feature of the registration process. The objective is to make registration more difficult because of the shady dealings of aerial drug smugglers. Be sure to check with the FAA procedures in effect at the time of your transaction; contact the nearest flight standards district office.

Radio station license

The airplane has to have a radio station license in your name; therefore, you have to fill out and mail to the Federal Communications Commission an application form (FCC 404) along with a fee. A section of the form is detached and must be placed on board the aircraft when you take possession.

Certified check for your equity portion

Most sellers will want payment from you in the form of a certified check. Be sure to have it prepared in the correct amount and the correct name. Have it made out in seller's and buyer's names and endorse it at the closing. It is a safety precaution. If the check is not endorsed by you, it cannot be cashed. If bank financing is involved, your check will have to be made out for the difference between the purchase price and the bank check plus the deposit you already paid.

TAKING POSSESSION

The actual closing of the transaction is the easiest part of buying the airplane. Be sure to have all the documents mentioned in this chapter with you; in the midst of all the excitement, do not forget your pilot and medical certificates. Take one more close look at the aircraft, especially if the seller has been flying it since you agreed to buy it. Review carefully once more the airframe and engine logs. Check to see that all the conditions laid out in the purchase and sale agreement have been met. Then it is time to make it happen.

You receive from the seller:

- Signed aircraft bill of sale
- Airworthiness certificate
- Airframe and engine logs
- Aircraft operating manual
- Weight and balance
- Seller's aircraft radio station license

You give the seller:

- Funds in the amount of the sale price (minus the deposit already given)
- Copy of the bill of sale for the seller's records. This is optional but most sellers will want one (you will have to make a copy because the FAA form is only in duplicate, the original to be sent in, the copy to be kept by you).

Place in the aircraft to meet FAA regulations:

- Airworthiness certificate
- New temporary registration
- New radio station license
- Operating manual
- Weight and balance

And now it is all done. Fire it up and fly away! Just be sure to mail at your earliest convenience the bill of sale, the registration application, and the aircraft radio station license application along with all the appropriate fees.

Appendices

A Financial analysis

Aircraft expenses worksheet
Aircraft expense data collection sheet
Aircraft and partnership financial analysis spreadsheet layout
Aircraft and partnership financial analysis spreadsheet formula template
Flying club financial analysis worksheet
Flying club financial analysis spreadsheet layout
Flying club financial analysis spreadsheet formula template

B Agreements and administration

Simple partnership agreement, three partners
Detailed partnership agreement, two partners
Simple partnership accounts worksheet
Detailed partnership accounting worksheet
Flying club articles of incorporation
Flying club bylaws
Flying club information and procedures statement
Flying club flight rules
Flying club continuing lease agreement
Flying club instructor scheduling information sheet
Flying club membership application

C Financing and insurance

Aircraft loan request worksheet
Aircraft loan application
Aircraft loan agreement, bank financing
Aircraft loan agreement, partner financing
Aircraft insurance request worksheet

D Aircraft flight records

Sample aircraft flight log

Aircraft flight and performance log
Aircraft squawk sheet
Aircraft schedule of recurrent inspections

E Preventative maintenance

FAR Part 43 authorization

F How to buy an airplane

Aircraft specifications comparison worksheet
Initial questions to ask
Prepurchase inspection checklist
Flight test checklist
Closing checklist
Sample documents

A

Financial analysis

Fig. A-1. Aircraft expenses worksheet.

AIRCRAFT COST WORKSHEET   Aircraft type:

(Calculate total cost for the aircraft in first cloumn, followed by costs per pilot for selected number of pilots.)

NUMBER OF PILOTS

ANNUAL FIXED EXPENSES

Tiedown/Hangar

Insurance

State Fees

Annual

Maintenance

Loan Payments

Cost of Capital (non-cash)

Total Fixed Expenses / yr

HOURLY OPERATING EXPENSES

Fuel

Oil

Engine Reserve

General Maint Res

Total Op Exp / hr

TOTAL HOURLY EXPENSES (annual fixed expenses/ hrs flown) + (hourly operating expenses*hrs flown)

50 Hours

100 Hours

150 Hours

Hourly Commercial Rental

TOTAL ANNUAL EXPENSES (total hourly expenses*hours flown)

50 Hours, Own

    *Own (cash only)

    Rent

100 Hours, Own

    *Own (cash only)

    Rent

150 Hours, Own

    *Own (cash only)

    Rent

Fig. A-2. Aircraft expense data collection sheet.

ASSUMPTIONS:

Aircraft Type:

Hangar/Month: Insurance/yr: State Fees/yr: Annual: Maintenance/yr:

Fuel Cons (gal/hr):   Fuel Cost ($/gal):   Oil Cons (qt/hr):   Oil Cost ($/qt):   Time Before OH:

Aircraft Value: Loan O/S: Loan Interest Rate: Loan/Inv Term (yrs):   Cost of Capital Rate:

Engine MOH Cost: Gen Maint Res/hr: Com. Rental/hr:

ASSUMPTIONS:

Aircraft Type:

Hangar/Month: Insurance/yr: State Fees/yr: Annual: Maintenance/yr:

Fuel Cons (gal/hr):   Fuel Cost ($/gal):   Oil Cons (qt/hr):   Oil Cost ($/qt):   Time Before OH:

Aircraft Value: Loan O/S: Loan Interest Rate: Loan/Inv Term (yrs):   Cost of Capital Rate:

Engine MOH Cost: Gen Maint Res/hr: Com. Rental/hr:

ASSUMPTIONS:

Aircraft Type:

Hangar/Month: Insurance/yr: State Fees/yr: Annual: Maintenance/yr:

Fuel Cons (gal/hr):   Fuel Cost ($/gal):   Oil Cons (qt/hr):   Oil Cost ($/qt):   Time Before OH:

Aircraft Value: Loan O/S: Loan Interest Rate: Loan/Inv Term (yrs):   Cost of Capital Rate:

Engine MOH Cost: Gen Maint Res/hr: Com. Rental/hr:

ASSUMPTIONS:

Aircraft Type:

Hangar/Month: Insurance/yr: State Fees/yr: Annual: Maintenance/yr:

Fuel Cons (gal/hr):   Fuel Cost ($/gal):   Oil Cons (qt/hr):   Oil Cost ($/qt):   Time Before OH:

Aircraft Value: Loan O/S: Loan Interest Rate: Loan/Inv Term (yrs):   Cost of Capital Rate:

Engine MOH Cost: Gen Maint Res/hr: Com. Rental/hr:

Fig. A-3. Aircraft and partnership financial analysis spreadsheet layout. (Continues through page 232.)

	B	C	D	E	F	G	H	I	J	K	L	M	N	O	P
FLYING EXPENSES PER PERSON, SINGLE ENGINED TWO SEAT TRAINER															
NUMBER OF PILOTS	1	2	3	4	5	6	7	8	9	10	11	12	13	14	15
ANNUAL FIXED EXPENSES															
Tiedown/Hangar	960.00	480.00	320.00	240.00	192.00	160.00	137.14	120.00	106.67	96.00	87.27	80.00	73.85	68.57	64.00
Insurance	750.00	375.00	250.00	187.50	150.00	125.00	107.14	93.75	83.33	75.00	68.18	62.50	57.69	53.57	50.00
State Fees	120.00	60.00	40.00	30.00	24.00	20.60	17.14	15.00	13.33	12.00	10.91	10.00	9.23	8.57	8.00
Annual	450.00	225.00	150.00	112.50	90.00	75.00	64.29	56.25	50.00	45.00	40.91	37.50	34.62	32.14	30.00
Maintenance	900.00	450.00	300.00	225.00	180.00	150.00	128.57	112.50	100.00	90.00	81.82	75.00	69.23	64.29	60.00
Loan Payments	1,189.36	594.68	396.45	297.34	237.87	198.23	169.91	148.67	132.15	118.94	108.12	99.11	91.49	84.95	79.29
Cost of Capital (non-cash)	525.00	262.50	175.00	131.25	105.00	87.50	75.00	65.63	58.33	52.50	47.73	43.75	40.38	37.50	35.00
Total Fixed Expenses / yr	4,894.36	2,447.18	1,631.45	1,223.59	978.87	815.73	699.19	611.79	543.82	489.44	444.94	407.86	376.49	349.60	326.29
HOURLY OPERATING EXPENSES															
Fuel	13.00	13.00	13.00	13.00	13.00	13.00	13.00	13.00	13.00	13.00	13.00	13.00	13.00	13.00	13.00
Oil	0.31	0.31	0.31	0.31	0.31	0.31	0.31	0.31	0.31	0.31	0.31	0.31	0.31	0.31	0.31
Engine Reserve	5.00	5.00	5.00	5.00	5.00	5.00	5.00	5.00	5.00	5.00	5.00	5.00	5.00	5.00	5.00
General Maint Res	2.00	2.00	2.00	2.00	2.00	2.00	2.00	2.00	2.00	2.00	2.00	2.00	2.00	2.00	2.00
Total Op Exp / hr	20.31	20.31	20.31	20.31	20.31	20.31	20.31	20.31	20.31	20.31	20.31	20.31	20.31	20.31	20.31
TOTAL HOURLY EXPENSES															
50 Hours	118.20	69.26	52.94	44.78	39.89	36.63	34.30	32.55	31.19	30.10	29.21	28.47	27.84	27.30	26.84
100 Hours	69.26	44.78	36.63	32.55	30.10	28.47	27.30	26.43	25.75	25.21	24.76	24.39	24.08	23.81	23.58
150 Hours	52.94	36.63	31.19	28.47	26.84	25.75	24.97	24.39	23.94	23.58	23.28	23.03	22.82	22.64	22.49
Hourly Commercial Rental	50.00	50.00	50.00	50.00	50.00	50.00	50.00	50.00	50.00	50.00	50.00	50.00	50.00	50.00	50.00
TOTAL ANNUAL EXPENSES															
50 Hours, Own	5909.98	3462.80	2647.08	2239.21	1994.50	1831.35	1714.82	1627.42	1559.44	1505.06	1460.57	1423.49	1392.11	1365.22	1341.92
Own (cash only)	5384.98	3200.30	2472.08	2107.96	1889.50	1743.85	1639.82	1561.79	1501.11	1452.56	1412.84	1379.74	1351.73	1327.72	1306.92
Rent	2500.00	2500.00	2500.00	2500.00	2500.00	2500.00	2500.00	2500.00	2500.00	2500.00	2500.00	2500.00	2500.00	2500.00	2500.00
100 Hours, Own	6925.61	4478.43	3662.70	3254.84	3010.12	2846.98	2730.44	2643.04	2575.07	2520.69	2476.19	2439.11	2407.74	2380.85	2357.54
Own (cash only)	6400.61	4215.93	3487.70	3123.59	2905.12	2759.48	2655.44	2577.42	2516.73	2468.19	2428.46	2395.36	2367.35	2343.35	2322.54
Rent	5000.00	5000.00	5000.00	5000.00	5000.00	5000.00	5000.00	5000.00	5000.00	5000.00	5000.00	5000.00	5000.00	5000.00	5000.00
150 Hours, Own	7941.23	5494.05	4678.33	4270.46	4025.75	3862.60	3746.07	3658.67	3590.69	3536.31	3491.82	3454.74	3423.36	3396.47	3373.17
Own (cash only)	7416.23	5231.55	4503.33	4139.21	3920.75	3775.10	3671.07	3593.04	3532.36	3483.81	3444.09	3410.99	3382.98	3358.97	3338.17
Rent	7500.00	7500.00	7500.00	7500.00	7500.00	7500.00	7500.00	7500.00	7500.00	7500.00	7500.00	7500.00	7500.00	7500.00	7500.00

ASSUMPTIONS:

Label	Value	Label	Value	Label	Value
Hangar/Month:	80.00	Insurance/yr:	750.00	State Fees/yr:	120.00
Annual:	450.00	Maintenance/yr:	900.00		
Fuel Cons (gal/hr):	6.50	Fuel Cost ($/gal):	2.00	Oil Cons (qt/hr):	0.13
Oil Cost ($/qt):	2.50	Time Before OH:	2000.00		
Aircraft Value:	15000.00	Loan O/S:	7500.00	Loan Interest Rate:	10.00%
Loan/Inv Term (yrs):	10	Cost of Capital Rate:	7.00%		
Engine MOH Cost:	10000.00	Gen Maint Res/hr:	2.00	Com. Rental/hr:	50.00

FLYING EXPENSES PER PERSON, SINGLE ENGINED TWO SEAT TRAINER.

NUMBER OF PILOTS	1	2	3	4	5	6	7	8	9	10	11	12	13	14	15
ANNUAL FIXED EXPENSES															
Tiedown/Hangar	960.00	480.00	320.00	240.00	192.00	160.00	137.14	120.00	106.67	96.00	87.27	80.00	73.85	68.57	64.00
Insurance	750.00	375.00	250.00	187.50	150.00	125.00	107.14	93.75	83.33	75.00	68.18	62.50	57.69	53.57	50.00
State Fees	120.00	60.00	40.00	30.00	24.00	20.00	17.14	15.00	13.33	12.00	10.91	10.00	9.23	8.57	8.00
Annual	450.00	225.00	150.00	112.50	90.00	75.00	64.29	56.25	50.00	45.00	40.91	37.50	34.62	32.14	30.00
Maintenance	900.00	450.00	300.00	225.00	180.00	150.00	128.57	112.50	100.00	90.00	81.82	75.00	69.23	64.29	60.00
Loan Payments	1,189.36	594.68	396.45	297.34	237.87	198.23	169.91	148.67	132.15	118.94	108.12	99.11	91.49	84.95	79.29
Cost of Capital (non-cash)	525.00	262.50	175.00	131.25	105.00	87.50	75.00	65.63	58.33	52.50	47.73	43.75	40.38	37.50	35.00
Total Fixed Expenses / yr	4,894.36	2,447.18	1,631.45	1,223.59	978.87	815.73	699.19	611.79	543.82	489.44	444.94	407.86	376.49	349.60	326.29
HOURLY OPERATING EXPENSES															
Fuel	13.00	13.00	13.00	13.00	13.00	13.00	13.00	13.00	13.00	13.00	13.00	13.00	13.00	13.00	13.00
Oil	0.31	0.31	0.31	0.31	0.31	0.31	0.31	0.31	0.31	0.31	0.31	0.31	0.31	0.31	0.31
Engine Reserve	5.00	5.00	5.00	5.00	5.00	5.00	5.00	5.00	5.00	5.00	5.00	5.00	5.00	5.00	5.00
General Maint Res	2.00	2.00	2.00	2.00	2.00	2.00	2.00	2.00	2.00	2.00	2.00	2.00	2.00	2.00	2.00
Total Op Exp / hr	20.31	20.31	20.31	20.31	20.31	20.31	20.31	20.31	20.31	20.31	20.31	20.31	20.31	20.31	20.31
TOTAL HOURLY EXPENSES															
50 Hours	118.20	69.26	52.94	44.78	39.89	36.63	34.30	32.55	31.19	30.10	29.21	28.47	27.84	27.30	26.84
100 Hours	69.26	44.78	36.63	32.55	30.10	28.47	27.30	26.43	25.75	25.21	24.76	24.39	24.08	23.81	23.58
150 Hours	52.94	36.63	31.19	28.47	26.84	25.75	24.97	24.39	23.94	23.58	23.28	23.03	22.82	22.64	22.49
Hourly Commercial Rental	50.00	50.00	50.00	50.00	50.00	50.00	50.00	50.00	50.00	50.00	50.00	50.00	50.00	50.00	50.00
TOTAL ANNUAL EXPENSES															
50 Hours, Own	5909.98	3462.80	2647.08	2239.21	1994.50	1831.35	1714.82	1627.42	1559.44	1505.06	1460.57	1423.49	1392.11	1365.22	1341.92
Own (cash only)	5384.98	3200.30	2472.08	2107.96	1889.50	1743.85	1639.82	1561.79	1501.11	1452.56	1412.84	1379.74	1351.73	1327.72	1306.92
Rent	2500.00	2500.00	2500.00	2500.00	2500.00	2500.00	2500.00	2500.00	2500.00	2500.00	2500.00	2500.00	2500.00	2500.00	2500.00
100 Hours, Own	6925.61	4478.43	3662.70	3254.84	3010.12	2846.98	2730.44	2643.04	2575.07	2520.69	2476.19	2439.11	2407.74	2380.85	2357.54
Own (cash only)	6400.61	4215.93	3487.70	3123.59	2905.12	2759.48	2655.44	2577.42	2516.73	2468.19	2428.46	2395.36	2367.35	2343.35	2322.54
Rent	5000.00	5000.00	5000.00	5000.00	5000.00	5000.00	5000.00	5000.00	5000.00	5000.00	5000.00	5000.00	5000.00	5000.00	5000.00
150 Hours, Own	7941.23	5494.05	4678.33	4270.46	4025.75	3862.60	3746.07	3658.67	3590.69	3536.31	3491.82	3454.74	3423.36	3396.47	3373.17
Own (cash only)	7416.23	5231.55	4503.33	4139.21	3920.75	3775.10	3671.07	3593.04	3532.36	3483.81	3444.09	3410.99	3382.98	3358.97	3338.17
Rent	7500.00	7500.00	7500.00	7500.00	7500.00	7500.00	7500.00	7500.00	7500.00	7500.00	7500.00	7500.00	7500.00	7500.00	7500.00

ASSUMPTIONS:

Hangar/Month:	80.00
Fuel Cons (gal/hr):	6.50
Aircraft Value:	15000.00
Engine MOH Cost:	10000.00
Insurance/yr:	750.00
Fuel Cost ($/gal):	2.00
Loan O/S:	7500.00
Gen Maint Res/hr:	2.00
State Fees/yr:	120.00
Oil Cons (qt/hr):	0.13
Loan Interest Rate:	10.00%
Com. Rental/hr:	50.00
Annual:	450.00
Oil Cost ($/qt):	2.50
Loan/Inv Term (yrs):	10
Maintenance/yr:	900.00
Time Before OH:	2000.00
Cost of Capital Rate:	7.00%

FLYING EXPENSES PER PERSON, SINGLE ENGINE FOUR SEAT FIXED GEAR, 150HP.

NUMBER OF PILOTS	1	2	3	4	5	6	7	8	9	10	11	12	13	14	15
ANNUAL FIXED EXPENSES															
Tiedown/Hangar	960.00	480.00	320.00	240.00	192.00	160.00	137.14	120.00	106.67	96.00	87.27	80.00	73.85	68.57	64.00
Insurance	1,000.00	500.00	333.33	250.00	200.00	166.67	142.86	125.00	111.11	100.00	90.91	83.33	76.92	71.43	66.67
State Fees	120.00	60.00	40.00	30.00	24.00	20.00	17.14	15.00	13.33	12.00	10.91	10.00	9.23	8.57	8.00
Annual	550.00	275.00	183.33	137.50	110.00	91.67	78.57	68.75	61.11	55.00	50.00	45.83	42.31	39.29	36.67
Maintenance	1,300.00	650.00	433.33	325.00	260.00	216.67	185.71	162.50	144.44	130.00	118.18	108.33	100.00	92.86	86.67
Loan Payments	2,220.13	1,110.07	740.04	555.03	444.03	370.02	317.16	277.52	246.68	222.01	201.83	185.01	170.78	158.58	148.01
Cost of Capital (non-cash)	980.00	490.00	326.67	245.00	196.00	163.33	140.00	122.50	108.89	98.00	89.09	81.67	75.38	70.00	65.33
Total Fixed Expenses / yr	7,130.13	3,565.07	2,376.71	1,782.53	1,426.03	1,188.36	1,018.59	891.27	792.24	713.01	648.19	594.18	548.47	509.30	475.34
HOURLY OPERATING EXPENSES															
Fuel	16.00	16.00	16.00	16.00	16.00	16.00	16.00	16.00	16.00	16.00	16.00	16.00	16.00	16.00	16.00
Oil	0.31	0.31	0.31	0.31	0.31	0.31	0.31	0.31	0.31	0.31	0.31	0.31	0.31	0.31	0.31
Engine Reserve	5.50	5.50	5.50	5.50	5.50	5.50	5.50	5.50	5.50	5.50	5.50	5.50	5.50	5.50	5.50
General Maint Res	2.50	2.50	2.50	2.50	2.50	2.50	2.50	2.50	2.50	2.50	2.50	2.50	2.50	2.50	2.50
Total Op Exp / hr	24.31	24.31	24.31	24.31	24.31	24.31	24.31	24.31	24.31	24.31	24.31	24.31	24.31	24.31	24.31
TOTAL HOURLY EXPENSES															
50 Hours	166.92	95.61	71.85	59.96	52.83	48.08	44.68	42.14	40.16	38.57	37.28	36.20	35.28	34.50	33.82
100 Hours	95.61	59.96	48.08	42.14	38.57	36.20	34.50	33.23	32.23	31.44	30.79	30.25	29.80	29.41	29.07
150 Hours	71.85	48.08	40.16	36.20	33.82	32.23	31.10	30.25	29.59	29.07	28.63	28.27	27.97	27.71	27.48
Hourly Commercial Rental	65.00	65.00	65.00	65.00	65.00	65.00	65.00	65.00	65.00	65.00	65.00	65.00	65.00	65.00	65.00
TOTAL ANNUAL EXPENSES															
50 Hours, Own	8345.76	4780.69	3592.34	2998.16	2641.65	2403.98	2234.22	2106.89	2007.86	1928.64	1863.82	1809.80	1764.10	1724.92	1690.97
Own (cash only)	7365.76	4290.69	3265.67	2753.16	2445.65	2240.65	2094.22	1984.39	1898.97	1830.64	1774.73	1728.14	1688.71	1654.92	1625.63
Rent	3250.00	3250.00	3250.00	3250.00	3250.00	3250.00	3250.00	3250.00	3250.00	3250.00	3250.00	3250.00	3250.00	3250.00	3250.00
100 Hours, Own	9561.38	5996.32	4807.96	4213.78	3857.28	3619.61	3449.84	3322.52	3223.49	3144.26	3079.44	3025.43	2979.72	2940.55	2906.59
Own (cash only)	8581.38	5506.32	4481.29	3968.78	3661.28	3456.27	3309.84	3200.02	3114.60	3046.26	2990.35	2943.76	2904.34	2870.55	2841.26
Rent	6500.00	6500.00	6500.00	6500.00	6500.00	6500.00	6500.00	6500.00	6500.00	6500.00	6500.00	6500.00	6500.00	6500.00	6500.00
150 Hours, Own	10777.01	7211.94	6023.59	5429.41	5072.90	4835.23	4665.47	4538.14	4439.11	4359.89	4295.07	4241.05	4195.35	4156.17	4122.22
Own (cash only)	9797.01	6721.94	5696.92	5184.41	4876.91	4671.90	4525.47	4415.64	4330.22	4261.89	4205.98	4159.39	4119.96	4086.17	4056.88
Rent	9750.00	9750.00	9750.00	9750.00	9750.00	9750.00	9750.00	9750.00	9750.00	9750.00	9750.00	9750.00	9750.00	9750.00	9750.00

ASSUMPTIONS:

Hangar/Month:	80.00	Insurance/yr:	1000.00	State Fees/yr: 120.00
Fuel Cons (gal/hr):	8.00	Fuel Cost ($/gal):	2.00	Oil Cons (qt/hr): 0.13
Aircraft Value:	28000.00	Loan O/S:	14000.00	Loan Interest Rate: 10.00%
Engine MOH Cost:	11000.00	Gen Maint Res/hr:	2.50	Com. Rental/hr: 65.00

Annual:	120.00	Maintenance/yr:	1300.00
Oil Cost ($/qt):	0.13	Time Before OH:	2000.00
Loan/Inv Term (yrs):	10	Cost of Capital Rate:	7.00%

FLYING EXPENSES PER PERSON, SINGLE ENGINE FOUR SEAT FIXED GEAR, 180HP.

NUMBER OF PILOTS	1	2	3	4	5	6	7	8	9	10	11	12	13	14	15
ANNUAL FIXED EXPENSES															
Tiedown/Hangar	960.00	480.00	320.00	240.00	192.00	160.00	137.14	120.00	106.67	96.00	87.27	80.00	73.85	68.57	64.00
Insurance	1,200.00	600.00	400.00	300.00	240.00	200.00	171.43	150.00	133.33	120.00	109.09	100.00	92.31	85.71	80.00
State Fees	120.00	60.00	40.00	30.00	24.00	20.00	17.14	15.00	13.33	12.00	10.91	10.00	9.23	8.57	8.00
Annual	650.00	325.00	216.67	162.50	130.00	108.33	92.86	81.25	72.22	65.00	59.09	54.17	50.00	46.43	43.33
Maintenance	1,300.00	650.00	433.33	325.00	260.00	216.67	185.71	162.50	144.44	130.00	118.18	108.33	100.00	92.86	86.67
Loan Payments	2,775.17	1,387.58	925.06	693.79	555.03	462.53	396.45	346.90	308.35	277.52	252.29	231.26	213.47	198.23	185.01
Cost of Capital (non-cash)	1,225.00	612.50	408.33	306.25	245.00	204.17	175.00	153.13	136.11	122.50	111.36	102.08	94.23	87.50	81.67
Total Fixed Expenses / yr	8,230.17	4,115.08	2,743.39	2,057.54	1,646.03	1,371.69	1,175.74	1,028.77	914.46	823.02	748.20	685.85	633.09	587.87	548.68
HOURLY OPERATING EXPENSES															
Fuel	19.00	19.00	19.00	19.00	19.00	19.00	19.00	19.00	19.00	19.00	19.00	19.00	19.00	19.00	19.00
Oil	0.31	0.31	0.31	0.31	0.31	0.31	0.31	0.31	0.31	0.31	0.31	0.31	0.31	0.31	0.31
Engine Reserve	6.00	6.00	6.00	6.00	6.00	6.00	6.00	6.00	6.00	6.00	6.00	6.00	6.00	6.00	6.00
General Maint Res	2.50	2.50	2.50	2.50	2.50	2.50	2.50	2.50	2.50	2.50	2.50	2.50	2.50	2.50	2.50
Total Op Exp / hr	27.81	27.81	27.81	27.81	27.81	27.81	27.81	27.81	27.81	27.81	27.81	27.81	27.81	27.81	27.81
TOTAL HOURLY EXPENSES															
50 Hours	192.42	110.11	82.68	68.96	60.73	55.25	51.33	48.39	46.10	44.27	42.78	41.53	40.47	39.57	38.79
100 Hours	110.11	68.96	55.25	48.39	44.27	41.53	39.57	38.10	36.96	36.04	35.29	34.67	34.14	33.69	33.30
150 Hours	82.68	55.25	46.10	41.53	38.79	36.96	35.65	34.67	33.91	33.30	32.80	32.38	32.03	31.73	31.47
Hourly Commercial Rental	75.00	75.00	75.00	75.00	75.00	75.00	75.00	75.00	75.00	75.00	75.00	75.00	75.00	75.00	75.00
TOTAL ANNUAL EXPENSES															
50 Hours, Own	9620.79	5505.71	4134.01	3448.17	3036.66	2762.32	2566.36	2419.40	2305.09	2213.64	2138.82	2076.47	2023.71	1978.49	1939.30
Own (cash only)	8395.79	4893.21	3725.68	3141.92	2791.66	2558.15	2391.36	2266.27	2168.98	2091.14	2027.46	1974.39	1929.48	1890.99	1857.64
Rent	3750.00	3750.00	3750.00	3750.00	3750.00	3750.00	3750.00	3750.00	3750.00	3750.00	3750.00	3750.00	3750.00	3750.00	3750.00
100 Hours, Own	11011.42	6896.33	5524.64	4838.79	4427.28	4152.94	3956.99	3810.02	3695.71	3604.27	3529.45	3467.10	3414.34	3369.12	3329.93
Own (cash only)	9786.42	6283.83	5116.31	4532.54	4182.28	3948.78	3781.99	3656.90	3559.60	3481.77	3418.08	3365.01	3320.11	3281.62	3248.26
Rent	7500.00	7500.00	7500.00	7500.00	7500.00	7500.00	7500.00	7500.00	7500.00	7500.00	7500.00	7500.00	7500.00	7500.00	7500.00
150 Hours, Own	12402.04	8286.96	6915.26	6229.42	5817.91	5543.57	5347.61	5200.65	5086.34	4994.89	4920.07	4857.72	4804.96	4759.74	4720.55
Own (cash only)	11177.04	7674.46	6506.93	5923.17	5572.91	5339.40	5172.61	5047.52	4950.23	4872.39	4808.71	4755.64	4710.73	4672.24	4638.89
Rent	11250.00	11250.00	11250.00	11250.00	11250.00	11250.00	11250.00	11250.00	11250.00	11250.00	11250.00	11250.00	11250.00	11250.00	11250.00

ASSUMPTIONS:

Hangar/Month:	80.00	Insurance/yr:	1200.00	State Fees/yr:	120.00
Fuel Cons (gal/hr):	9.50	Fuel Cost ($/gal):	2.00	Oil Cons (qt/hr):	0.13
Aircraft Value:	35000.00	Loan O/S:	17500.00	Loan Interest Rate:	10.00%
Engine MOH Cost:	12000.00	Gen Maint Res/hr:	2.50	Com. Rental/hr:	75.00

Annual:	120.00	Maintenance/yr:	1300.00
Oil Cost ($/qt):	2.50	Time Before OH:	2000.00
Loan/Inv Term (yrs):	10	Cost of Capital Rate:	7.00%

FLYING EXPENSES PER PERSON, SINGLE ENGINE FOUR SEAT COMPLEX, 200HP.

NUMBER OF PILOTS	1	2	3	4	5	6	7	8	9	10	11	12	13	14	15
ANNUAL FIXED EXPENSES															
Tiedown/Hangar	960.00	480.00	320.00	240.00	192.00	160.00	137.14	120.00	106.67	96.00	87.27	80.00	73.85	68.57	64.00
Insurance	1,500.00	750.00	500.00	375.00	300.00	250.00	214.29	187.50	166.67	150.00	136.36	125.00	115.38	107.14	100.00
State Fees	120.00	60.00	40.00	30.00	24.00	20.00	17.14	15.00	13.33	12.00	10.91	10.00	9.23	8.57	8.00
Annual	750.00	375.00	250.00	187.50	150.00	125.00	107.14	93.75	83.33	75.00	68.18	62.50	57.69	53.57	50.00
Maintenance	1,500.00	750.00	500.00	375.00	300.00	250.00	214.29	187.50	166.67	150.00	136.36	125.00	115.38	107.14	100.00
Loan Payments	3,568.07	1,784.03	1,189.36	892.02	713.61	594.68	509.72	446.01	396.45	356.81	324.37	297.34	274.47	254.86	237.87
Cost of Capital (non-cash)	1,575.00	787.50	525.00	393.75	315.00	262.50	225.00	196.88	175.00	157.50	143.18	131.25	121.15	112.50	105.00
Total Fixed Expenses / yr	9,973.07	4,986.53	3,324.36	2,493.27	1,994.61	1,662.18	1,424.72	1,246.63	1,108.12	997.31	906.64	831.09	767.16	712.36	664.87
HOURLY OPERATING EXPENSES															
Fuel	21.00	21.00	21.00	21.00	21.00	21.00	21.00	21.00	21.00	21.00	21.00	21.00	21.00	21.00	21.00
Oil	0.63	0.63	0.63	0.63	0.63	0.63	0.63	0.63	0.63	0.63	0.63	0.63	0.63	0.63	0.63
Engine Reserve	7.50	7.50	7.50	7.50	7.50	7.50	7.50	7.50	7.50	7.50	7.50	7.50	7.50	7.50	7.50
General Maint Res	3.00	3.00	3.00	3.00	3.00	3.00	3.00	3.00	3.00	3.00	3.00	3.00	3.00	3.00	3.00
Total Op Exp / hr	32.13	32.13	32.13	32.13	32.13	32.13	32.13	32.13	32.13	32.13	32.13	32.13	32.13	32.13	32.13
TOTAL HOURLY EXPENSES															
50 Hours	231.59	131.86	98.61	81.99	72.02	65.37	60.62	57.06	54.29	52.07	50.26	48.75	47.47	46.37	45.42
100 Hours	131.86	81.99	65.37	57.06	52.07	48.75	46.37	44.59	43.21	42.10	41.19	40.44	39.80	39.25	38.77
150 Hours	98.61	65.37	54.29	48.75	45.42	43.21	41.62	40.44	39.51	38.77	38.17	37.67	37.24	36.87	36.56
Hourly Commercial Rental	95.00	95.00	95.00	95.00	95.00	95.00	95.00	95.00	95.00	95.00	95.00	95.00	95.00	95.00	95.00
TOTAL ANNUAL EXPENSES															
50 Hours, Own	11579.32	6592.78	4930.61	4099.52	3600.86	3268.43	3030.97	2852.88	2714.37	2603.56	2512.89	2437.34	2373.41	2318.61	2271.12
Own (cash only)	10004.32	5805.28	4405.61	3705.77	3285.86	3005.93	2805.97	2656.01	2539.37	2446.06	2369.71	2306.09	2252.26	2206.11	2166.12
Rent	4750.00	4750.00	4750.00	4750.00	4750.00	4750.00	4750.00	4750.00	4750.00	4750.00	4750.00	4750.00	4750.00	4750.00	4750.00
100 Hours, Own	13185.57	8199.03	6536.86	5705.77	5207.11	4874.68	4637.22	4459.13	4320.62	4209.81	4119.14	4043.59	3979.66	3924.86	3877.37
Own (cash only)	11610.57	7411.53	6011.86	5312.02	4892.11	4612.18	4412.22	4262.26	4145.62	4052.31	3975.96	3912.34	3858.51	3812.36	3772.37
Rent	9500.00	9500.00	9500.00	9500.00	9500.00	9500.00	9500.00	9500.00	9500.00	9500.00	9500.00	9500.00	9500.00	9500.00	9500.00
150 Hours, Own	14791.82	9805.28	8143.11	7312.02	6813.36	6480.93	6243.47	6065.38	5926.87	5816.06	5725.39	5649.84	5585.91	5531.11	5483.62
Own (cash only)	13216.82	9017.78	7618.11	6918.27	6498.36	6218.43	6018.47	5868.51	5751.87	5658.56	5582.21	5518.59	5464.76	5418.61	5378.62
Rent	14250.00	14250.00	14250.00	14250.00	14250.00	14250.00	14250.00	14250.00	14250.00	14250.00	14250.00	14250.00	14250.00	14250.00	14250.00

ASSUMPTIONS:

Hangar/Month:	80.00	Insurance/yr:	1500.00	State Fees/yr:	120.00
Fuel Cons (gal/hr):	10.50	Fuel Cost ($/gal):	2.00	Oil Cons (qt/hr):	0.25
Aircraft Value:	45000.00	Loan O/S:	22500.00	Loan Interest Rate:	10.00%
Engine MOH Cost:	15000.00	Gen Maint Res/hr:	3.00	Com. Rental/hr:	95.00

Maintenance/yr:	1500.00	Annual:	750.00
Time Before OH:	2000.00	Oil Cost ($/qt):	0.25
Cost of Capital Rate:	7.00%	Loan/Inv Term (yrs):	10

FLYING EXPENSES PER PERSON, SINGLE ENGINE SIX SEAT COMPLEX, 300HP.

NUMBER OF PILOTS	1	2	3	4	5	6	7	8	9	10	11	12	13	14	15
ANNUAL FIXED EXPENSES															
Tiedown/Hangar	960.00	480.00	320.00	240.00	192.00	160.00	137.14	120.00	106.67	96.00	87.27	80.00	73.85	68.57	64.00
Insurance	3,000.00	1,500.00	1,000.00	750.00	600.00	500.00	428.57	375.00	333.33	300.00	272.73	250.00	230.77	214.29	200.00
State Fees	120.00	60.00	40.00	30.00	24.00	20.00	17.14	15.00	13.33	12.00	10.91	10.00	9.23	8.57	8.00
Annual	1,000.00	500.00	333.33	250.00	200.00	166.67	142.86	125.00	111.11	100.00	90.91	83.33	76.92	71.43	66.67
Maintenance	3,000.00	1,500.00	1,000.00	750.00	600.00	500.00	428.57	375.00	333.33	300.00	272.73	250.00	230.77	214.29	200.00
Loan Payments	11,893.57	5,946.78	3,964.52	2,973.39	2,378.71	1,982.26	1,699.08	1,486.70	1,321.51	1,189.36	1,081.23	991.13	914.89	849.54	792.90
Cost of Capital (non-cash)	5,250.00	2,625.00	1,750.00	1,312.50	1,050.00	875.00	750.00	656.25	583.33	525.00	477.27	437.50	403.85	375.00	350.00
Total Fixed Expenses / yr	25,223.57	12,611.78	8,407.86	6,305.89	5,044.71	4,203.93	3,603.37	3,152.95	2,802.62	2,522.36	2,293.05	2,101.96	1,940.27	1,801.68	1,681.57
HOURLY OPERATING EXPENSES															
Fuel	30.00	30.00	30.00	30.00	30.00	30.00	30.00	30.00	30.00	30.00	30.00	30.00	30.00	30.00	30.00
Oil	0.63	0.63	0.63	0.63	0.63	0.63	0.63	0.63	0.63	0.63	0.63	0.63	0.63	0.63	0.63
Engine Reserve	13.13	13.13	13.13	13.13	13.13	13.13	13.13	13.13	13.13	13.13	13.13	13.13	13.13	13.13	13.13
General Maint Res	6.00	6.00	6.00	6.00	6.00	6.00	6.00	6.00	6.00	6.00	6.00	6.00	6.00	6.00	6.00
Total Op Exp / hr	49.75	49.75	49.75	49.75	49.75	49.75	49.75	49.75	49.75	49.75	49.75	49.75	49.75	49.75	49.75
TOTAL HOURLY EXPENSES															
50 Hours	554.22	301.99	217.91	175.87	150.64	133.83	121.82	112.81	105.80	100.20	95.61	91.79	88.56	85.78	83.38
100 Hours	301.99	175.87	133.83	112.81	100.20	91.79	85.78	81.28	77.78	74.97	72.68	70.77	69.15	67.77	66.57
150 Hours	217.91	133.83	105.80	91.79	83.38	77.78	73.77	70.77	68.43	66.57	65.04	63.76	62.69	61.76	60.96
Hourly Commercial Rental	145.00	145.00	145.00	145.00	145.00	145.00	145.00	145.00	145.00	145.00	145.00	145.00	145.00	145.00	145.00
TOTAL ANNUAL EXPENSES															
50 Hours, Own	27711.07	15099.28	10895.36	8793.39	7532.21	6691.43	6090.87	5640.45	5290.12	5009.86	4780.55	4589.46	4427.77	4289.18	4169.07
Own (cash only)	22461.07	12474.28	9145.36	7480.89	6482.21	5816.43	5340.87	4984.20	4706.79	4484.86	4303.28	4151.96	4023.93	3914.18	3819.07
Rent	7250.00	7250.00	7250.00	7250.00	7250.00	7250.00	7250.00	7250.00	7250.00	7250.00	7250.00	7250.00	7250.00	7250.00	7250.00
100 Hours, Own	30198.57	17586.78	13382.86	11280.89	10019.71	9178.93	8578.37	8127.95	7777.62	7497.36	7268.05	7076.96	6915.27	6776.68	6656.57
Own (cash only)	24948.57	14961.78	11632.86	9968.39	8969.71	8303.93	7828.37	7471.70	7194.29	6972.36	6790.78	6639.46	6511.43	6401.68	6306.57
Rent	14500.00	14500.00	14500.00	14500.00	14500.00	14500.00	14500.00	14500.00	14500.00	14500.00	14500.00	14500.00	14500.00	14500.00	14500.00
150 Hours, Own	32686.07	20074.28	15870.36	13768.39	12507.21	11666.43	11065.87	10615.45	10265.12	9984.86	9755.55	9564.46	9402.77	9264.18	9144.07
Own (cash only)	27436.07	17449.28	14120.36	12455.89	11457.21	10791.43	10315.87	9959.20	9681.79	9459.85	9278.28	9126.96	8998.93	8889.18	8794.07
Rent	21750.00	21750.00	21750.00	21750.00	21750.00	21750.00	21750.00	21750.00	21750.00	21750.00	21750.00	21750.00	21750.00	21750.00	21750.00

ASSUMPTIONS:

Hangar/Month:	80.00	State Fees/yr:	120.00
Fuel Cons (gal/hr):	15.00	Oil Cons (qt/hr):	0.25
Aircraft Value:	150000.00	Loan Interest Rate:	10.00%
Engine MOH Cost:	21000.00	Com. Rental/hr:	145.00
Insurance/yr:	3000.00	Annual:	1000.00
Fuel Cost ($/gal):	2.00	Oil Cost ($/qt):	2.50
Loan O/S:	75000.00	Loan/Inv Term (yrs):	10
Gen Maint Res/hr:	6.00	Maintenance/yr:	3000.00
		Time Before OH:	1600.00
		Cost of Capital Rate:	7.00%

FLYING EXPENSES PER PERSON, FOUR SEAT LATE MODEL LIGHT TWIN.

NUMBER OF PILOTS	1	2	3	4	5	6	7	8	9	10	11	12	13	14	15
ANNUAL FIXED EXPENSES															
Tiedown/Hangar	960.00	480.00	320.00	240.00	192.00	160.00	137.14	120.00	106.67	96.00	87.27	80.00	73.85	68.57	64.00
Insurance	2,250.00	1,125.00	750.00	562.50	450.00	375.00	321.43	281.25	250.00	225.00	204.55	187.50	173.08	160.71	150.00
State Fees	120.00	60.00	40.00	30.00	24.00	20.00	17.14	15.00	13.33	12.00	10.91	10.00	9.23	8.57	8.00
Annual	1,000.00	500.00	333.33	250.00	200.00	166.67	142.86	125.00	111.11	100.00	90.91	83.33	76.92	71.43	66.67
Maintenance	2,500.00	1,250.00	833.33	625.00	500.00	416.67	357.14	312.50	277.78	250.00	227.27	208.33	192.31	178.57	166.67
Loan Payments	515.39	257.69	171.80	128.85	103.08	85.90	73.63	64.42	57.27	51.54	46.85	42.95	39.65	36.81	34.36
Cost of Capital (non-cash)	4,322.50	2,161.25	1,440.83	1,080.63	864.50	720.42	617.50	540.31	480.28	432.25	392.95	360.21	332.50	308.75	288.17
Total Fixed Expenses / yr	11,667.89	5,833.94	3,889.30	2,916.97	2,333.58	1,944.65	1,666.84	1,458.49	1,296.43	1,166.79	1,060.72	972.32	897.53	833.42	777.86
HOURLY OPERATING EXPENSES															
Fuel	40.00	40.00	40.00	40.00	40.00	40.00	40.00	40.00	40.00	40.00	40.00	40.00	40.00	40.00	40.00
Oil	0.83	0.83	0.83	0.83	0.83	0.83	0.83	0.83	0.83	0.83	0.83	0.83	0.83	0.83	0.83
Engine Reserve	12.50	12.50	12.50	12.50	12.50	12.50	12.50	12.50	12.50	12.50	12.50	12.50	12.50	12.50	12.50
General Maint Res	2.00	2.00	2.00	2.00	2.00	2.00	2.00	2.00	2.00	2.00	2.00	2.00	2.00	2.00	2.00
Total Op Exp / hr	55.33	55.33	55.33	55.33	55.33	55.33	55.33	55.33	55.33	55.33	55.33	55.33	55.33	55.33	55.33
TOTAL HOURLY EXPENSES															
50 Hours	288.69	172.01	133.67	113.67	102.00	94.23	88.67	84.50	81.26	78.67	76.55	74.78	73.28	72.00	70.89
100 Hours	172.01	113.67	94.23	84.50	78.67	74.78	72.00	69.92	68.30	67.00	65.94	65.06	64.31	63.67	63.11
150 Hours	133.12	94.23	81.26	74.78	70.89	68.30	66.45	65.06	63.98	63.11	62.40	61.82	61.32	60.89	60.52
Hourly Commercial Rental	120.00	120.00	120.00	120.00	120.00	120.00	120.00	120.00	120.00	120.00	120.00	120.00	120.00	120.00	120.00
TOTAL ANNUAL EXPENSES															
50 Hours, Own	14434.55	8600.61	6655.96	5683.64	5100.24	4711.31	4433.51	4225.15	4063.10	3933.46	3827.38	3738.99	3664.20	3600.09	3544.53
Own (cash only)	10112.05	6439.36	5215.13	4603.01	4235.74	3990.90	3816.01	3684.84	3582.82	3501.21	3434.43	3378.78	3331.70	3291.34	3256.36
Rent	6000.00	6000.00	6000.00	6000.00	6000.00	6000.00	6000.00	6000.00	6000.00	6000.00	6000.00	6000.00	6000.00	6000.00	6000.00
100 Hours, Own	17201.22	11367.28	9422.63	8450.31	7866.91	7477.98	7200.17	6991.82	6829.77	6700.12	6594.05	6505.66	6430.86	6366.75	6311.19
Own (cash only)	12878.72	9206.03	7981.80	7369.68	7002.41	6757.56	6582.67	6451.51	6349.49	6267.87	6201.10	6145.45	6098.36	6058.00	6023.03
Rent	12000.00	12000.00	12000.00	12000.00	12000.00	12000.00	12000.00	12000.00	12000.00	12000.00	12000.00	12000.00	12000.00	12000.00	12000.00
150 Hours, Own	19967.89	14133.94	12189.30	11216.97	10633.58	10244.65	9966.84	9758.49	9596.43	9466.79	9360.72	9272.32	9197.53	9133.42	9077.86
Own (cash only)	15645.39	11972.69	10748.46	10136.35	9769.08	9524.23	9349.34	9218.17	9116.15	9034.54	8967.76	8912.12	8865.03	8824.67	8789.69
Rent	18000.00	18000.00	18000.00	18000.00	18000.00	18000.00	18000.00	18000.00	18000.00	18000.00	18000.00	18000.00	18000.00	18000.00	18000.00

ASSUMPTIONS:

Hangar/Month: 80.00	Insurance/yr: 2250.00	State Fees/yr: 120.00	Annual: 1000.00	Maintenance/yr: 2500.00
Fuel Cons (gal/hr): 20.00	Fuel Cost ($/gal): 2.00	Oil Cons (qt/hr): 0.33	Oil Cost ($/qt): 2.50	Time Before OH: 2.50
Aircraft Value: 65000.00	Loan O/S: 3250.00	Loan Interest Rate: 10.00%	Loan/Inv Term (yrs): 10	Cost of Capital Rate: 7.00%
Engine MOH Cost: 25000.00	Gen Maint Res/hr: 2.00	Com. Rental/hr: 120.00		

Fig. A-4. Aircraft and partnership financial analysis spreadsheet formula template. (Microsoft EXCEL)

Columns H through P on page 234.

	A	B	C	D	E	F	G
3		1	2	3	4	5	6
4	NUMBER OF PILOTS						
5							
6	ANNUAL FIXED EXP						
7	Tiedown/Hangar	=D49*12	=B7/2	=B7/3	=B7/4	=B7/5	=B7/6
8	Insurance	=G49	=B8/2	=B8/3	=B8/4	=B8/5	=B8/6
9	State Fees	=J49	=B9/2	=B9/3	=B9/4	=B9/5	=B9/6
10	Annual	=M49	=B10/2	=B10/3	=B10/4	=B10/5	=B10/6
11	Maintenance	=P49	=B11/2	=B11/3	=B11/4	=B11/5	=B11/6
12	Loan Payments	=PMT(J53/12,M53*12,-G53)*12	=B12/2	=B12/3	=B12/4	=B12/5	=B12/6
13							
14	Cost of Capital (non-cash)	=(D53-G53)*P53	=B14/2	=B14/3	=B14/4	=B14/5	=B14/6
15							
16	Total Fixed Exp / yr	=SUM(B7:B14)	=SUM(C7:C14)	=SUM(D7:D14)	=SUM(E7:E14)	=SUM(F7:F14)	=SUM(G7:G14)
17							
18	HOURLY OP EXP						
19	Fuel	=G51*D51	=B19	=C19	=D19	=E19	=F19
20	Oil	=J51*M51	=B20	=C20	=D20	=E20	=F20
21	Engine Reserve	=D55/P51	=B21	=C21	=D21	=E21	=F21
22	General Maint Res	=G55	=B22	=C22	=D22	=E22	=F22
23							
24	Total Op Exp / hr	=SUM(B19:B22)	=SUM(C19:C22)	=SUM(D19:D22)	=SUM(E19:E22)	=SUM(F19:F22)	=SUM(G19:G22)
25							
26	TOTAL HOURLY EXP						
27	50 Hours	=B16/50+B24	=C16/50+C24	=D16/50+D24	=E16/50+E24	=F16/50+F24	=G16/50+G24
28	100 Hours	=B16/100+B24	=C16/100+C24	=D16/100+D24	=E16/100+E24	=F16/100+F24	=G16/100+G24
29	150 Hours	=B16/150+B24	=C16/150+C24	=D16/150+D24	=E16/150+E24	=F16/150+F24	=G16/150+G24
30							
31	Hourly Comml Rental	=J55	=J55	=J55	=J55	=J55	=J55
32							
33	TOTAL ANNUAL EXP						
34	50 Hours, Own	=B27*50	=C27*50	=D27*50	=E27*50	=F27*50	=G27*50
35	Own (cash only)	=B34-B14	=C34-C14	=D34-D14	=E34-E14	=F34-F14	=G34-G14
36	Rent	=B31*50	=C31*50	=D31*50	=E31*50	=F31*50	=G31*50
37							
38	100 Hours, Own	=B28*100	=C28*100	=D28*100	=E28*100	=F28*100	=G28*100
39	Own (cash only)	=B38-B14	=C38-C14	=D38-D14	=E38-E14	=F38-F14	=G38-G14
40	Rent	=B31*100	=C31*100	=D31*100	=E31*100	=F31*100	=G31*100
42							
43	150 Hours, Own	=B29*150	=C29*150	=D29*150	=E29*150	=F29*150	=G29*150
44	Own (cash only)	=B43-B14	=C43-C14	=D43-D14	=E43-E14	=F43-F14	=G43-G14
45	Rent	=B31*150	=C31*150	=D31*150	=E31*150	=F31*150	=G31*150
49	ASSUMPTIONS:	Hangar/Month:	75		Insurance/yr:		1500
51		Fuel Cons (gal/hr):	10		Fuel Cost ($/gal):		2
53		Aircraft Value:	45000		Loan O/S:		20000
55		Engine MOH Cost:	10000		Gen Maint Res/hr:		2

	H	I	J	K	L	M	N	O	P
4	7	8	9	10	11	12	13	14	15
7	=B7/7	=B7/8	=B7/9	=B7/10	=B7/11	=B7/12	=B7/13	=B7/14	=B7/15
8	=B8/7	=B8/8	=B8/9	=B8/10	=B8/11	=B8/12	=B8/13	=B8/14	=B8/15
9	=B9/7	=B9/8	=B9/9	=B9/10	=B9/11	=B9/12	=B9/13	=B9/14	=B9/15
10	=B10/7	=B10/8	=B10/9	=B10/10	=B10/11	=B10/12	=B10/13	=B10/14	=B10/15
11	=B11/7	=B11/8	=B11/9	=B11/10	=B11/11	=B11/12	=B11/13	=B11/14	=B11/15
12	=B12/7	=B12/8	=B12/9	=B12/10	=B12/11	=B12/12	=B12/13	=B12/14	=B12/15
14	=B14/7	=B14/8	=B14/9	=B14/10	=B14/11	=B14/12	=B14/13	=B14/14	=B14/15
16	=SUM(H7:H14)	=SUM(I7:I14)	=SUM(J7:J14)	=SUM(K7:K14)	=SUM(L7:L14)	=SUM(M7:M14)	=SUM(N7:N14)	=SUM(O7:O14)	=SUM(P7:P14)
19	=G19	=H19	=I19	=J19	=K19	=L19	=M19	=N19	=O19
20	=G20	=H20	=I20	=J20	=K20	=L20	=M20	=N20	=O20
21	=G21	=H21	=I21	=J21	=K21	=L21	=M21	=N21	=O21
22	=G22	=H22	=I22	=J22	=K22	=L22	=M22	=N22	=O22
24	=SUM(H19:H22)	=SUM(I19:I22)	=SUM(J19:J22)	=SUM(K19:K22)	=SUM(L19:L22)	=SUM(M19:M22)	=SUM(N19:N22)	=SUM(O19:O22)	=SUM(P19:P22)
27	=H16/50+H24	=I16/50+I24	=J16/50+J24	=K16/50+K24	=L16/50+L24	=M16/50+M24	=N16/50+N24	=O16/50+O24	=P16/50+P24
28	=H16/100+H24	=I16/100+I24	=J16/100+J24	=K16/100+K24	=L16/100+L24	=M16/100+M24	=N16/100+N24	=O16/100+O24	=P16/100+P24
29	=H16/150+H24	=I16/150+I24	=J16/150+J24	=K16/150+K24	=L16/150+L24	=M16/150+M24	=N16/150+N24	=O16/150+O24	=P16/150+P24
31	=J55	=J55	=J55	=J55	=J55	=J55	=J55	=J55	=J55
34	=H27*50	=I27*50	=J27*50	=K27*50	=L27*50	=M27*50	=N27*50	=O27*50	=P27*50
35	=H34-H14	=I34-I14	=J34-J14	=K34-K14	=L34-L14	=M34-M14	=N34-N14	=O34-O14	=P34-P14
36	=H31*50	=I31*50	=J31*50	=K31*50	=L31*50	=M31*50	=N31*50	=O31*50	=P31*50
38	=H28*100	=I28*100	=J28*100	=K28*100	=L28*100	=M28*100	=N28*100	=O28*100	=P28*100
39	=H38-H14	=I38-I14	=J38-J14	=K38-K14	=L38-L14	=M38-M14	=N38-N14	=O38-O14	=P38-P14
40	=H31*100	=I31*100	=J31*100	=K31*100	=L31*100	=M31*100	=N31*100	=O31*100	=P31*100
43	=H29*150	=I29*150	=J29*150	=K29*150	=L29*150	=M29*150	=N29*150	=O29*150	=P29*150
44	=H43-H14	=I43-I14	=J43-J14	=K43-K14	=L43-L14	=M43-M14	=N43-N14	=O43-O14	=P43-P14
45	=H31*150	=I31*150	=J31*150	=K31*150	=L31*150	=M31*150	=N31*150	=O31*150	=P31*150

State Fees/yr:	120	Annual:		750	Maintenance/yr:		1000
Oil Cons (qt/hr):	0.25	Oil Cost ($/qt):		2.5	Time Before OH:		2000
Loan Interest Rate:	0.12	Loan/Inv Term (yrs):		10	Cost of Capital Rate:		0.07
Com. Rental/hr:	90						

Fig. A-5. Flying club financial analysis worksheet.

FLYING CLUB FINANCIAL ANALYSIS WORKSHEET ($)

(To obtain a surplus of income over expenses, set annual fees and dues and hourly aircraft rental to exceed corresponding expenses by the desired percentage.)

EXPENSES	TOTAL	AIRCRAFT #1 Type Hrs/Yr	AIRCRAFT #2 Type Hrs/Yr	AIRCRAFT #3 Type Hrs/Yr	AIRCRAFT #4 Type Hrs/Yr	AIRCRAFT #5 Type Hrs/Yr

ANNUAL FIXED EXPENSES

AIRCRAFT RELATED
Tiedown/Hangar
Insurance, Aircraft
Fees and Taxes
100 Hour and Annual Inspections
Maintenance
Loan Payments
Depreciation

GENERAL EXPENSES
Insurance, Club
Office rent
Accountant's Fee
Manager's Salary
Mechanic's Salary
Supplies/Administrative
Other

Total Fixed Expenses/yr

HOURLY OPERATING EXPENSES

Fuel
Oil
Engine Reserve
General Maint Res

Total Op Exp/hr

Total Op Exp/yr (op exp per hr*hrs per yr)

TOTAL ANNUAL EXPENSES
(total fixed exp per yr + total op exp per yr)

INCOME (Set fees and dues to equal or exceed total fixed expenses, set hourly aircraft rental income to equal or exceed hourly aircraft op expenses)

FIXED: Annual Fees and Dues
OPERATING: Annual Aircraft Rental Income
(hourly aircraft rental*hrs flown)

TOTAL ANNUAL INCOME

SURPLUS/DEFICIT (to general reserve)

NUMBER OF MEMBERS (enter)

ANNUAL FEES AND DUES PER MEMBER PER YEAR:

Fig. A-6. Flying club financial analysis spreadsheet layout.

FLYING CLUB FINANCIAL ANALYSIS, FIVE AIRPLANE CLUB ($)

	TOTAL	AIRCRAFT #1		AIRCRAFT #2		AIRCRAFT #3		AIRCRAFT #4		AIRCRAFT #5	
EXPENSES		Type	C-150	Type	C-150	Type	C-150	Type	C-172	Type	PA28-201
		Hrs/Yr	500	Hrs/Yr	500	Hrs/Yr	500	Hrs/Yr	350	Hrs/Yr	300
ANNUAL FIXED EXPENSES											
AIRCRAFT RELATED											
Tiedown/Hangar	4,500		900		900		900		900		900
Insurance, Aircraft	7,400		1,300		1,300		1,300		1,500		2,000
Fees and Taxes	600		120		120		120		120		120
100 Hour and Annual Inspections	7,050		1,350		1,350		1,350		1,500		1,500
Maintenance	0		0		0		0		0		0
Loan Payments	5,788		0		0		0		2,220		3,568
Depreciation	7,000		1,000		1,000		1,000		1,500		2,500
GENERAL EXPENSES											
Insurance, Club	1,000										
Office rent	1,200										
Accountant's Fee	500										
Manager's Salary	5,200										
Mechanic's Salary	4,160										
Supplies/Administrative	500										
Other	1,000										
Total Fixed Expenses/yr	45,898		4,670		4,670		4,670		7,740		10,588
HOURLY OPERATING EXPENSES											
Fuel	70		12		12		12		14		20
Oil	5		1		1		1		1		1
Engine Reserve	25		4		4		4		5		8
General Maint Res	14		2		2		2		3		5
Total Op Exp/hr	114		19		19		19		23		34
Total Op Exp/yr	46,750		9,500		9,500		9,500		8,050		10,200
TOTAL ANNUAL EXPENSES	92,648		14,208		14,208		14,208		15,836		20,856
INCOME											
FIXED: Annual Fees and Dues	52,783										
OPERATING: Annual Aircraft Rental Income	53,763		10,925		10,925		10,925		9,258		11,730
								NUMBER OF MEMBERS (enter)		75	
TOTAL ANNUAL INCOME	106,545										
SURPLUS/DEFICIT (to general reserve)	13,897						ANNUAL FEES AND DUES PER MEMBER PER YEAR:				704

Fig. A-7. Flying club financial analysis spreadsheet formula template. (Microsoft EXCEL)

	A	D	F	H	J	L	N	O
4	EXPENSES	TOTAL	AIRCRAFT #1	AIRCRAFT #2	AIRCRAFT #3	AIRCRAFT #4	AIRCRAFT #5	
5								
6	ANNUAL FIXED EXPENSES							
7	AIRCRAFT RELATED							
8	Tiedown/Hangar	=SUM(F8:N8)						
9	Insurance, Aircraft	=SUM(F9:N9)						
10	Fees and Taxes	=SUM(F10:N10)						
11	100 Hour and Annual Inspections	=SUM(F11:N11)						
12	Maintenance	=SUM(F12:N12)						
13	Loan Payments	=SUM(F13:N13)						
14	Depreciation	=SUM(F14:N14)						
15								
16	GENERAL EXPENSES							
17	Insurance, Club							
18	Office rent							
19	Accountant's Fee							
20	Manager's Salary							
21	Mechanic's Salary							
22	Supplies/Administrative							
23	Other							
24								
25	Total Fixed Expenses/yr	=SUM(D8:D24)	=SUM(F8:F24)	=SUM(H8:H24)	=SUM(J8:J24)	=SUM(L8:L24)	=SUM(N8:N24)	
26								
27	HOURLY OPERATING EXPENSES							
28	Fuel		=SUM(F28:N28)					
29	Oil		=SUM(F29:N29)					
30	Engine Reserve		=SUM(F30:N30)					
31	General Maint Res		=SUM(F31:N31)					
32								
33	Total Op Exp/hr	=SUM(D28:D31)	=SUM(F28:F31)	=SUM(H28:H31)	=SUM(J28:J31)	=SUM(L28:L31)	=SUM(N28:N31)	
34								
35	Total Op Exp/yr	=SUM(F35:N35)	=F33*F6	=H33*H6	=J33*J6	=L33*L6	=N33*N6	
36								
37	TOTAL ANNUAL EXPENSES	=D25+D35	=SUM(F25:F35)	=SUM(H25:H35)	=SUM(J25:J35)	=SUM(L25:L35)	=SUM(N25:N35)	
38								
39	INCOME							
40	FIXED: Annual Fees and Dues	=D25+D25*0.15						
41	OPERATING: Annual Aircraft Rental Income	=SUM(F41:N41)	=F35+(F35*0.15)	=H35+(H35*0.15)	=J35+(J35*0.15)	=L35+(L35*0.15)	=N35+(N35*0.15)	
45	TOTAL ANNUAL INCOME	=SUM(D40:D41)						
47	SURPLUS/DEFICIT (to general reserve)	=D45-D37					=D40/N45	

B

Agreements
and administration

Fig. B-1. Simple partnership agreement, three partners. (Continues through page 242.)

Appendix 2.1: Simple Partnership Agreement, Three Partners

AIRCRAFT PARTNERSHIP AGREEMENT

Introduction

The following agreement, entered into by Timothy F. Smith, Fran D. Serge, and Donald Wooly, hereinafter referred to as "the partners", applies to the conduct of their partnership in experimental aircraft model Concept-70, serial number 8, FAA registration number N8BM, hereinafter referred to as the "aircraft".

1. Ownership.

The three partners agree that they own three equal shares of the aircraft, and related accessory equipment. (Exhibit A)

2. Decisions.

All decisions including decisions to operate away from home base shall be unanimous except as follows:

2.1 Decisions pertaining to the operation of the aircraft as pilot in command including pre- and post-flight activities may be made without the consent of the other partners.

3. Legality of Operations.

Each partner is individually responsible, when pilot in command, to insure that the operation of the aircraft and related auxiliary activities by the partner and by obtained help are within legal and insurance limits.

4. Persons authorized to fly.

No one except the herein mentioned partners may be permitted to fly the aircraft, except for test flights by a person who has the appropriate insurance clearance and is unanimously acceptable to all the partners.

5. Loan Payments.

5.1 The partners agree to share the loan payments under the bank agreement (Exhibit B) in three equal parts.

5.2 The partners agree to make all payments by the due date.

5.3 Each partner is individually responsible for charges incurred by his failure to make payments on time.

5.4 In the event of individual default resulting in foreclosure, the defaulting partner(s) agrees to reimburse the other partner(s) for all their losses incurred by the foreclosure relative to the original purchase price plus improvements.

6. Expenses.

6.1 All expenses will be shared equally by the three partners.

6.2 In relation to new equipment purchases, said purchases shall not be considered an expense if unanimous agreement to make the purchase is lacking. However, if a partner individually decides to purchase a piece of new equipment, he may install it upon unanimous approval, and retains sole rights to it.

7. Insurance.

7.1 Insurance deductibles are to be paid by the pilot in command if the incident/accident is a result of his or her negligence. if individual negligence is undeterminable, the deductible will be shared equally by the partners.

7.2 Insurance receivables in case of incident/accident are to be divided equally among the partners or their inheritors, except for 7.1.

8. Rights of Related Parties.

Parties related to the partners possess no rights whatsoever except as follows:

8.1 In case of a partner's death, his inheritors shall be obligated to promptly dispose of his share with the remaining partners having first right of refusal under the terms of the original purchase price plus improvements.

9. Collateralization Exclusion.

The partners agree not to put up the said aircraft as any form of collateral whatsoever, jointly and severally, except as collateral under the terms of Exhibit B.

10. Departure of Partner(s) from Partnership.

10.1 In event of a partner's departure from the partnership, the remaining partner(s) have the first right of refusal for a 45-day period at the original purchase price plus improvements.

10.2 If a partner departs from the partnership and the remaining partners exercise their option under 10.1, the departed partner is to receive a one-third share of any gains on the subsequent sale of the aircraft by the other two partners at any time during the first 24 months after the original purchase of the aircraft.

10.3 If a partner departs from the partnership and the remaining partners do not exercise their option under 10.1, the departing partner may sell his share to a third party for any gain, provided that the third party undertakes to unconditionally abide by this agreement.

11. Amendments.

This agreement may be amended at any time upon unanimous agreement of the partners. The partners are obligated to review the agreement 24 calendar months after its existence.

Dated this _____ day of _____ , 1992.

Witness:_____

_____
Timothy F. Smith

_____
Fran D. Worsted

_____
Donald Wooley

EXHIBIT A

EXPERIMENTAL AIRCRAFT MODEL "CONCEPT 70", SERIAL NUMBER 8,
N-NUMBER N8BM, EQUIPMENT LIST

The above aircraft is complete with the following instruments:

o Altimeter

o Airspeed Indicator

o Moore Variometer with audio

o PZL Rate of Climb

o 12-hour panel mounted stop watch clock

o Mentor Radio

o G Meter

o Turn and Bank Indicator

o Compass and Batteries

o Clamp-on Swivel tail wheel for ground handling

o Gear Warning buzzer with test button

o Water Ballast plumbing

o Oxygen control unit mounted in panel, oxygen bottle not mounted

o One extra pair of wing pins

o The trailer includes all the extra dolleys and stands for holding the aircraft in the trailer and also included are two wing stands and electric brake.

The price of the above combination of trailer instruments and aircraft is $11,500.

AIRCRAFT PARTNERSHIP AGREEMENT

This document memorializes an agreement between:

HARRIS G. STURGEON
of 69 Elm Lane, Lincoln, Maine

and

GEORGE H. SALMON
of 179 Frog Pond Road, Wilcox, Maine

(referred to hereafter as the Partners).

1. General.

The Partners own a 1978 Piper Cherokee, Archer aircraft, Model PA 28-181, Serial Number 28-6947032, registered as N4968X (referred to as the "Aircraft"). Each Partner owns an undivided fifty percent (50%) interest in the aircraft, and each Partner is responsible for fifty percent (50%) of the expenses associated with the aircraft.

2. Concerning Certain Financing Obligations.

The Partners agree and acknowledge that Mr.Salmon's interest in the aircraft has been financed by Mr. Sturgeon pursuant to the terms of a note attached to this agreement as Exhibit A. The current principal balance (excluding accrued interest) due on such note is $10,000. Mr. Sturgeon agrees that upon receipt of all future principal payments by Mr. Salmon, he will execute an appropriate payments chart appendix modification to this document to reflect the principal payments by Mr. Salmon. Mr. Salmon acknowledges that his rights in the aircraft and in the aircraft partnership are subordinate to the terms of that note and that in the event of loss of the aircraft, death of a partner or dissolution of this partnership, the note (together with all accrued interest and principal) shall first be paid before he receives any insurance or sale proceeds. Further, Mr. Salmon acknowledges that in the event of any uninsured loss or damage to the aircraft, such uninsured loss or damage shall not serve to reduce or extinguish the note, which will remain as an independent financial obligation.

3. Concerning Use of the Aircraft.

Each Partner shall have full use and benefit of the aircraft upon a schedule to be mutually agreed. Neither Partner will use (or permit the use of) the aircraft under conditions which could have the effect of voiding the hull or liability insurance on the aircraft.

4. Concerning Expenses of the Aircraft.

With the exception of fuel expenses, all expenses arising from the ownership or operation of the aircraft, including but not limited to tiedown or hangar charges, insurance charges, property taxes, oil or other expendables, inspections, maintenance and overhauls, shall be borne equally by the Partners. The Partners agree to maintain a careful record for payment of the aircraft expenses and to meet, review and reconcile all aircraft expenditures at least every six months. Neither partner may unilaterally commit the partnership to any expenditure in excess of $50.00.

5. Concerning Loss or Damage to the Aircraft.

In the event of damage to the aircraft for any reason, the Partner using the aircraft at the time the damage is incurred will be responsible for payment of the uninsured portion or deductible of the claim. If the aircraft is damaged under circumstances where it was not in use by one of the Partners, then the uninsured or deductible portion of the claim shall be borne equally.

6. Annual Statement of Value.

The Partners agree that as of the date of this agreement, the aircraft's fair market value is $44,000. The Partners agree that they shall prepare an addendum to this agreement signed by each of them stating the fair market value of the aircraft (to be defined according to a mutually acceptable method) every six months commencing from the date of this agreement in form attached as Exhibit B.

7. Concerning Death or Disability of a Partner.

In the event of the death or disability of a Partner, the remaining Partner may purchase the other Partner' s interest for fifty percent (50%) of the most recent agreed-upon fair market value pursuant to paragraph 6 and exhibit B. Such purchase, however, shall be subject to the provisions of paragraph 2 above and the promissory note attached as exhibit A.

8. Termination of the Partnership.

This partnership may be terminated by written notice given to each of the partners at the address indicated above. Such notice shall also state whether the Partner electing to terminate desires to buy the aircraft outright or sell his interest to the remaining Partner. The Partner receiving such notice shall then inform the other Partner as to his desires to buy or sell the aircraft. In this situation, the following rules will apply:

a. If both Partners desire to self the aircraft, it shall be sold to a third party and the proceeds divided equably (following a final accounting between the Partners).

b. If one Partner desires to sell and one Partner desires to buy, the purchase price shall be fifty percent (50%) of the most recent agreed upon fair market vague pursuant to paragraph 6 above and Exhibit B.

c. If one Partner desires to sell and the other Partner desires to maintain ownership through a new partnership with a third party, the Partner desiring to sell will give the other Partner 60 days to find a new partner.

d. If both Partners desire to buy the aircraft, then both Partners shall submit simultaneously to an independent umpire a sealed bid representing the highest figure that he will pay to purchase the other Partner's interest in the aircraft. The independent umpire will review both figures, determine which Partner has offered the higher figure, and the aircraft shall be sold to the Partner making the higher offer at the amount of that offer.

Any purchase or sale under this paragraph is subject to the provisions of paragraph 2 and the promissory note attached as Exhibit A.

9. Arbitration.

In the event that any dispute should arise concerning the partnership or the construction of this partnership agreement, such dispute shall be submitted to arbitration in accordance with the rules of the American Arbitration Association. The location of such arbitration shall be Lincoln, Maine, and the costs of such arbitration proceeding shall be born equally by the parties.

Dated this _____ day of _____ , 1992.

_____
Harris G, Sturgeon

Witness:_____

_____
George H. Salmon

Fig. B-3. Simple partnership accounts worksheet. (Continues on page 247.)

N1786L PARTNERSHIP FINANCIAL STATEMENT 1990

HOURLY RATE ☐

BEGINNING BALANCE ☐

CURRENT BALANCE ☐

INCOME

Date	Amount	Description	Chk#

Date	Amount	Description	Chk#

EXPENSE

Date	Amount	Payee	Chk#

FINANCIAL SUMMARY 1990

	SZUROVY	SCHUETTE	HOWARD	TOTAL
HOURS				
CASH EXPENSES ($)				
COST OF CAPITAL ($)				
$ PER HOUR				

ENGINE AND AIRFRAME RESERVE

BEGINNING HOURS

ENDING HOURS

BEGINNING E & A RESERVE ($)

ADDITIONAL E& A RESERVE ($)

ASSESSMENTS

ENDING E & A RESERVE ($)

Fig. B-4. Detailed partnership accounting worksheet. (Continues on page 249.)

N1786L PARTNERSHIP FINANCIAL STATEMENT 1990

HOURLY RATE

BEGINNING BALANCE

CURRENT BALANCE

INCOME

Date	Hrs	Op Inc	Oth Inc	Description	Chk#
		57.60			

Date	Hrs	Op Inc	Oth Inc	Description	Chk#

Date	Hrs	Op Inc	Oth Inc	Description	Chk#

N1786L PARTNERSHIP FINANCIAL STATEMENT 1990

Account Types: Hangar, Insurance, Fees, Annual Maintenance, Op/Res, Other

EXPENSE

Date	Amount	Payee	Chk#	Account

FINANCIAL SUMMARY 1990 ($)

	TOTAL
FLIGHT HOURS	
HANGAR	
INSURANCE	
FEES	
ANNUAL	
MAINTENANCE	
OP/RES	
OTHER	
TOTAL CASH	
COST OF CAPITAL	
TOTAL EXPENSES	
$/HOUR	

ENGINE AND AIRFRAME RESERVE

BEGINNING HOURS	
ENDING HOURS	
BEGINNING E & A RESERVE ($)	
ADDITIONAL E & A RESERVE ($)	
ASSESSMENTS	
ENDING E & A RESERVE ($)	

Fig. B-5. Flying club articles of incorporation. (AOPA)

SAMPLE ARTICLES OF INCORPORATION, FLYING CLUB

1. The name of this corporation is the _____ Flying Club, hereinafter referred to as the "Club."

2. The purposes for which this Club is formed are:

   a. To own or lease and maintain one or more aircraft for the education, transportation, and general use of the members of the Club or their families or such individuals as the Board of Directors may designate pursuant to any bylaws which may hereafter be adopted.

   b. To acquire, own, hold, sell, lease, pledge, mortgage or otherwise dispose of any property, real or personal, necessary to the operation of the Club.

   c. To borrow money, contract debts, make contracts and to exercise any and all other powers as a natural person could lawfully make, do, perform or exercise which may be necessary, convenient or expedient for the accomplishment of any of its objects or purposes, providing the same be not inconsistent with the laws of the State of_____ and to that end, enumeration of such powers shall not be deemed inclusive.

3. The term of existence of the Club shall be perpetual or until such time as it is dissolved as provided by the laws of the State of_____.

4. The principal office for the transaction of the business of this Club is to be located at: _____

5. The names and addresses of the incorporators of this Club are: _____

6. The names and addresses of the persons who are hereby appointed to act as the first directors to manage the affairs of this Club are: _____

7. The Club is organized without shares.

8. The property rights of the members of this Club shall be equal.

9. The Club shall be operated not for profit, and no part of the: net earnings of the Club will inure to the benefit of any member.

10. Upon dissolution of the Club as provided by the laws of the State of _____, three members of this Club shall be designated as trustees who shall liquidate the assets thereof and after paying all debts and liabilities of the Club, shall distribute the surplus equally among the members thereof.

11. IN WITNESS WHEREOF, for the purpose of forming this Club, under the laws of the State of _____, we the undersigned, constitute the incorporators including the persons named hereinabove, as the first Directors of this Club and execute these Articles this _____
(date)

Notary's paragraph of acknowledgment

Notary's Seal

Fig. B-6. Flying club bylaws. (AOPA) **(Continues through page 260.)**

SAMPLE FLYING CLUB BYLAWS

ARTICLE I - PURPOSE

1. The purpose of this Club shall be to provide for its members convenient means for flying at the most economical rates.

ARTICLE II - MEETING OF MEMBERS

1. All meetings of the members, except as herein otherwise provided, shall be held at a place to be determined by the President.

2. The annual meeting of the Club shall be held during the first week at such time as the Board of Directors shall determine.

3. Notice of the annual meetings of the members shall be given by written notice mailed to each member at his last known place of business or residence at least ten (10) days before such annual meeting.

4. Special meetings of the members may be held at such time and place as the President may determine, or may be called by a majority of the Directors or by written petition of at least (__) members. It shall be the duty of the Secretary to call such meetings within thirty (30) days after such demand.

5. Notice of general meeting of members, stating the time and, in general terms, the purpose thereof, shall be given in a like manner as the notice required for the regular annual meetings. If all the members shall be present at any gathering, any business may be transacted without previous notice.

6. At any meeting of the members, a quorum shall consist of one-half of the members who are in good standing.

7. The President, or in his absence the Vice-President, or in the absence of the President and Vice-President, a Chairman elected by the members present shall call the meeting of the members to order and shall act as the presiding officer thereof.

8. At the annual meeting of the members, the members shall elect by ballot a Board of Directors as constituted by these bylaws.

9. At every meeting of the members, each member shall have only one vote. Votes cast by mail will be accepted provided they are received by the Secretary at least (__) days prior to the meeting when the vote is to be taken. Proxy votes in writing will be accepted.

10. A majority vote of the members present is necessary for the adoption of any resolution and for the election of a member to the Board of Directors.

11. Parliamentary procedures will be followed and minutes will be kept at all meetings.

ARTICLE III - BOARD OF DIRECTORS

1. The powers, business and property of the Club shall be exercised, conducted and controlled by a Board of Directors of (__) members.

2. Each Director shall be elected annually from the membership of the Club at the regular meeting of the members.

3. In case of a vacancy in the Board, the remaining Directors shall fill such vacancy by appointment from the Club membership. If (__) or more vacancies occur at any one time, they shall be filled by vote of the members at a meeting duly called.

4. No later than one week after each annual meeting of members, the newly elected Directors shall hold a meeting and organize by the election of a President, Vice-President, Secretary, Treasurer and Aircraft Maintenance Officer; and transact any other business.

5. Regular meetings of the Board of Directors shall be called at a time and place to be determined by the President.

6. Special meetings of the Board of Directors shall be called at any time on the order of the President or on the order of (__) Directors.

7. Notice of special meetings of the Board of Directors stating the time and, in general terms, the purpose shall be mailed or personally given to each Director not later than three days before the day appointed for the meeting. If all Directors shall be present at any meeting, any business may be transacted without previous notice.

8. (__) Directors shall constitute a quorum of the Board at all meetings and the affirmative vote of at least (__) Directors

shall be necessary to pass any resolution or authorize any act of the Club.

9. Each member of the Board of Directors shall serve without any compensation or reward, except as otherwise provided in these bylaws.

10. The Board of Directors shall cause to be kept a complete record of all its acts and proceedings of its meetings and to present a full statement at the regular meeting of the members, showing in detail the condition of the affairs of the Club.

11. The Board of Directors may assign to any member any duty or office which the Board deems appropriate and necessary to the conduct of the Club and which is not otherwise expressly provided for in these bylaws.

12. The Board of Directors may engage salaried personnel from outside the Club membership to perform such services in behalf of the Club as the Board deems appropriate and necessary.

13. The Board of Directors shall have the power and authority to promulgate and enforce all rules and regulations pertaining to the use and operation of Club property and to do and perform or cause to be done and performed any and every act which the Club may lawfully do and perform.

ARTICLE IV – OFFICERS

1. The Executive Office of the Club shall have a President, Vice-President, Secretary, Treasurer and an Aircraft Maintenance Officer.

2. The President, Vice-President, Secretary, Treasurer and Aircraft Maintenance Officer shall be elected by the Board of Directors from their own number at the first meeting after organization of the corporation and thereafter at the first meeting after the regular annual meeting of the members and shall hold office for _____ (__) months and until their successors are elected and qualified.

3. The President and Vice-President shall serve without compensation or reward. The Secretary, Treasurer and Aircraft Maintenance Officer shall each receive two (2) hours of flying time per month as compensation for their services.

4. The Treasurer shall be bonded, the premium therefore to be at the expense of the Club.

IV.1 President

1. The President shall be the Chief Executive Officer of the Club. He shall preside at all meetings of the Club and the Board of Directors. He may call any special meeting of the members or the Board of Directors and shall have, subject to the advice and control of the Directors, general charge of the business of the Club, and shall execute with the Secretary, in the name of the Club, all certificates of membership, contracts and instruments other than checks which have been first approved by the Board of Directors.

2. The President shall co-sign all checks executed in the name of the Club.

3. The President shall be responsible to the Board of Directors for the operation of the Club. He shall make and enforce decisions regarding the suitability of all equipment and the qualifications of all members for each type of flight operation. He shall recommend for approval to the Board of Directors all operational rules of the Club and shall report with recommendations all violation of such rules by any member of the Club.

IV.2 Vice President

1. The Vice-President shall be vested with all the powers and shall perform the duties of the President in case of the absence or disability of the President.

2. The Vice-President shall also perform such duties connected with the operation of the Club as he may undertake at the suggestion of the President.

IV.3 Secretary

1. The Secretary shall keep the minutes of all proceedings of the members and of the Board of Directors in books provided for that purpose. He shall attend to the giving and serving of notices of all meetings of the members and of the Board of Directors and otherwise. He shall keep a proper membership book showing the name of each member of the Club, the book of bylaws, .the Club Seal, if any, and such other books and papers as the Board of Directors may direct. He shall execute with the President, in the name of the Club, all certificates of membership, contracts and instruments which have been first approved by the Board of Directors. In the absence or disability of the Treasurer and under the direction of the President he shall execute in the name of the Club checks for expenditures authorized by the Board of Directors. He shall

also maintain an appointment book for the operation of the aircraft.

2. The Secretary shall perform all duties incident to the Office of the Secretary, subject to the control of the Board of Directors.

3. The Secretary shall also perform such duties connected with the operation of the Club as he may undertake at the suggestion of the President.

IV.4 Treasurer

1. The Treasurer shall co-sign with the President, in the name of the Club, all checks for the expenditures authorized by the Board of Directors. He shall receive and deposit all funds of the Club in the bank selected by the Board of Directors, which funds shall be paid out only by check as hereinbefore provided. He shall also account for all receipts, disbursements and balance on hand.

2. The Treasurer will provide a monthly report of the financial status of the Club to the Board of Directors and a quarterly report to every member.

3. The Treasurer will inform the President on the 15th day of each month if any members are delinquent and will notify him when such delinquency plus any fines have been paid.

4. The Treasurer shall perform all duties incident to the Office of the Treasurer, subject to the control of the Board of Directors.

5. The Treasurer shall also perform such duties connected with the operation of the club as he may undertake at the suggestion of the President.

IV.5 Aircraft Maintenance Officer

1. The Aircraft Maintenance Officer shall be responsible for maintaining current information in the logbooks of the aircraft.

2. The Aircraft Maintenance Officer shall be responsible for maintaining the aircraft in proper operating condition, by or under the supervision of a properly certificated aircraft and powerplant mechanic, and for obtaining all inspections, major overhauls and for compliance with all service bulletins for the aircraft.

3. The Aircraft Maintenance Officer shall be responsible for all papers required to be carried in the aircraft and for the execution of all papers required upon the completion of inspections and major repairs.

ARTICLE V - VACANCIES

1. If any Office, other than that of President, becomes vacant for any reason, the President shall appoint an interim successor until such time as the Board of Directors shall elect a successor from the membership who shall hold office for the unexpired term. If the Office of President becomes vacant, the Vice-President shall become President and the Board of Directors shall elect a new Vice-President from the membership.

ARTICLE VI - SAFETY BOARD

1. A Safety Board shall be designated by the Board of Directors for each aircraft accident involving either a member of the Club or any equipment belonging to the Club, providing such accident resulted in damage to equipment exceeding a sum of_____ (__) dollars.

2. The Safety Board shall consist of (__) members of the Club who were not involved in the accident.

3. The Safety Board shall take all steps necessary to ascertain the facts, conditions and circumstances for the accident; shall arrive at conclusions regarding the probable cause and the responsibility for said accident; and shall make known to the Board of Directors, and to all parties involved in the accident, its findings in the form of a written report.

ARTICLE VII - HEARINGS

1. The Board of Directors, upon receipt of the findings of the Safety Board shall offer to all parties involved in the accident the opportunity of a hearing. After the hearing, or if such hearing is waived by all the parties involved in the accident, the Board of Directors shall decide the financial responsibility. The decision of the Board of Directors shall be final.

2. The Board of Directors shall not impose financial responsibility on any one member in excess of _____ (__) dollars for any one accident, unless the damage results from a violation which is not covered by insurance carried on the aircraft; then the party responsible for the damage shall

be liable for the full amount. Recommendation of the Board should be approved by recorded vote of all Club members.

3. All financial obligations imposed on any member as a result of the decision of the Board of Directors shall be satisfied within thirty (30) days of written notice. Otherwise, in the case of a member, all unsatisfied monies may be deducted from the membership fee, the remainder of which shall be returned to the member with a cancellation of membership in the Club.

ARTICLE VIII - MEMBERSHIP

1. New members may be admitted to the Club only after being approved by a unanimous vote of the members. Membership shall be limited to _____ (__) per aircraft.

2. Upon receipt of the initiation fee, the Club shall issue to each member a certificate of membership on a form approved by the Board of Directors.

3. A member may withdraw from the Club upon notification to the Secretary in writing thirty (30) days in advance and said member may make withdrawal final within the next ninety (90) days without further notification provided that the withdrawing member has disposed of all share in the assets of the Club to a new member acceptable to the Club. The Club shall have the first option to Purchase the share of a member wishing to withdraw from the Club and the Club shall have thirty (30) days from the withdrawal notice to exercise this option.

4. A member may be expelled by a two-thirds vote of the members voting at any regular or special meeting of the members. Ten (10) days notice shall be given to each member who shall have the right to be heard either in person or by counsel at a meeting of the Club called for this purpose, A member so expelled shall receive from the Club a sum equal to his/her share in the assets of the Club less any monies, dues or fines owing to the Club.

5. In the event of the death of a member, the Club shall have the first option to purchase from the estate the member's share in the assets of the Club. If a member wishes to name in his/her will a beneficiary of his/her share in the assets of the Club, the named beneficiary must be acceptable to the Club.

ARTICLE IX - MEMBER PAYMENTS

1. **Initiation Fees.** A person duly elected to the Club as

provided for by these bylaws shall be deemed a member upon payment of an initial fee of _____ (__) dollars.

2. **Dues.** Each member shall be assessed monthly dues in the amount of (__) dollars, said dues to be payable one (1) month in advance, due on the (15th) day of each month. The monthly dues may be charged from time to time at the discretion of the Board of Directors.

3. **Hourly Aircraft Rate.** The hourly aircraft rates shall be (__) dollars for _____ aircraft (list each type and rates applicable). Members will forward payment for aircraft use to the Treasurer immediately following each flight. Payments will be made by check via the club lock box or mailed directly to the Treasurer. The hourly aircraft rate may be changed from time to time at the discretion of the Board of Directors.

4. **Delinquency.** Any member who has failed to pay the dues, hourly aircraft rate charges or any other sum due the Club within fifteen (15) days after said sums shall be due, shall be considered a delinquent member and shall be automatically suspended from flying the Club aircraft and engaging in any other Club activity. A ten percent (10%) penalty of the delinquent amount shall be charged after one (1) month's delinquency unless the Board of Directors waives the penalty upon a showing of good cause by the member. When a delinquent member fails to pay any sum owed to the Club, or at the discretion of the Board of Directors, to make suitable arrangements with the Board for payment thereof within sixty (60) days of the due date, the member shall automatically be considered as indicating an intention to withdraw from the Club.

ARTICLE X - CLUB FINANCES

1. No member may authorize expenditures or otherwise incur financial obligations in the name of the Club except as expressly provided for in these bylaws or other regulations duly promulgated by the Club membership.

2. The Treasurer is authorized to expend Club funds in payment for all normal fixed costs of the Club and all operating costs not in excess of (__)dollars. The Treasurer must obtain approval from the Board of Directors for any unusual expenditure and all expenditures in excess of (__)dollars.

3. The Maintenance Officer may authorize work on Club aircraft in an amount of (__) dollars without seeking approval from the Board of Directors. The Maintenance Officer must consult

with the Treasurer before authorizing any work to determine whether there are sufficient funds to pay for the work.

4. Individual members will be reimbursed for any personal expenditures not in excess of (__) dollars when such expenditures are for club aircraft repairs or maintenance necessary to safely complete a trip back the Club's home base.

5. No member, officer, Director or any other individual shall obligate the Club to any purchase, repair, service or in any manner in an amount in excess of (__)dollars without the approval of a majority of the Club members.

ARTICLE XI - FLIGHT RULES AND PROFICIENCY

1. The Board of Directors shall develop, or cause to be developed, a set of Flight Rules. The Flight Rules will take into consideration varying levels of members' experience and proficiency and the type of aircraft to be flown.

2. The Board of Directors shall develop, or cause to be developed, a Flight Proficiency Program for all members to include, but not necessarily limited to, periodic check rides with qualified flight instructors, minimum number of flight hours per month, minimum number of landings per month, and periodic refresher courses. The Flight Proficiency Program must be approved by a majority of the Club members.

ARTICLE XII - SURPLUS

1. The net savings or surplus remaining after all operating costs and other expenses have been paid shall remain in the Club's treasury for the purchase of new equipment, for engine overhaul, for contingencies or for the purpose of reducing the hourly rates for flying as shall be determined by the Board of Directors. The net savings in any event shall not be distributed to the members for their individual use.

ARTICLE XIII - AMENDMENTS

1. These bylaws may be repealed or amended or new bylaws adopted at any meeting of the members called for that purpose or any regular meeting of the members by a two-thirds majority vote of such members.

2. (__%) of the members shall be considered a quorum.

**Fig. B-7. Flying club information and
procedures statement. (Continues through page 263.)**

B&C FLYING CLUB
ANDERSON AIRPORT
762 BENTON DRIVE
ANDERSON, NEBRASKA, 43019
TEL: (   )

The B&C Flying Club is a non-profit corporation founded in 1982 and dedicated to providing well equipped, professionally maintained aircraft at reasonable cost, excellent flight instruction for both new and experienced pilots, and other aviation related activities for its members.

B&C has a fleet of late model, single and multi-engine aircraft available for rent on an hourly basis. For specifics on the current fleet check our aircraft rate sheet.

Certificated Flight Instructors are available for private, instrument and commercial instruction and check-out flights. The club contracts maintenance to a full time certified FAA repair station to insure that all aircraft are maintained in the safest flying condition.

MEMBERSHIP

Membership is open to the public subject to qualification requirements and membership level limits established by the Board of Directors. To apply for membership, a completed application form and non-refundable application fee of $30.00 must be submitted along with a $50.00 deposit and first and last month's dues of $30.00/mo. to the club office. After a 90 day probationary period a member will be considered to be a full member in good standing. The credit deposit will be returned or applied to the closing bill when membership is terminated.

Each new member is issued a copy of the Club Bylaws and Operations Rules and is required to read and comply with those Bylaws and Rules. Members must also sign a continuing Lease Agreement and Liability Statement (on the back of the attached application) prior to their first flight.

CHECK OUT AND CURRENCY

With our emphasis on safety, all pilots must be checked out by a Club Check Pilot in each type of aircraft they desire to fly. A member may check out in a high performance aircraft and also be signed off for lower horsepower aircraft of the same manufacturer. To maintain currency in each type, pilots are required to fly at least 1 hour and 3 takeoffs and landings to a full stop in a Club airplane within the preceding 90 days. In tailwheel aircraft the currency must be within the preceding 60 days.

SCHEDULING

Aircraft rental and instruction are scheduled via phone ( ) or in person at the Club's counter on Anderson Airport. The counter is open 7 days a week (by arrangement with Executive Aviation), 8:30 AM through 5:00 PM and later on certain evenings. After hours scheduling requests are recorded by an answering machine and confirmed the following day. Cancellations must be made at least four hours prior to scheduled departure time or a scheduling penalty fee will be imposed. Cancellations after hours may also be recorded on the answering machine. Aircraft will not be scheduled if a member's bill is in arrears.

INSURANCE

All B&C Club pilots and aircraft are amply insured. Club members, Club Flight instructors, Club check pilots, and Designated FAA Examiners are covered by the insurance policy for Club aircraft operation as per the following:

o $2,000,000.00 per occurrence for property damage, liability, passenger legal liability, and passenger bodily injury liability.

o   All risk while not-in-motion after a $250,00 deductible and risk while in-motion after a $500.00 deductible. The pilot in command is responsible for the deductible.

BILLING

All club members are billed on the first day of the month for the previous month's aircraft rental. In addition, members that exceed $100.00 in rental billing between the 1st and the 15th of the month are billed on the 16th of the month. Payments are due within 10 days of the bill mailing date. All bills not paid by the due date are subject to a 10% late charge. New members without a qualifying local credit record may be placed on a "cash prior to takeoff " basis until financial responsibility is confirmed.

DISCOUNTS ON SIMULATORS AND PILOT SUPPLIES

The Club has two Pacer Mark II aircraft simulators and an AST 300, multi engine simulator available to members at a discount for IFR training and currency. In addition, all Club members may purchase pilot or aircraft supplies at a discount. Certain pilot supplies and charts are stocked at the Club counter and other purchases may be specially ordered from suppliers.

ADDITIONAL INFORMATION

For more information please call the Club at (   )

Fig. B-8. Flying club flight rules. (AOPA)

FLIGHT RULES

1. All members of the Club shall comply with all Federal Aviation Regulations, state, airport and Club rules while operating Club aircraft.

2. A violation of any of the Club's rules by a member renders him or her liable to either a temporary flight suspension of not more than (__) days and/or a monetary fine not to exceed (__)dollars. Repeated violations shall result in a recommendation by the Board of Directors that the member be expelled from the Club, such recommendation to be voted on by the membership. A majority vote shall be necessary for expulsion.

3. All members must be checked out and approved for solo by a flight instructor designated by the Board of Directors before soloing any Club aircraft.

4. A member must perform a thorough preflight inspection of the aircraft, including a visual inspection of the fuel quantity, prior to commencing flight. Any damage or discrepancies discovered by a member will be assumed to be the responsibility of the last user unless it has been reported previously to the Maintenance Officer and entered in the aircraft's squawk log. If a condition is discovered which may affect the airworthiness of the aircraft, the aircraft shall not be flown until cleared by the Maintenance Officer and signed off in the squawk log as resolved.

5. Each member must ascertain that the airworthiness and registration certificates, appropriate operating limitations information, current aircraft radio station license and operator's manual are in the aircraft prior to commencing flight.

6. All aircraft operating limitations must be observed. Aerobatic maneuvers are prohibited except those which are permissible under the operating limitations when the aircraft is operated in the utility category.

7. Flight plans must be filed with the FAA for flights over sparsely populated areas; mountainous, wooded or desert terrain; or for extended overwater flight; and for all student solo cross-country flights in excess of fifty (50) miles.

8. All flights must be booked in accordance with the Club's current scheduling policies.

9. Except in emergencies, Club aircraft shall be flown from and landed on airfields approved by the Board of Directors only. Any member with less than (__)hours total flying time who lands on an unapproved field due to an emergency must call the President before attempting a takeoff from the field. The President shall decide whether the member should attempt the takeoff alone or wait until a better qualified pilot arrives.

10. No member may fly Club aircraft after sunset unless checked out for night flying by a Club instructor.

11. Members with less than (__)hours shall not fly Club aircraft when weather conditions are less than (__) feet ceiling and (__) miles visibility, or when the surface winds exceed (__) miles per hour.

12. Upon completion of a flight, the pilot must tidy up the aircraft. Ash trays will be emptied, waste paper and extra charts (a sectional chart for the local area should be kept in the aircraft) will be removed, seat belts will be straightened, etc.

13. All tanks will be topped at the end of every flight.

14. All members must take a proficiency check ride every (__) months with a flight instructor designated by the Board of Directors. Following a proficiency check, the flight instructor shall approve the member by a logbook entry for either continued solo privileges or additional dual or ground instruction.

15. No member (except the Maintenance Officer) may perform any maintenance on Club aircraft, other than preflight inspection, without authorization from the Maintenance Officer.

16. Club aircraft may not be used to give flight instruction to anyone except Club members and, upon approval by the Board of Directors, members of their immediate family.

Fig. B-9. Flying club continuing lease agreement.

Continuing Lease Agreement
B&C FLYING CLUB
(a non-profit organization)

In consideration of my membership and of aircraft made available to me by B&C Flying Club under this lease, I agree that on each and all subsequent flights in Club aircraft, I shall:

1. Observe and comply with all Federal, State and local air regulations and manufacturers operational procedures.

2. Inspect and make a ground check of the aircraft, its equipment and accessories, before takeoff and not accept such aircraft until 1 am satisfied it is airworthy and all equipment and accessories are operating properly for the flight to be under taken.

3. Allow no one else to fly the aircraft.

4. Land only at public airports approved by the Club and published in the FAA airports and Facilities Directory, except as a precautionary or emergency measure, when reasonably necessary.

5. Return the aircraft to the Club's place of business at the agreed time, weather permitting, in the same condition 1 received it, normal wear and tear excepted.

6. Report all accidents to such aircraft, whether major or minor, to the club at once, together with the names and addresses of witnesses, and all involved parties; in the event of accident involving it, not to move aircraft unless expressly authorized to do so by the Club.

7. Indemnify and hold the Club harmless from any and all loss, damages and attorneys' fees resulting from operating Club aircraft in my possession and control.

8. Pay all bills based on established and adjusted Club rates within ten (10) days of mailing date unless the Club specifically agrees to other arrangements in writing.

9. Have read, will comply with and be bound by; the Club Bylaws and their Amendments, the Club Membership Regulations and their Amendments, and the terms of this lease until my membership in the Club terminates.

10. Notify the Club in writing upon wishing to terminate my membership. I understand my bill MUST be paid IN FULL prior to terminating membership and that Club dues and late charges continue to accrue until my bill is paid.

Signature of Lessee _____   Date _____

By my signature I acknowledge receiving a copy of this Agreement.

Fig. B-10. Flying club instructor scheduling information sheet.

B&C FLYING CLUB
FLIGHT INSTRUCTION SCHEDULING AND BILLING INFORMATION

1. Please do all scheduling directly through the B&C scheduling system. The schedule reflects the most recent information about the date and time you want.

2. While 2 hours is adequate for most lessons, some instructors prefer to allocate 2.5-3.0 hours, so please check with your CFI.

3. Billing is $20-35 per instructor hour depending on the individual CFI and includes all time associated with the lesson; pre and post flight discussions, aircraft preflight, etc. Payment is due at the end of each lesson unless prior arrangement is made with the CFl concerned. Some CFI's offer savings on prepaid blocks. CFI's can accept checks and cash, but not credit cards.

4. When in doubt about the weather, assume the lesson is on, unless you hear from your CFl who may have an alternate lesson plan in mind.

5. If you need to cancel a lesson, please give as much notice as you can. For cancellations received 24 hours prior to scheduled time there is no charge. Cancellations without 24 hours notice are subject to a charge equal to 2 hours of the CFI's time or 70% of the lesson scheduled, whichever is greater. If the CFl can schedule someone in your place, there will be no charge.

6. If your CFI fails to show, or cancels at the last minute, you will be credited the loss of time against your next lesson. Weather and maintenance problems are exempt. CFI's and students occasionally get "mismatched". Please see the Chief Flight Instructor if you have any questions or problems.

8. The counter is manned from 8:30 to 17:30 seven days a week. After hours an answering machine is available for messages. The Club number is (   )

Fig. B-11. Flying club membership application.

B&C FLYING CLUB
Membership Application

PERSONAL

Name:_____

Address: _____

City:_____State:____ Zip:_____

Home Ph:(____)_____ Driv. Lic#:_____

Office Use

Emp:__ Flt:__

Chk:__ Sav:__

App:_____

EMPLOYMENT

Employer: _____

Work Address:_____

City: _____ State:____ Zip: _____

Work Phone:(____)_____X_____ Occupation:_____

Employed Since:_____ Supervisor:_____

FLYING AND MEDICAL HISTORY

Certificate #:_____ Total Hours:_____

Ratings:_____

FAA Medical: Class:_____ Date:_____ Restrictions:_____

BFR Due Date:_____ Aircraft Flown:_____

Previous Flying at: _____ Date Last Flight:_____

How Did You Learn About B&C:_____

REFERENCES

Name (Pers. Ref.)	Relationship	Phone:	Known Since:

Landlord/Mtge Holder:_____ Phone: _____

Bank Ref: Bank   Phone: Account #

Checking:_____

Savings: _____

Other Credit Ref: _____

I hereby apply to the B&C Flying Club and certify that all information is true and correct.

Signature:_____ Date:_____

C

Financing and insurance

Fig. C-1. Aircraft loan request worksheet.

	BANK:	BANK:	BANK:
LOAN TERMS — Have ready for bankers: Aircraft make, model, year, total time, time since major overhaul, detailed equipment list, damage history, annual date, hours per year to be flown. If specific aircraft is not yet located, define the specs you are looking for.			
Minimum loan amount			
Max % of value financed, new a/c			
Max % of value financed, used a/c			
How value determined?			
Min downpayment requirements			
Max loan maturity, new a/c			
Max loan maturity, used a/c			
Fixed or variable interest rate?			
Annual Percentage Rate (APR)			
Must all partners co-sign for full amount?			
Closing and other fees			
Preapproval available?			
LOAN AMOUNT REQUESTED:			
MATURITY REQUESTED			
MONTHLY PAYMENT			
COLLATERAL REQUIREMENTS			
First lien on aircraft			
Additional collateral requirements			
BORROWER STRENGTH, INFO			
Should each partner be able to carry total loan?			
Application form is sufficient information			
Tax returns also required (how many years?)			
Other evidence of income (W 2, paystubs, etc)			
INSURANCE REQUIREMENTS			
All risk?			
Bank named as loss payee?			
Market value or stated value?			
Maximum deductible			
Waiver of subrogation?			

Fig. C-2. Aircraft loan application.

BANK LOAN APPLICATION

The Applicant is applying ☐ Individually ☐ Jointly with
(If joint, a separate application is required.)

Choice of Due Date (check one)   1 ☐   5 ☐   10 ☐   15 ☐   20 ☐   25 ☐

Name (Print) _____   Amt. of Loan $ _____   Repayable in _____ months
              LAST NAME   FIRST   MIDDLE

Present Address _____   Zip Code _____   Years There _____

Former Address _____   Years There _____

Date of Birth _____   Social Security # _____   No. of Dependents _____   Home Phone No. _____

INCOME INFORMATION

Employer _____   Position/Department _____

Years There _____   Business Phone No. _____   Present Monthly Take Home Salary/Wages (Net) $ _____

Former Employer _____
                        NAME   ADDRESS

Alimony, child support, or separate maintenance income need not be revealed if you do not wish to have it considered as a basis for repaying this obligation.

If considered, is alimony, child support, separate maintenance received under: court order ☐   written agreement ☐   oral understanding ☐
Is this type of income listed likely to continue for the duration of the loan?   Yes ☐   No ☐

Other Income (Source) _____   per ☐ Week ☐ Month $ _____

Checking Account _____   _____   _____
                        BANK   BRANCH   ACCOUNT NUMBER   BALANCE

Savings Account _____   _____   _____
                        BANK   BRANCH   ACCOUNT NUMBER   BALANCE

☐ Rent   Landlord's Name _____   Monthly Payment $ _____

Real Estate owned in the name of _____   Date Acquired _____   Purchase Price $ _____

Mortgage Holder _____   Mortgage Balance $ _____   Monthly Pmt. $ _____
                                Account No. _____

Auto owned (Make and Year) _____   Purchased from _____

Financed by _____   Balance owing $ _____   Monthly Pmt. $ _____

DEBT INFORMATION AND CREDIT REFERENCES

Include all charge accounts, installment contracts, education loans, liability for support/alimony/separate maintenance, or any other debt upon which you are individually or jointly liable. Include paid credit references. Use separate sheet if necessary.

Creditor	Address	Type of Debt or Acct. No.	Name(s) in Which Acct. Carried	Original Debt	Present Balance	Monthly Payments
1.				$	$	$
2.				$	$	$
3.				$	$	$
4.				$	$	$
5.				$	$	$

Are you a co-maker, endorser, or guarantor on any loan or contract?   Yes ☐   No ☐   If "Yes," for whom? _____   To whom? _____

Have you ever had any judgements, or legal proceedings against You?   Yes ☐   No ☐   If "Yes," to whom owed? _____

Have you been declared bankrupt in the last 14 years?   Yes ☐   No ☐   If "Yes," Court _____   Year _____

PLEASE COMPLETE BOTH SIDES. FOLD AND TAPE FOR PRIVACY. POSTAGE IS PREPAID

FINANCIAL STATEMENT—Attach supplemental schedules if necessary

ASSETS		LIABILITIES	
Cash	$	Notes Payable—Banks—Secured	$
Cash Value—Life Insurance	$		
Securities—Stocks & Bonds—Itemize	$	Notes Payable—Banks—Unsecured	$
		Notes Payable—Other—Describe	
Autos and Other Personal Property		Accounts and Bills Due	
		Mortgage Held By	Monthly Payment
Real Estate—Type and Address	Value		Mortgage Balance
		Other Debts—Itemize	
Other Asset—Itemize		TOTAL LIABILITIES	
		NET WORTH	
TOTAL ASSETS	$	Total Liabilities & Net Worth	$

PILOT HISTORY DATA

Name and Address

F.A.A. Pilot Rating	When Issued	Class	Ever Revoked or Suspended?	Total Hours Logged	Solo	Last 90 Days
Date Last Physical			Doctor—Name and Address			

INSURANCE

Company Name and Address

Coverage Provided

Hull $ Property Damage $ Personal Liability $ Annual Premium

POLICY MUST NAME _____ AS LOSS PAYEE INCLUDING BREACH OF WARRANTY IN BANK'S FAVOR AND 30 DAYS' NOTICE OF CANCELLATION

Agent's Name and Address

AIRCRAFT INFORMATION

Year and Make		☐ New	☐ Used	Manufacturer of Engine(s)		☐ New	☐ Remanufactured
Model				Engine Model Number(s)			H.P.
Hull Serial Number	F.A.A. Registration N-			Engine Serial Number(s)			
Radios, Extra Equipment and Value							
Aircraft Will Be Used For: ☐ Business	☐ Pleasure		☐ Both	Aircraft Will Be Based At:			

		TERMS OF SALE	
Total Engine Time	Engine Time Since Major O/H	Total Delivered Price	
Airframe Time	Engine Time Since Top O/H	Including Extra Equipment, Etc.	$
Name of Present Owner		Less—Cash Down Payment	$
Aircraft Licensed Until		Trade-In Allowance	
		Unpaid Cash Balance	$

Name of Relative or Friend not living with you _____ Address _____ Relationship _____

Signature _____

Date _____

Fig. C-3. Aircraft loan agreement, bank financing. (Continues through page 282.)

This loan agreement is a typical example of aircraft bank loan agreements. It is an actual agreement (the names of the borrowers and the bank have been changed) documenting a loan for a Piper Warrior. The loan was fixed rate for seven years, the maximum maturity this bank was willing to grant for used aircraft. The Warrior's total purchase price was $18,000. Note the terrible "boilerplate" language of the Guaranty. It is important to study the loan documents thoroughly, preferably before you show up to sign on the dotted line. Many borrowers make the mistake of not seeing these documents until closing.

FIRST COMMUNITY BANK

CONSUMER AIRCRAFT LOAN

PROMISSORY NOTE, DISCLOSURE STATEMENT

AND SECURITY AGREEMENT

George H. Salmon and Hilda Jackoo

The undersigned, residing at 149 Frog Pond Road, Wilcox, Maine; heinafter called "Debtor", hereby grants to First Community Bank, 2300 Adams Street, Hiller, Massachusetts 01390, hereinafter called "Secured Party," a security interest in the aircraft described below and all accessories and equipment now owned or hereafter acquired by Debtor and attached to, located in, or used in connection with, such aircraft, including without limitation the engines and avionics equipment described below, all logs and similar books relating to such aircraft and all proceeds of any of the foregoing, all hereinafter called the "Collateral":

Year Manufactured:	1976
New or Used:	Used
Manufacturer of Aircraft:	Piper
Model No.:	Pa28-151
Serial No.:	28-7615026
FAA No.:	N4539X

The avionics equipment includes the following: Dual KX 170B, 2 VOR/LOC, G/S, King Audio Panel, King XPD, King ADF, King DME.

Home Airport Address: Wilcox Municipal, Wilcox, Maine

Said security interest is hereby granted as security for the payment of the Total of Payments hereinafter stated and any substitutions for, or renewals or extension thereof and for the payment and performance of any and all other liabilities and obligations of Debtor to Secured Party under this Agreement, all hereinafter called the "Obligations".

For value received, Debtor agrees and promises to pay to Secured Party at its principal office in Hiller, Massachusetts the total of Payments ($20,477.52), consisting of the Amount Financed and the Finance Charge described below, in consecutive monthly installments in the amounts and at the times described below,

DISCLOSURES OF THE COST OF DEBTOR'S LOAN

AMOUNT FINANCED - The amount of credit provided to Debtor or on his behalf:

$12,000.00

FINANCE CHARGE - The dollar amount the credit will cost Debtor:

$8,402.52

TOTAL OF PAYMENTS - The amount Debtor will have paid when all scheduled payments have been made:

$20,477.52

ANNUAL PERCENTAGE RATE - The cost of Debtor's credit as a yearly rate:

16.50%

Debtor's payment schedule will be:

Number of Payments: 84

Amount of Each Payment: $243.78

When Payments are Due: Monthly, beginning 12/15/82

Late Charges: If the Amount Financed is $6,000 or less and Debtor's payment is more than 10 days late, Debtor will be charged 5% of the overdue installment or $5.00, whichever is less. If the Amount Financed is over $6,000 and Debtor's payment is more than 10 days late, Debtor will be charged 5% of the overdue installment.

Prepayment: If the Obligations are prepaid in full, Debtor may be entitled to a refund of part of the Finance Charge.

Security Interest: Obligor is giving a security interest in the aircraft, related equipment and other assets described above.

Filing Fees in connection with the Security Interest: $52.50

Property insurance may be obtained by Debtor through any duly licensed insurance agent of Debtor's choice, subject only to the Secured Party's right to refuse to accept any insurer offered by Debtor for reasonable cause.

See the portions of this Agreement below for additional information about nonpayment, default, the right to accelerate the maturity of the Obligations and prepayment refunds.

The Amount Financed is made up of:

Amount paid to Debtor directly:	$12,000.00
Amount paid to others on Debtor's behalf to public officials:	$22.50
TOTAL:	$12,022.50

ADDITIONAL AGREEMENTS

Debtor further agrees that:

Late Payment: If any installment of the Total of Payments is not paid within ten days of the due date thereof, Debtor agrees to pay Secured party a late charge equal to 5% of such overdue installment, which shall not exceed $5.00 if the Amount Financed hereunder is $6,000 or less.

Set-Off Rights: Any and all deposits or other sums at any time credited by, or due from, Secured Party to Debtor shall at all times constitute additional security for the Obligations and may be set off against any Obligations upon the occurrence of any event of default, and at any time thereafter.

Prepayment: Prepayment in full of the Obligations may be made at any time without penalty. Upon prepayment in full, Debtor will receive a rebate of the unearned interest, if any, computed according to the actuarial method, except that no refunds will be made in amounts less than $1 to the extent permitted by law.

Default: If an event of default occurs hereunder, and the Secured Party declares the balance Debtor owes immediately due and payable, Debtor will pay interest on that balance (a) for one year following the date Debtor's balance is declared due and payable at the Annual Percentage Rate set forth above, and from one year thereafter at the rate of 6% per annum, until such obligations are fully paid, if the Amount Financed is $6,000 or less or (b) at the Annual Percentage Rate set forth above. until such obligations are fully paid, if the Amount Financed is over $6,000.

Debtor hereby warrants and covenants that except for the security interest granted hereby Debtor is the owner of the Collateral free from any restriction, lien, encumbrance, or right, title or interest of others, and that Debtor will defend the Collateral against all claims of all persons at any time claiming any interest therein; that no financing statement covering the Collateral or any portion thereof is on file in any public office and that no document covering the Collateral and representing a lien, encumbrance or any right, title or interest of any party other than Debtor or Secured Party is recorded with the Federal Aviation Administration Aircraft Registry, that Debtor will pay all title search, title report, escrow, and filing fees and charges incurred by Secured Party in connection with the Collateral and the perfection of its Security interest therein, and that at the request of Secured Party, Debtor will join Secured Party in executing one or more documents confirming Secured Party's security interest hereunder, in form satisfactory to Secured Party and will pay the cost of recording or filing the same in all public offices whenever filing is deemed by Secured Party to be necessary or desirable.

DEBTOR UNDERSTANDS AND AGREES THAT THE PROVISIONS APPEARING ON THE REVERSE SIDE HEREOF CONSTITUTE A PART OF THIS AGREEMENT AS FULLY AS IF THEY WERE PRINTED ON THE FACE HEREOF ABOVE DEBTOR'S SIGNATURE. IF THIS AGREEMENT IS SIGNED BY TWO OR MORE DEBTORS, THE TERM "DEBTOR" SHALL REFER TO EACH PERSON SIGNING THIS AGREEMENT, JOINTLY AND SEVERALLY. DEBTOR HEREBY ACKNOWLEDGES RECEIPT OF A COPY OF THIS AGREEMENT.

"IN WITNESS WHEREOF, Debtor has hereunto set its hand and seal this 10th day of November, 1982:

WITNESS:

_____   _____
                                  George H. Salmon (co-owner)

_____   _____
                                  Hilda Jackoo   (co-owner)

GUARANTY

For valuable consideration, the receipt and sufficiency of which are hereby acknowledged, the undersigned, jointly and severally if more than one, hereby guarantees to Secured Party the due payment and fulfillment by Debtor of all obligations pursuant to the above Promissory Note, Disclosure Statement and Security Agreement ("Agreement") and agrees that on the default by Debtor under the Agreement to pay to Secured Party on demand the full amount unpaid under the Agreement. Undersigned consents to any renewal, extension, or postponement of the time of payment of Debtor's obligations under the Agreement or to any other forebearance or indulgence with respect thereto and consents to any substitution, exchange, modification or release of any security therefor or the release of any other person primarily or secondarily liable under the Agreement whether or not notice thereof shall be given to the undersigned, and the enforcement of Secured Party's rights hereunder shall not be affected by the neglect or failure of Secured Party to take any action with respect to any security, right, obligation, endorsement or guaranty which it may at any time hold. The undersigned waives all requirements of notice, (including notice of acceptance of this guaranty), demand, presentment or protest and any right which the undersigned might otherwise have to require Secured Party first to proceed against Debtor or against any other guarantor or any other person or first to realize on any security held by it before proceeding against the undersigned for the enforcement of this guaranty. An action on this guaranty may be brought in an appropriate court of Massachusetts and service may be had on the undersigned by registered mail.

DATE:

WITNESS:

_____   _____
                                      George H. Salmon (co-owner)

_____   _____
                                      Hilda Jackoo   (co-owner)

(Additional Provisions)

IT IS FURTHER AGREED: Debtor will not sell, transfer or otherwise dispose of, or offer to sell, transfer or otherwise dispose of, any or all of the collateral, or any interest therein; that Debtor will furnish and keep in force and on deposit with Secured Party at all times the originals of all risks - ground and flight, liability and such other insurance policies as Secured Party may require, payable to Secured Party and Debtor as their interests may appear, with such supplementary endorsements, coverages and amounts, and in such form as Secured Party may require, with insurance companies approved by Secured Party and non-cancellable except on thirty days prior written notice to Secured Party; that upon failure of Debtor to do so, Secured Party may procure such insurance, and Debtor agrees to pay the premiums therefor upon demand, or, if the premiums should have been paid by Secured Party at its option, to repay the amount thereof to Secured Party on demand, together with interest thereon at the same rate described herein, but Secured Party shall be under no duty to procure such insurance or pay such premiums; that insurance proceeds shall be applied toward replacement of the Collateral or payment of the Obligations at Secured Party's option, and Secured Party may act as attorney for Debtor in obtaining, adjusting, settling and cancelling such insurance and endorsing any drafts; and that in case of any default hereunder, Secured Party is hereby authorized to cancel such insurance and Debtor hereby assigns to Secured Party any moneys, not in excess of the unpaid balance of the Obligations, payable under such insurance, including return of unearned premiums, and directs any insurance company to make such payments direct to Secured Party, to be applied,to said unpaid balance; that Debtor will pay all taxes, assessments and other charges on or levied against the Collateral, will keep the Collateral free from any restriction, lien, encumbrance, or right, title or interest of others and in first-class order and repair and certified for flying at all times, will have the Collateral, including all engines and the air-frame, thoroughly inspected, overhauled and repaired as required by the Federal Aviation Administration standards or by the manufacturer and at least once in every period of twelve consecutive months, will report to Secured Party promptly any damage to the Collateral, and will n@t waste or destroy the Collateral or any part thereof or remove any accessories or equipment therefrom; that the Collateral will at all times be duly registered with the Federal Aviation Administration and all other federal and state authorities having jurisdiction, that no such registration will at any time expire, or be suspended, revoked, cancelled or terminated, and that the Collateral and the use thereof will at all times comply with all laws, rules, regulations and requirements of the Federal Aviation Administration and all other federal and state authorities having jurisdiction, and the terms and conditions of all said policies of insurance; that Secured Party may examine and inspect the Collateral and all log and similar books and records relating thereto, at any time, wherever located; that the Collateral will be used only for the purpose stated above; that the Collateral will be kept at all times when not in use for more than fourteen days at the home airport address stated herein, and that Debtor will not permit removal of any of the Collateral from the states to which use of the Collateral is restricted by the liability insurance policy required hereunder; that Secured Party may at its option discharge taxes, assessments, restrictions, liens, encumbrances, rights, title and interests of others on or in the Collateral, and make any reasonable expenditure for maintenance or preservation of the Collateral, and Debtor will on demand repay the amount thereof to Secured Party together with interest thereon at the Annual Percentage Rate described above.

The happening of any of the following events, conditions, or occurrences shall constitute an event of default under this Agreement; (a) default in the payment or performance of any of the Obligations, (b) any warranty, representation or statement made.or furnished to Secured Party by or on behalf of Debtor proves to have been false in any material respect when made or furnished; (c)any loss, theft, damage, destruction or sale to or of any of the Collateral, or the making or suffering of any levy, seizure or attachment thereof or thereon or the incurring of any restriction, lien, encumbrance, or right, title or interest of others thereon or therein; or (d) death or insolvency of the Debtor, the appointment of a receiver, trustee or creditor's committee of or for any part of the property of the Debtor, the assignment, trust, or mortgage for the benefit of creditors by Debtor, or the commencement of any proceeding for a composition of debts or reorganization, or arrangement with creditors, or any proceeding under any federal or state law relating to bankruptcy, insolvency, or the relief or rehabilitation of debtors, by or against Debtor.

Upon any such default, which is material under the circumstances and involves either the non-payment of one or more payments provided for herein or a substantial impairment of the value of the Collateral, or at any time thereafter, Secured Party may, after giving such notice and opportunity to cure as may be required by applicable law, declare the Obligations to be immediately due and payable, and exercise, to the extent permitted by applicable law, the rights and remedies of a secured party under the Uniform Commercial Code, including without limitation the sale of the Collateral at public.or private sale, and any other tights or remedies provided herein. If the Secured Party sells the Collateral at a public or private sale or otherwise disposes of it, and the proceeds of such disposition are insufficient to pay the Obligations in full, Debtor shall, to the extent permitted by applicable law, remain liable"to the Secured Party for the deficiency with interest thereon at the Annual Percentage Rate described above. If any event of default occurs hereunder, Debtor agrees, to the extent permitted by applicable law, to pay Secured Party's reasonable costs of collection, including court costs and attorney's fees.

Any condition or restriction hereinabove imposed with respect to Debtor may be waived, modified or suspended by Secured Party but only on secured Party's prior action in writing and only as so expressed in such writing and not otherwise. Secured Party shall not be deemed to have waived any of its other rights hereunder or under any other agreement, instrument or paper signed by Debtor unless such waiver be in writing and signed by Secured Party. No delay or omission on the part of Secured Party in exercising any right shall operate as a waiver of such right or any other right. A waiver on any one occasion shall not be construed as a bar to, or waiver of, any right or remedy on any future occasion. All Secured Party's rights and remedies, whether evidenced hereby or by any other agreement, instrument or paper, shall be cumulative and may be exercised separately or concurrently. Any demand upon, or notice to, Debtor that Secured Party may elect to give shall be effective when deposited in the mails addressed to Debtor at the address shown herein or as modified by any notice given after the date hereof. Demands or notices addressed to any other address at which Secured Party customarily communicates with Debtor shall also be effective. This Agreement and all rights and obligations hereunder, including matters of construction, validity and performance, shall be governed by the laws of Massachusetts. This Agreement shall be delivered in Massachusetts by Debtor for acceptance by Secured Party.

If and to the extent that applicable law confers any rights or imposes any duties inconsistent with or in addition to any provisions of this Agreement, the affected provisions hereof shall be considered amended to conform thereto but all other provisions hereof shall remain in full force and effect.

**Fig. C-4. Aircraft loan agreement,
partner financing. (Continues through page 286.)**

This sample promissory note is an example of a loan agreement documenting the financing of one partner by another. To maintain the "arms' length" business-like nature of the transaction, the loan is based entirely upon the terms and conditions on which an area bank (the alternative) was providing aircraft financing at the time. The language about how the interest rate is set and varies is similar to what the borrowing partner would have found in a loan agreement required by the bank. The interest rate on this note is variable.

One difference from the bank loan agreement is the percentage point above the "contract interest rate." This percentage is the "spread" the bank charges above a reference rate such as the "contract interest rate" (another common reference rate is the prime rate). Had the borrowing partner gone to the bank, he would have had to pay 2.5 percent over the "contract interest rate," resulting in an all in rate of 11.80 percent, a full percentage point above the rate of this note. For the lending partner, there is also an advantage. The 10.80 percent the lending partner is making on this transaction is higher than the return to be had on alternative investments, such as certificates of deposit.

PROMISSORY NOTE

$10,000.00

Lincoln, ME
April 15, 1992

FOR VALUE RECEIVED, the undersigned GEORGE H. SALMON, promises to pay to HARRIS G. STURGEON or order the sum of **TEN THOUSAND ($10,000.00) DOLLARS** with interest from the date of this note on the unpaid principal at the rate of 10.80% per annum, amortized over 120 months, said interest and principal to be paid in consecutive monthly installments of **ONE HUNDRED THIRTY SIX AND 75/100 DOLLARS**, ($136.75), commencing April 15, 1992, until the amount of such consecutive monthly installments is increased or decreased as hereinafter provided. The entire unpaid balance of this note together with accrued interest shall be paid on March 15, 2002.

As of October 15, 1992, the interest rate shall be adjusted to 1.5 percentage points over the "Contract Interest Rate, Purchase of Previously Occupied Homes National Average for All Major Types of Lenders" published by the Federal Home Loan Bank Board or successor agencies, as prevailing 45 days preceding each adjustment date. The interest rate shall thereafter be adjusted in the manner described above every six months during the term of this note. In the event of a change of the interest rate, the amount of the monthly principal and interest installment will be changed so that the then unpaid balance of the loan will be completely paid in 120 months from the date of this note.

The entire unpaid balance of this note, together with any interest due thereon, shall become immediately due and payable at the option of the holder hereof upon the happening of any of the following events:

(a) failure of the undersigned to make any payment required to be paid hereunder within thirty (30) days after such payment shall be due; or

(b) in the event that any of the terms, conditions, covenants or provisions of the mortgage or any other instrument given as collateral security for this note are not fully performed within any applicable grace period; or

(c) upon dissolution or termination of the nominee trust, the trustee of which is the maker of the note herein; or

(d) upon the appointment of a receiver for any part or all of the property of, or an assignment for the benefit of creditors by, or the commencement of any proceedings under any bankruptcy or insolvency laws by or against the maker hereof, other than an involuntary petition which is removed within thirty (30) days.

The maker of this note hereby waives presentment for payment, demand, notice of dishonor, notice of protest, and any other defense, legal or equitable, except payment, which might otherwise be available, and expressly consents to and waives notice of

(a) any extension or postponement of the time for payment or any other indulgence and to the addition or release (whether by operation of law or otherwise) of any other party or person primarily and secondarily liable hereunder; and

(b) any and all impairment, release, substitution or exchange by the holder hereof of any property securing this obligation.

In the event of any default hereunder, the holder hereof may, at its option, set off against the payment of this note any sums due from the holder to the maker, and may hold, as additional security for the payment of this note any property, real or personal, of the maker in the possession of the holder.

This note is secured in collateral by a 1978 Piper PA 28-181 Archer aircraft, United States Federal Aviation Administration (hereinafter FAA) registration number N4968X, Manufacturers serial number 28-694032. The collateral security agreement shall be a lien placed on the title documents of the aircraft and registered with the FAA, Oklahoma City, Oklahoma.

In the event that the ownership of the aircraft granted as collateral security for this note, or any part thereof, becomes vested in anyone other than the debtor named in said collateral security agreement, the whole sum of principal and interest then remaining unpaid shall become immediately due without notice at the option of the holder hereof.

The maker of this note hereby agrees to pay all costs, charges and expenses of collection, including reasonable attorney's fees, in the event this note is placed into the hands of any attorney for collection or enforcement hereof.

The rights and obligation hereunder shall be governed by the laws of the State of Maine. In the event that any provision or clause of this note or the collateral security therefor conflicts with applicable law, such conflict shall not affect other provisions of this note or said collateral security which can be given effect without the conflicting provisions, and to this end the provisions of this note and said collateral security are declared severable.

This note has been executed under seal on the day and year first above written.

_____   _____
WITNESS   George H. Salmon

Fig. C-5. Aircraft insurance request worksheet.

Have for insurers each partner's age, licences and ratings , total hours logged, hours in type, hours of relevant experience (R/G;tailwheel,multi, etc).

	DESIRED LIMIT	INSURER 1:		INSURER 2:		INSURER 3:	
		COVERAGE	COST	COVERAGE	COST	COVERAGE	COST
HULL							
All risk							
All risk in motion							
All risk not in motion							
Deductibles							
TOTAL HULL COST							
LIABILITY							
Per occurrence							
Per person per occurrence							
Per occupant per occurrence							
Bodily injury sublimit							
Spouse sublimit							
Child (a/c owners') sublimit							
TOTAL LIABILITY COST							
MEDICAL							
Per occurrence							
Per person per occurrence							
TOTAL INSURANCE COST							

EXCLUSIONS (use above insurer numbers for YES/NO)	YES	NO
FAR violations		
Flights on legal airworthiness cert. waivers		
Instruction for owners or non-owners		
In flight operation by non-owner		
Intentional off airport landings		
Ops under govt. liability waiver		
Other exclusions:		

Note: Only generally undesirable exclusions are listed above. Check policies carefully for other exclusions

OTHER TERMS, CONDITIONS AND ISSUES
Flights by non-owners:
Geographic coverage:
Experience needed to reduce policy cost:
Insurance provider rating:
Other:
Other:
Other:

D

Aircraft flight records

Fig. D-1. Sample aircraft flight log.

DATE	PILOT	TACH	FLT TIME	ROUTE

Fig. D-2. Aircraft flight and performance log.

TACH END:	DATE:		N:		PILOT:		
	ROUTE:						
(-) TACH START:	OAT	ALTITUDE	IAS	MP	RPM	MIXTURE	
= FLIGHT TIME:	OIL PRESS	OIL TEMP	EGT	CHT	GAL/HR	TAS	
REMARKS							

TACH END:	DATE:		N:		PILOT:		
	ROUTE:						
(-) TACH START:	OAT	ALTITUDE	IAS	MP	RPM	MIXTURE	
= FLIGHT TIME:	OIL PRESS	OIL TEMP	EGT	CHT	GAL/HR	TAS	
REMARKS							

Fig. D-3. Aircraft squawk sheet.

AIRCRAFT SQUAWK REPORT		N:	TACH:
DATE NOTED:	PILOT:	DATE RESOLVED:	BY:
SQUAWK:		RESOLUTION:	
SIGNATURE:		SIGNATURE:	

AIRCRAFT SQUAWK REPORT		N:	TACH:
DATE NOTED:	PILOT:	DATE RESOLVED:	BY:
SQUAWK:		RESOLUTION:	
SIGNATURE:		SIGNATURE:	

Fig. D-4. Aircraft schedule of recurrent inspections.

RECURRENT CHECKS DUE	N:	
Enter date or Tach hours when **next** check due. Cross out superseded date.		
ANNUAL INSPECTION:		
100 HOUR INSPECTION:		
TRANSPONDER CHECK:		
STATIC/ALTIMETER CHECK:		
FCC RADIO LICENSE (renewal):		

VOR CHECKS:				

E

Preventative maintenance

Part 43 of the Federal Aviation Regulations authorizes the holder of a pilot's license to perform certain preventative maintenance on the aircraft owned or operated by the pilot, provided that the aircraft is not used for Part 121, 127, 129, or 135 operations.

It is the sole responsibility of anyone performing any maintenance on any aircraft to be fully informed of and adhere to current maintenance regulations.

Fig. E-1. Preventative maintenance authorized by FAR Part 43.

Appendix A of FAR Part 43 defines preventative maintenance authorized by Part 43:

1. Removal, installation, and repair of landing gear tires.
2. Replacing elastic shock absorber cords on landing gear.
3. Servicing landing gear shock struts by adding oil, air, or both.
4. Servicing landing gear wheel bearings, such as cleaning and greasing.
5. Replacing defective safety wiring or cotter keys.
6. Lubrication not requiring disassembly other than removal of nonstructural items such as cover plates, cowlings, and fairings.
7. Making simple fabric patches not requiring rib stitching or the removal of structural parts or control surfaces. In the case of balloons, the making of small fabric repairs to envelopes (as defined in, and in accordance with, the balloon manufacturer's instructions) not requiring load tape repair or replacement.
8. Replenishing hydraulic fluid in the hydraulic reservoir.
9. Refinishing decorative coating of fuselage, balloon baskets, wings, tail group surfaces (excluding balanced control surfaces), fairings, cowling,

landing gear, cabin, or cockpit interior when removal or disassembly of any primary structure or operating system is not required.

10. Applying preservative or protective material to components where no disassembly of any primary structure or operating system is involved and where such coating is not prohibited or is not contrary to good practices.

11. Repairing upholstery and decorative furnishings of the cabin, cockpit, or balloon basket interior when the repairing does not require disassembly of any primary structure or operating system or interfere with an operating system or affect primary structure of the aircraft.

12. Making small simple repairs to fairings, nonstructural cover plates, cowlings, and small patches and reinforcements not changing the contour so as to interfere with proper air flow.

13. Replacing side windows where that work does not interfere with the structure or any operating system such as controls, electrical equipment, etc.

14. Replacing safety belts.

15. Replacing seats or seat parts with replacement parts approved for the aircraft, not involving disassembly of any primary structure or operating system.

16. Troubleshooting and repairing broken circuits in landing light wiring circuits.

17. Replacing bulbs, reflectors, and lenses of position and landing lights.

18. Replacing wheels and skis where no weight and balance computation is involved.

19. Replacing any cowling not requiring removal of the propeller or disconnection of flight controls.

20. Replacing or cleaning spark plugs and setting of spark plug gap clearance.

21. Replacing any hose connection except hydraulic connections.

22. Replacing prefabricated fuel lines.

23. Cleaning fuel and oil strainers or filter elements.

24. Replacing and servicing batteries.

25. Removing and installing glider wings and tail surfaces that are specifically designed for quick removal and installation and when such removal and installation can be accomplished by the pilot.

26. Cleaning of balloon burner pilot and main nozzles in accordance with the balloon manufacturer's instructions.

27. Replacing or adjustment of nonstructural standard fasteners incidental to operations.

28. Removing and installing balloon baskets and burners that are specifically designed for quick removal and installation and when such removal and installation can be accomplished by the pilot, provided that baskets are

not interchanged except as provided in the type certificate data sheet for that balloon.

29. The installation of anti-misfueling devices to reduce the diameter of fuel tank filler openings provided the specific device has been made a part of the aircraft type certificate data by the aircraft manufacturer, the aircraft manufacturer has provided FAA-approved instructions for installation of the specific device, and installation does not involve the disassembly of the existing tank filler opening.

30. Removing, checking, and replacing magnetic chip detectors.

F

How to buy an airplane

Fig. F-1. Aircraft specifications comparison worksheet.

	Aircraft (model/yr)	Aircraft (model/yr)	Aircraft (model/yr)	Aircraft (model/yr)
Seats and configuration				
Powerplant make, model				
Horsepower				
Type fuel used (80, 100LL, auto, etc)				
Propeller make and model				
Gross weight				
Empty weight				
Useful load				
Payload, full fuel and oil				
Fuel capacity				
Baggage capacity				
Maximum speed, sea level				
Cruise speed 75% power				
65% power				
55% power				
Range 75% power				
65% power				
55% power				
Rate of climb, sea level				
Service ceiling				
Best angle of climb speed				
Best rate of climb speed				
Stall speed, clean				
Stall speed gear and flaps down				
Approach speed				
Takeoff distance over 50 ft obstacle				
Landing distance over 50 ft obstacle				

Fig. F-2. Initial questions to ask.

Aircraft:
Owner:
Telephone:
Address:
Aircraft home base:
Date of conversation:

- ☐ How many owners has the airplane had?
- ☐ Where has it been based geographically during its life?
- ☐ Has it ever been used for training or rental flying?
- ☐ Total time airframe
- ☐ Total time engine
- ☐ Total time engine since major overhaul
- ☐ How many times has the engine been overhauled?
- ☐ Who performed the overhaul?
- ☐ Was the overhaul to factory-new tolerances or service limits?
- ☐ Has there been a top overhaul since the major overhaul?
- ☐ Were the accessories also overhauled? If not, how many hours are on the accessories: starter, alternator, magnetos, vacuum pump, and the like?
- ☐ Are all ADs complied with and entered into the appropriate logbook?
- ☐ Are the airframe and engine logbooks original and complete?
- ☐ Does the airplane have EGT and CHT gauges?
- ☐ Is there any damage history?
- ☐ How old is the paint and interior?
- ☐ Separately rate the exterior and interior on a scale of 1 to 10
- ☐ Has the airplane been hangared?
- ☐ When was the last annual?
- ☐ Who did the last annual?
- ☐ Was the oil sent out for analysis at oil change, and are the results available?
- ☐ How many hours has the airplane flown since the last annual?
- ☐ How many hours has the airplane flown in the last 12 months?
- ☐ When was the most recent transponder and static/altimeter check?
- ☐ Describe major maintenance performed in the last 12 months?
- ☐ What make and model avionics does the airplane have: navcom, HSI, ADF, loran, area navigation, GPS, and the like?
- ☐ Are there any maintenance issues with the avionics?

☐ Does the airplane have an intercom? Does it work?

☐ Are pictures—exterior, interior, and instrument panel—available?

☐ What is the asking price?

☐ Notes:

Fig. F-3. Prepurchase inspection checklist.

Aircraft:
Location:
Date:

Documentation inspection

☐ Certificate of airworthiness
☐ Registration
☐ Radio station license
☐ Examine airframe and engine logbooks for:
  ~ Proper annual entries
  ~ Evidence of 100-hour inspections indicating commercial use
  ~ Compression (most recent and history)
  ~ Amount of hours flown per year
  ~ Evidence of unscheduled repair work
  ~ Airworthiness directive compliance
  ~ Engine major overhaul entry (when and where done, to what tolerances)
  ~ Record of geographic movements

Mechanical inspection

Airframe
☐ Check for wrinkled skin, loose rivets, dings, cracks, and corrosion.
☐ Check for mismatched paint, which could be a sign of repairs.
☐ Check all controls for free and correct movement.
☐ Check all control hinges (ailerons, elevator, rudder, flaps) for looseness, play, and hairline cracks.
☐ Check vertical and horizontal stabilizer attach points for looseness, play, and hairline cracks.
☐ Check wing attach points for hairline cracks and corrosion (loose attach points might be a cause for immediate rejection)
☐ Check control cables for looseness and chafing. Look inside fuselage and wings through inspection panels with a flashlight.
☐ Check fuel caps, quick drains and fuel tank areas for signs of fuel leaks (brownish stains)

- [ ] Check fuselage underside for cleanliness and signs of leaks from engine area
- [ ] Check wing struts for any signs of damage, corrosion, or hairline cracks.
- [ ] On fabric covered aircraft do fabric test, and check for loose or peeling fabric.
- [ ] Check engine cowling for looseness, play, and cracks, especially at attach points.

Landing gear
- [ ] Check landing gear struts for leaks.
- [ ] Check tires for wear and bald spots.
- [ ] Check brake pads for wear, brake disks for corrosion, pitting, and warping, and brake hydraulic lines for signs of seeping or leaking fluid.

Cockpit
- [ ] Check cabin doors and windows for signs of water leaks.
- [ ] Check windows for crazing.
- [ ] Check seat belts for wear and tear. They can get caught and damaged in the seat rails.
- [ ] Move all controls and trim to verify full control movement and check for binding.
- [ ] Move all other knobs and switches to check for proper operation.
- [ ] Check ELT for proper operation.
- [ ] Check entire aircraft for proper display of placards and limitations.

Engine and propeller
- [ ] Compression check
- [ ] Check baffles for damage or deformation. Baffle irregularities can cause cooling problems
- [ ] Check for any sign of leaks, especially around the various gaskets. Look for oil and fuel stains.
- [ ] Check lower spark plugs for proper condition (take them out and examine them)
- [ ] Check wiring harness for signs of brittleness and fraying.
- [ ] Check the induction/exhaust system for leaks, cracks, corrosion, and looseness.
- [ ] Check engine controls running to the cockpit for free and easy movement.
- [ ] Check the battery for fluid level and signs of overheating.
- [ ] Check accessory attachments (alternator, mags, vacuum pump, starter, electric fuel pump, etc). Check alternator belt for fraying and tightness.
- [ ] Check propeller for nicks, and spinner for cracks.

Fig. F-4. Flight test checklist.

Aircraft:
Location:
Weather conditions:
Date:

☐ Preflight. Do a detailed preflight per the operating manual. Follow the detailed manual checklist to be sure of covering everything.

☐ Engine start. Note how easily the engine cranks and turns over.

☐ Taxi. Perform radio checks on both coms. Test brakes. Notice engine response, steering, suspension.

☐ Pretakeoff checks. Perform careful pretakeoff checks and runup verifying aircraft behavior to operating manual standards.

☐ Takeoff. Note if power settings reach required levels. Climb to a convenient maneuvering altitude.

☐ Basic VFR maneuvers, handling checks. Perform steep turns, slow flight, stalls. Cycle flaps and gear. Note if aircraft is in trim.

☐ Cruise checks. Set up various cruise configurations. Note performance compared to operating manual standards. Check engine gauges.

☐ Avionics checks. Check all avionics in flight. Do in-flight radio checks. Track VORs localizer and glideslope on all appropriate navs. Compare needle indication of each VOR set to the same radial. Check ADF and marker beacons as appropriate. Establish radar contact with ground control, compare transponder altitude readout reported by ground control to altimeter indication.

☐ Miscellaneous checks. Check cabin lights, vents, heating system

☐ Touch and goes. Perform two or three touch and goes to feel fully comfortable with the handling of the aircraft.

☐ Postflight check. Uncowl engine, check for evidence of any leaks. Turn on all nav lights, landing lights, strobes, and flashing beacon, and check for operation.

Fig. F-5. Closing checklist.

Aircraft:
Location:
Witnesses/notary:
Date:

You receive from the seller:

- ☐ Signed aircraft bill of sale
- ☐ Airworthiness certificate
- ☐ Airframe and engine logbooks
- ☐ Aircraft operating manual
- ☐ Weight and balance
- ☐ Seller's aircraft radio station license

You give the seller:

- ☐ Funds in the amount of the sale price (minus the deposit already given)
- ☐ Copy of the bill of sale for the seller's records. This is optional but most sellers will want one (you will have to make a copy because the FAA form is only in duplicate, the original to be sent in, the copy to be kept by you).

Place in the aircraft to meet FAA regulations

- ☐ Airworthiness certificate
- ☐ New temporary registration
- ☐ New radio station license
- ☐ Operating manual
- ☐ Weight and balance information

Fig. F-6. Sample documents.

FORM APPROVED
OMB NO. 2120-0042

UNITED STATES OF AMERICA
DEPARTMENT OF TRANSPORTATION FEDERAL AVIATION ADMINISTRATION

AIRCRAFT BILL OF SALE

FOR AND IN CONSIDERATION OF **$**   THE
UNDERSIGNED OWNER(S) OF THE FULL LEGAL
AND BENEFICIAL TITLE OF THE AIRCRAFT DES-
CRIBED AS FOLLOWS:

UNITED STATES
REGISTRATION NUMBER **N**

AIRCRAFT MANUFACTURER & MODEL

AIRCRAFT SERIAL No.

DOES THIS   DAY OF   **19**

HEREBY SELL, GRANT, TRANSFER AND

DELIVER ALL RIGHTS, TITLE, AND INTERESTS

IN AND TO SUCH AIRCRAFT UNTO:

Do Not Write In This Block
FOR FAA USE ONLY

PURCHASER

NAME AND ADDRESS
(IF INDIVIDUAL(s), GIVE LAST NAME, FIRST NAME, AND MIDDLE INITIAL.)

DEALER CERTIFICATE NUMBER

AND TO   EXECUTORS, ADMINISTRATORS, AND ASSIGNS TO HAVE AND TO HOLD
SINGULARLY THE SAID AIRCRAFT FOREVER, AND WARRANTS THE TITLE THEREOF.

IN TESTIMONY WHEREOF   HAVE SET   HAND AND SEAL THIS   DAY OF   **19**

SELLER

NAME (S) OF SELLER (TYPED OR PRINTED)	SIGNATURE (S) (IN INK) (IF EXECUTED FOR CO-OWNERSHIP, ALL MUST SIGN.)	TITLE (TYPED OR PRINTED)

ACKNOWLEDGMENT   (NOT REQUIRED FOR PURPOSES OF FAA RECORDING: HOWEVER, MAY BE REQUIRED
BY LOCAL LAW FOR VALIDITY OF THE INSTRUMENT.)

ORIGINAL: TO FAA

AC FORM 8050-2 (8-85) (0052-00-629-0002)

FORM APPROVED
OMB NO. 2120-0029
EXP. DATE 10/31/84

UNITED STATES OF AMERICA DEPARTMENT OF TRANSPORTATION
FEDERAL AVIATION ADMINISTRATION-MIKE MONRONEY AERONAUTICAL CENTER
AIRCRAFT REGISTRATION APPLICATION

UNITED STATES REGISTRATION NUMBER **N**	CERT. ISSUE DATE
AIRCRAFT MANUFACTURER & MODEL	
AIRCRAFT SERIAL No.	FOR FAA USE ONLY

TYPE OF REGISTRATION (Check one box)

☐ 1. Individual   ☐ 2. Partnership   ☐ 3. Corporation   ☐ 4. Co-owner   ☐ 5. Gov't.   ☐ 8. Foreign-owned Corporation

NAME OF APPLICANT (Person(s) shown on evidence of ownership. If individual, give last name, first name, and middle initial.)

TELEPHONE NUMBER: (   )   _

ADDRESS (Permanent mailing address for first applicant listed.)

Number and street: _____

Rural Route: _____   P.O. Box: _____

CITY	STATE	ZIP CODE

☐   **CHECK HERE IF YOU ARE ONLY REPORTING A CHANGE OF ADDRESS**

ATTENTION! Read the following statement before signing this application.

A false or dishonest answer to any question in this application may be grounds for punishment by fine and / or imprisonment (U.S. Code, Title 18, Sec. 1001).

CERTIFICATION

I/WE CERTIFY:

(1) That the above aircraft is owned by the undersigned applicant, who is a citizen (including corporations) of the United States.

    (For voting trust, give name of trustee: _____), or:

    CHECK ONE AS APPROPRIATE:

    a. ☐ A resident alien, with alien registration (Form 1-151 or Form 1-551) No. _____

    b. ☐ A foreign-owned corporation organized and doing business under the laws of (state or possession) _____, and said aircraft is based and primarily used in the United States. Records of flight hours are available for inspection at _____

(2) That the aircraft is not registered under the laws of any foreign country; and
(3) That legal evidence of ownership is attached or has been filed with the Federal Aviation Administration.

    NOTE: If executed for co-ownership all applicants must sign. Use reverse side if necessary.

TYPE OR PRINT NAME BELOW SIGNATURE

EACH PART OF THIS APPLICATION MUST BE SIGNED IN INK.	SIGNATURE	TITLE	DATE
	SIGNATURE	TITLE	DATE
	SIGNATURE	TITLE	DATE

NOTE: Pending receipt of the Certificate of Aircraft Registration, the aircraft may be operated for a period not in excess of 90 days, during which time the PINK copy of this application must be carried in the aircraft.

AC FORM 8050-1 (1-83) (0052-00-628-9005)

Aircraft registration application serves as temporary registration.

Index

financial recordkeeping *cont.*
  periodic reporting to partners, 102
  statement, 98
  statement, more informative, 99-102
prepurchase inspection, 210-214
  mechanical, 211-213
    airframe, 211
    checklist, 299-300
    cockpit, 212
    engine and propeller, 212
    landing gear, 211
    test flight, 212-213
  papers, examining of, 210-211
preventative maintenance, list of, 293-295

Q

questions, 31-38

R

radio station license, 219

recordkeeping, financial, partnership, 95-102
records, 89-103, 183-191
  flying club, 183-191
  partnership, 89-103
recurrent inspections, schedule of, 292
researching and finding plane, 201-207

S

safety, flying club, 173-175
scheduling, aircraft operations, partnership, 89-90
special requirements, 32
squawk sheet, 293
state fees, 16
statistics, flying club records, 190-191
structure
  partnership, 34-35
    accounting, 35
    annual expenses, 35

equal shares, 34-35
meetings, 35
partners, how many, 34
resolving disputes, 35

T

tiedown hangar, 16
training partnership, 116
two partner partnership, 104-107
typical partnership agreement, 50-59

U

underwriters, 81-82
upkeep and costs, 26

V

volunteer time, 27

W

warbird partnership, 114-116

SOFTWARE ORDER INFORMATION

The partnership and flying club financial analysis
templates are available on 3.5" or 5.25" disk, ready for
your immediate use (both templates on one disk). In order to
use the templates you will need the following systems and
software:

o IBM or compatible computer capable of running
  Microsoft Excel 3.0 and Microsoft Windows 3.0.

o Microsoft Excel 3.0 and Microsoft Windows 3.0
  installed on your computer.

To receive your disk containing the partnership and
flying club financial analysis templates, please send **$19.95**
(Massachusetts residents please add 5% sales tax of $1.00
per disk) and the coupon below to:

LF Associates
Department D
PO Box 173
Sudbury, MA 01776

LF Associates, Department D, PO Box 173, Sudbury, MA 01776

Please send____ copies of the Partnership and Flying Club Financial Analysis Template Disk.
Enclosed is a check or money order for **$19.95 per disk**. Circle disk size: 3.5" 5.25"
Massachusetts residents add 5% sales tax [$1.00 per disk]

Name:_____

Street:_____

City:_____ State:_____ Zip: _____

Please allow up to 4 weeks for delivery. Sorry, no cash or credit cards.